EMOTIONAL ALIGNMENT IS EASY

By

Leslie van Oostenbrugge

The Awakening Dentist

MAKE YOUR MARK GLOBAL

MAKE YOUR MARK GLOBAL PUBLISHING, LTD
USA & Monaco
Emotional Alignment is Easy © 2019 Leslie van Oostenbrugge
Published by Make Your Mark Global Publishing, LTD

The purpose of this book is not to give medical advice, nor to give a prescription for the use of any technique as a form of treatment for any physical, medical, psychological, or emotional condition. The information in this book does not replace the advice of a physician, either directly or indirectly. It is intended only as general information and education. In the event that you use any of the information in this book for yourself, as is your constitutional right, the author and publisher assume no responsibility for your actions. No expressed or implied guarantee of the effect of use of any of the recommendations can be given. The author and publisher are not liable or responsible for any loss or damage allegedly arising from any information in this book. All of the names and details have been changed to protect the privacy of individuals.

Without limiting the rights under copyright reserved above, no part of this publication may be reproduced, stored in, or introduced into a retrieval system, or transmitted in any form or by any means (electronic, mechanical, photocopying, recording, or otherwise), without the prior written permission of the copyright owner.

The scanning, uploading, and distribution of this book via the Internet or any other means without the permission of the publisher is illegal and punishable by law. Please purchase only authorized electronic editions and do not participate in or encourage any electronic piracy of copyrightable materials. Your support of the author's rights is appreciated. And karma will get you if you violate this anyway!

While the author has made every effort to provide accurate information regarding references and Internet addresses at the time of publication, the author does not assume responsibility for errors or changes that occur after publication. The author also does not assume any responsibility for third-party websites and/or their content.

Book cover design concept by Ronald van Oostenbrugge

Emotional Alignment is Easy
Publisher: Make Your Mark Global, LTD
Fernley, Nevada
p.452
Trade Paperback ISBN 978-0-9994949-7-4
Subjects: Health
Summary: Blending professional insights from holistic dentistry with practical wisdom from the Law of Attraction, Leslie van Oostenbrugge makes the link between dental disease, health and emotional wellbeing.

MAKE YOUR MARK GLOBAL PUBLISHING, LTD
USA & Monaco
Emotional Alignment is Easy © 2019 Leslie van Oostenbrugge

For information on bulk purchase orders of this book or to book Leslie to speak at your event or on your program, send an email to Leslie@TheAwakeningDentist.com

Praise for Emotional Alignment is Easy

This amazing book is the missing link between dentistry and holistic healing. Leslie van Oostenbrugge is the dentist you always wish you had, here offering deep wisdom, compassion, and new hope for your dental health and spiritual well-being. I am deeply inspired by Leslie's vision of how positive and healing a visit to the dentist can be, merged with soul awakening. I have the highest regard for this courageous visionary woman who is making a major contribution to upgrading spiritual consciousness through dental service and healing.

~ Alan Cohen, bestselling author of *A Course in Miracles Made Easy*

This brilliant book brings a forward-thinking, refreshing, and honest outlook that make people think differently about their teeth and the importance of good health. Whatever your relationship with your teeth – or with your dentist! – read this book!

~ Taz Thornton, UK's Best Female Coach

Leslie is such an amazing light and energy! She brings such an intriguing and life-changing perspective to not just the dental world, but to anyone and everyone. She is definitely a pioneer in her field and in life!

~ Jill Stocker, D.O., Age Management Medicine & Hormone Optimization Expert

You are not your profession

I AM

For my fabulous children,
Keij, Max and Eef

In loving memory of Patty Fitzpatrick

Energy

They…
told me to stop studying dentistry

They…
told me to not ask such bold questions.
All answers were to be found in the books, they said. But they weren't my answers…

A <u>few years later</u>:
I…
graduated with honors from Dental School
graduated with honors from a School of Physical Therapy

Dear Friend,

I appreciate your interest in my work and online consultations. Many people have asked: "For whom are you writing this book?" I've felt pressured to give an answer that would fit into someone's neat little box. Let me just say this: I am so happy it is YOU, but... who are you? Are you a carpenter, are you a housewife, are you a marathon runner, are you a nurse, are you a dog lover, are you a criminal, are you a dentist, are you a son, are you a...

Well, guess what? That is not what you are! What are you, then? You are a soul experiencing life in a body. You chose this experience. You just forgot. See... we are all the same. We just express consciousness in a different way. This philosophy, however, needs to be translated into daily life and action.

I am hoping to give you tools to 'live' your life in your own way so you can develop your own unique gifts, for that is what you are, a unique gift to the world.

There are a lot of people you can turn to for help; friends, confidants, doctors, dentist, healers, psychics, you name it. According to 'where you are' you choose who might be of assistance.

My most cherished wish is to remind you that you are a multidimensional personality and within you lies ALL the knowledge and the knowing to live your life to the fullest.

Every single person you choose to help you can only be a mediator or intermediary, to link you back to where you came from: Source.

I am honored you chose me to be your intermediary.

(You, hanging on the edge of a cliff yelling)

You: "Help! Is anybody out there?"

Source: "Yes, hello. It is me, Source."

You: "… Is anybody else out there?"

Contents

Foreword & Forward 1

Introduction 2

The dentist 10

Responsibilities 12

Communication 14

Call them names 18

Tooth 21

It is sugar, babe! 24

Treat or defeat? 27

Drill 31

Fear! 35

Jim 38

Bliss? 41

Cry if you want to 42

The dental exam 45

The dentist can help you overcome your fear 47

The gum: SOUL of the mouth! 49

The dentist saved my life 51

Wrong tooth pulled 54

Anamnesis 58

Your teeth are *living* body parts 61

To the bone 64

Chemistry of stress 69

The lymphatic system	71
Love your K9's!	74
GPS	77
Shopping cart	80
'…and Fill'	85
Filling materials.	90
®	95
Physical Pain, Mental Pain	99
House of teeth	105
'House' with teeth	107
Metaphysical meaning of pain	110
Your body as a manifestation	114
Mechanisms of oral pain	122
4 x ¼	125
Be-cause	130
Love at first bite	134
Exercise	139
My cell phone is your placebo	145
A bitter pill to swallow	148
SALIVA, your holy tooth water	152
Tongue tied	155
OUCH	157
Until death do us not part	162
About me	177
About myself	182

You form history; it doesn't form you	185
More of the same	189
Homeless	193
The accountant	201
Colleague	202
It is law!	203
One for the money	208
Think and grow! It is Law	212
New Thought is New Life	215
New data	217
Are you out of your mind?	237
A new dimension	242
Conscious	246
Bridge over troubled water	248
LinkedIn	250
Crystal clear	253
Parents	255
Past life	258
Your family is your gift	261
The sacred privilege to be a mom	264
Healing is the portal to abundance	267
I love me	270
Affirmations for you	275
Chemistry of "feeling good"	277
What's (the) matter?	280

Spirit meets science, hi!..284

Mind boggle. 287

Your experience is your proof! 290

Trick or treat? 293

Off course...297

Source energy...300

Sleeping beauty..305

Calibration 306

Emotional alignment...309

Practice no force...311

Be still...315

Ask..322

*Sign*ature 326

Flying high² 329

Timing is on your side 336

Emotions are manifestations...338

The Miracle..341

Dent-art-ist...345

Office Spirit #1...351

Survival guide for the dentist 354

MWM® (Meditate While Medicate) 358

High energy..361

The $100 bill...367

Mind my own business...371

Court...374

Reptility	380
222	382
The meaning of 222	388
Armed to the teeth	391
Emotions have colors	399
You are the rainbow: the colors are in you	402
The spiritual meaning of teeth	406
Spiritual meaning of teeth problems	408
Meridians	412
Tap into your canines	417
Let's get physical	420
Psychodontics	422
Archangel Michael	424
Aftermath	428
'Who am I grateful for?' list	430
About the Author	431
Get Published Share Your Message with the World	432

Foreword & Forward

"Don't die with the music still in you", Wayne Dyer said. Wayne Dyer was an American philosopher, self-help author and motivational speaker.

In April 2015, I attended a spiritual World Summit in Denver. Dr. Dyer was the keynote speaker. How happy I was to be able to listen to his story.

With all my respect to late Dr. Dyer, his beautiful and brilliant story did not reveal any 'new' stuff to me. I was in tears discovering I had already found my path years prior to that talk.

Wayne Dyer, and I didn't learn anything new? Was I out of my mind? Of course, he had a lot of fascinating insights that were new to many people, but it wasn't new for me. I was so happy about that because it showed that I was already on the path of enlightenment.

Because of a <u>lack</u> of self-love, <u>lack</u> of money, <u>lack</u> of self-worth, I had miraculously stepped into a world of miracles.

You'd better read that again...

Did you get it? Because of those things, yes, I'd stepped into a world full of miracles and successes.

So here follows this **'freakingboringohyeahIknowthiscrap'** subject: other people's success story can be your own!

"Believe it and you will see it!" is my statement. (Rather than "see it and believe it").

This book is my music.

Introduction

When you align with Source, or awaken from the dream life gets easier than you've probably ever imagined was possible.

From childhood on I have been tremendously aware of other people's emotions. I could feel them. As a result, I have often had an indefinable insight and intuition in specific matters.

For instance, my mother carried the grief about her own mother's death until the day she died herself. When I was about 14, I said to her: "Mom, your grief is selfish; your mother is having a great time in Heaven." Now, where in the world does a child get this belief or information from?

My life turned around when my mom died… I felt I 'needed' her to die to be able to grow myself. I felt very guilty feeling this. However, lives and deaths are cycles. We serve a huge, bigger picture which will be revealed when we die. Compare life to a huge poster consisting of hundreds of pictures, then view that poster from up above - there is the bigger picture.

Because of my mom's upbringing, I was brought up in a way that caused me to live conditionally until the age of 45.

You can only grow in your profession when you grow or expand emotionally.

This book is a combination of the know-how of a dentist and the 'knowing' of being a human. I am aware that I am aware. Yay!

PART I of this book will give you knowledge and a lot of background information on dentistry. I will provide information about why and how some dental procedures are done.

It is <u>not</u> my goal to direct you to specific treatments or to criticize others. I merely want to show you some of the different angles of dental treatment. After all, any one of them 'must' lead to your problem being solved.

I have always been funny. I love to make people laugh. That is why I wrote this part with a funny twist. Matters concerning dental issues are serious enough already.

Have you ever had the urge to pick up a *book* about dentistry? Let me guess… NO? Because it reminded you of the dentist? Or most dental books are boring textbooks? You probably would've been bored by page 3.

In many cases I really do understand why pictures in dental books cause distress. If you flip through one and remember that you have an appointment in three days, you'll probably end up sick to your stomach.

But, hey, dentists can be very lovely people! As much as 'we dentists' (most of us) do our best to be kind, empathic, and passionate in providing your dental care…we seem to 'never get it right, and 'never get you over it'. But… we cannot be held responsible for that on our own. You are too, as well as the assistant.

We are a team.

The dental triangle; you, me and the assistant.

Have you ever read a book about teeth?

Good for you! You have shown you are eager to learn or study about a subject few want to understand.

Generally speaking, books about dentistry are very tough for the average reader to understand.

So, I hope the humor with which Part I is written might make it easier for you to read along. You can find more serious and detailed information on the internet or in other books, if you wish. I will refer to specific books and websites.

Please visit my website: www.theawakeningdentist.com for more information. Feel free to interact with me and ask questions by emailing leslie@theawakeningdentist.com

I invite you to go ahead and read about how to be your own dental health creator. It is easier than you might think!! And yes, dental health is *within* your reach…

PART II this book will guide you through **my** personal transformation as a human being. This influenced my dentist-being for the better.

I discovered the journey to find anything *outside* yourself is a waste of time. There is no 'journey'. There is actually nothing 'outside' yourself. Now isn't that odd?

We often think we 'need' a disaster to finally decide to change our lives. It is as if we cannot decide to change just because we want to; we seem to 'need' to have an excuse. Often that excuse is the loss of a loved one, a divorce, an accident, you name it. To me, indeed, the excuse was the loss of my mother.

Finally, I realized: I myself am the creator of my own life.

I found out that being the creator of your own life means:

Desire to begin and desire to allow!

I realize this sounds very abstract right now. I'd love to 'tell' you all about it. Dare to desire!

It has brought me miracles; however, miracles have always been here. I had just not seen them.

Part II of this book is also a <u>Practical guide to how to change your consciousness!!</u>

Q: Why would you want to change your consciousness?

A's:

- You haven't found your dream job
- You are in financial debt
- You haven't found your mate yet
- You tend to be jealous
- You worry too much
- You think it is everybody else's fault
- You think you are perfect
- You think you are not perfect!
- You don't know why life is meant to be
- You feel attacked easily by other people
- And so on

I have read many books about life change, self-care, self-help and consciousness. What I missed was a practical guide (or maybe I didn't search enough?). The books I found were beautifully written but I knew I couldn't fit the 'programs' they presented into my daily routine.

I just needed it to be different so I would indeed start breaking the vicious cycle I was in. Break the cycle in my head of flawed ideas and thoughts.

Just like creating the new habit of interdental cleaning, this process is creating a new habit of thinking.

I thank you so much for devoting your precious time to reading my book.

Have fun!

Leslie Van O, the Awakening Dentist
www.theawakeningdentist.com

This book is kind of a documentary
This book is a dental tale
This book will not contain bloody pictures
This book will contain <u>bloody interesting</u> drawings
This book is written for YOU!
This book will contain teaching moments
This book will leave space to get your handkerchief
This book will contain exercise pages; please use them
This book will contain drawings I made myself
This book will contain easy-to-understand language
This book will contain short chapters to keep your focus
This book will help you to love your dentist
This book will help you to love your UNIVERSE
This book will help you to love your teeth
This book will show you the miracles of the Universe
This book is NOT a dental textbook
This book is to realize to respect each other
This book will help you love yourself
This book will help you remember who you really are
This book will contain a lot of funny phrases
This book will show that teeth are alive!
This book will show **that gums** are the **soul** of the mouth
This book will show you that life is no struggle at all
This book will show you that the Law of Attraction really exists
This book will show you life-changing affirmations

'As Within, So Without'

Change within and your outer world will change.

For me it, for instance, meant: I doubled the number of clients in my practice, I received a giant financial gift, I got divorced and I got to write this book.

Mind your teeth:

A practical guide to dental health

The dentist

A dentist is she or he who specializes in dentistry.

Dentistry is the prevention and treatment of diseases and conditions of the oral cavity.

The oral cavity is also known as the mouth, the opening where you put your chocolate bars and your beer!

The dentist's 'working area' reaches from the outside of the lips to the very top of the pharynx[1].

The *very* moment you cannot taste the chocolate and the beer anymore, the stuff might have reached your pharynx. Now swallow!

By the way: the word 'FEAR' didn't show up in the dictionary anywhere near the word 'dentist'. So, in the most literal sense, it is not associated with us.

Education: the course in Dental School will take 4-8 years of your life.

The curriculum will vary per country! Required courses to gain admission to dental programs include, for instance, chemistry, biology and physics.

---

[1] Pharynx: the tube or cavity, with its surroundings membrane and muscles, that connects the mouth and nasal passages with the esophagus. The esophagus connects the mouth through the pharynx with the stomach.

What problems could poor dental health cause?

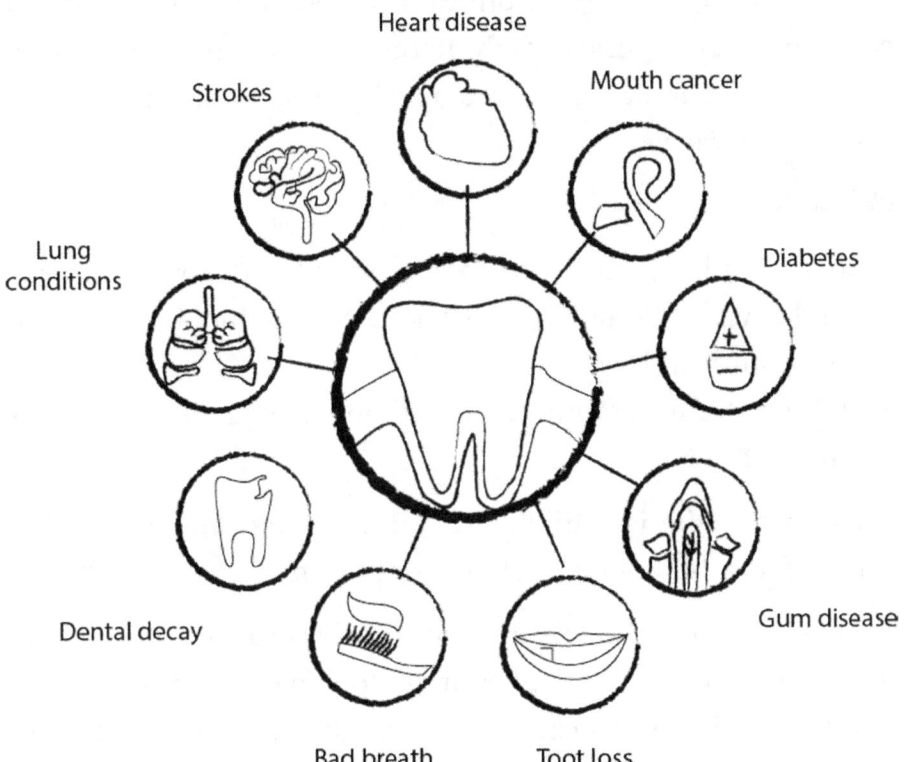

Responsibilities

A newly licensed dentist is able to carry out *most* dental treatments, such as teeth cleaning, restorative work (fillings/ crowns/ bridges), orthodontics (braces), endodontics (root canal therapy), periodontal therapy (gum and bone), oral surgery (pulling of teeth), and administering anesthetic (*lucky you AND lucky me*).

Of course, we start with:

1. Examination (I check the inside as well as the outside of the oral cavity, I do not only check for sick tissue, I also love to see your healthy gums.
2. (Often) X-Ray examination and then, of course, a diagnosis follows!

Diagnosis is the identification of the nature and (hopefully) cause of a certain phenomenon/symptoms.

As a recently qualified dentist, you really learn your profession by *doing* the work! It takes courage to expand. Many (but not all) dentists have this courage. Fortunately, I am one of those who do!

Another huge responsibility is **communication**! (This is the #1 responsibility, actually!)

Talk to your clients and give them room to react, preferably without all your tools sticking in and out of their mouth, dear mouth workers! (I know it's hard sometimes!)

Talk _to_ your kiddie patients! Not over their heads _about_ them.

Responsibility does not belong to the dentist only.

You, as the client/patient, are also very much responsible for your own dental health!

The dentist is only the tour guide to show you how to reach achieve and maintain this state of well-being.

Dental health conditions can lead to conditions in the rest of the body, and vice versa!

Communication

According to the Oxford English Dictionary communication is:

"The imparting or exchanging of information by speaking, writing, or using some other medium."

Non-verbal communication is the process of conveying meaning in the form of NON-word messages.

Verbal communication is effective verbal or spoken communication, dependent on a number of factors and cannot be fully isolated from other important interpersonal skills such as non-verbal communication, *listening skills* and clarification.

Examples of non-verbal communication include: haptic communication, gesture, body language, facial expression, handshake, eye contact and: **color!**

Color is used to communicate a lot of things. You will learn more about this subject later.

Additionally, speech contains non-verbal elements known as *paralanguage* (e.g. rhythm, intonation, tempo and stress).

Communication plays a fundamental role in our lives and society. Most of us, however, don't realize to what extent. From the very beginning of our lives, we participate in the process of acquiring rules about communication. These rules are embedded into our relationships, though we aren't necessarily aware of it. Communication is a complicated process and we automate it almost without conscious effort.

"One cannot not communicate" was a statement of Paul Watzlawick (1921-2007). He developed the theory of human communication.

My communication always starts immediately when I *personally* invite my clients into my office, no bells, chimes, or number tickets needed.

I shake hands and look everybody in the eye before they step into my office. Before you've even entered the office, I have already read you all. I do not forget the kids! I will sit on my knees to greet them (depending how tall they are, LOL, some 12-year-olds might be mighty high!)

Personally; because I want them to feel welcome and to know I will take the necessary time for their treatment.

Personally; because I do not like to 'buzz, beep or beam' them up like a cashier in a food market or like Captain Kirk[2].

I think it is part of appreciating the people who choose to come to YOUR office.

When friends, family, and relatives come to be treated by me, the handshake also non-verbally means a lot: "I am in a different role now. At this moment, I am your dentist and I am responsible for the health of your teeth". It is a dividing line between chit-chat and professional talk.

---

[2] Beam me up Scotty is a catchphrase from the science fiction television series *Star Trek*. Captain Kirk gives his chief engineer Montgomery 'Scotty' Scott a command to transport him back to the Starship Enterprise

Do not misunderstand me; of course, there is a lot of humor in my office! Lot of times we have to get a handkerchief to wipe happy tears from everyone's face. (At the dentists? Yes!)

Our handshake will 'tell' me a lot! Is it firm, sloppy and perhaps… sweaty?

Firm: client may be very clear and assertive in describing their problems.

Sloppy: client may be unsure of him/herself. They might look up to you. So sometimes it is tougher to get a diagnosis because they do not want to bother you…

Sweaty: client IS nervous, no doubt.

Now, of course I invite them to lie down in the chair.

This is *the moment* people think(!) they have to give their power away to me and let go of their own.

I always tell them: "You are the boss. You are the owner of your teeth. I am merely your guide and advisor. If you do not want anything to happen, it won't happen. I will take good care of you."

This doesn't mean all fear is lost but it takes some of the stress away.

I think non-verbal communication includes *color*. That's why the colors of my office are red and orange.

Red is the color of energy, passion and strength.

Orange symbolizes health, attraction and happiness.

Clients more than often compliment me about the colors in my office; "Not like a hospital or dental office", they say.

LESS WHITE = LESS FRIGHT

Then I push the button for the chair to tilt backwards; I always warn people first so they won't be startled.

It may sound silly but some people are already so stressed out that this might help them to ease a little bit.

After I ask whether they are comfortable (as far as one can be comfortable in a dental chair), I am ready to start my exam.

I am eager to find healthy teeth and gums; if something appears different, I will explain this to the patients and have them look with me into a mirror. Of course, if they don't want to do that they don't have to. Usually I am able to convince them, however. Not always within the first few appointments, though.

We will discuss the problems that I detect, and I will suggest <u>treatment options with their prognosis and costs.</u> Note the plural form; there is hardly ever only one solution to the problem. Clients need to know this.

Many dentists give the impression there is just one option available.

Also, the X-rays are always shown and discussed.

If the client does not want the treatment for some reason, I always make a note in their file and tell them that while I do not agree with their decision, I accept it. Clients are free to make their own choice. This is also communication.

TALK BECAUSE YOU CARE

Call them names

Hydroxyapatite, glucosamine, triglyceride, Osteocyte, chondrocyte, epithelium, submandibular, occlusal, distal, thrombocytes, nerves, Glycerophospholipids, carbohydrate, pyruvic Acid, calcium, globulin, alpha-2-, beta- and gamma globulin, albumin, Streptococcus Mutans, Porphyromonas Gingivalis, fungus, microsporidia, Prevotella intermedia, Fusobacterium nucleatum, Enterococcus faecalic, Staphylococcus aureus, Candida, Actinobacillus actinomycetemcomitans, Streptococcus constellatus, Enteric gram negative rods,

Aerobic (_nothing to do with your 7-8pm session at the gym_),

An-aerobic (_unrelated to cancelling this session_).

Campylobacter rectus, M. Masseter,

Streptococcus Salivarius, sublingual glands,

M. Orbicularis Oris, buccal branche, maxilla, Mandible, M. Incisivus Labii, mucus, mesial, peripheral, rubor, calor, dolor, attrition, friction, Buccal cusp, mesial root, apex, intraligamental, ligament, peripheral nerve, Excavation, endodontic rescue kit, extraction, decapitation, gingivitis, bruxism, parodontitis, Augmentin, dentin conditioner, bond-strength, polyacrylic acid, amelogenesis imperfecta, hyperglottis hypoglottis, white poison, second opinion, root deformation, frames, pulp, pulp stones, pulp chamber, vascular, interradicular, intraradicular, splint, eruption, Impaction, inversion, eversion, abfraction, sinus lift, odontoblasts, remission, Calcification, Tartar, scaler, burr, finishing rubber, M. Pterygoideus, M. Genioglossus, N. Facialis, N. Mandibularis. Clavulanate, luxate, avulsion, CMD, DMFT, cavity, caries profunda, exponation, decay, composite, Hg, Au, Mercury, H2O2, paracetamol, veneer, constriction, finishing.

Emotional Alignment Is Easy

Hey, you! Why did you turn the last page so quickly? I knew you would! Wasn't it interesting? Too boring maybe? Awful? Out of reach?

I understand; it took me 4.5 years to learn about the ins and outs of the former page and it is only a fraction of the theoretical knowledge we have to drill into our brains as dental students. And this isn't taking into account the practical side of (the) course, which is the most important part. So why did I bother you with page 18 and 19… I said I was going to use easy-to-understand-language and I didn't keep my promise…

It was to remind you all that most of you regard your oral cavity and your teeth the same as my abundant lists of dental terms!

Something that is out of reach, miles away, far away, unverifiable!

A 'far, far away Kingdom', like in the Shrek[3] Universe!

Patients think that cavities are mysterious things that just appear in one's teeth, without any reason. Like they just happen … overnight.

That is not true!

I am here to show you how to LOVE, care for and cherish YOUR teeth. It is easy…just grin and bear with me.

Take care of your teeth: they are living parts of your body!

---

[3] Shrek: a fictional character in a computer animation movie made by DreamWorks Animation. He is a green ogre who loves his swamp.

Tooth

Now, there's a lot of stuff worth chewing on concerning this subject.

Your front teeth are situated between the cuspid teeth (or K9's).

The next drawing represents your front tooth cross-sectioned from the side.

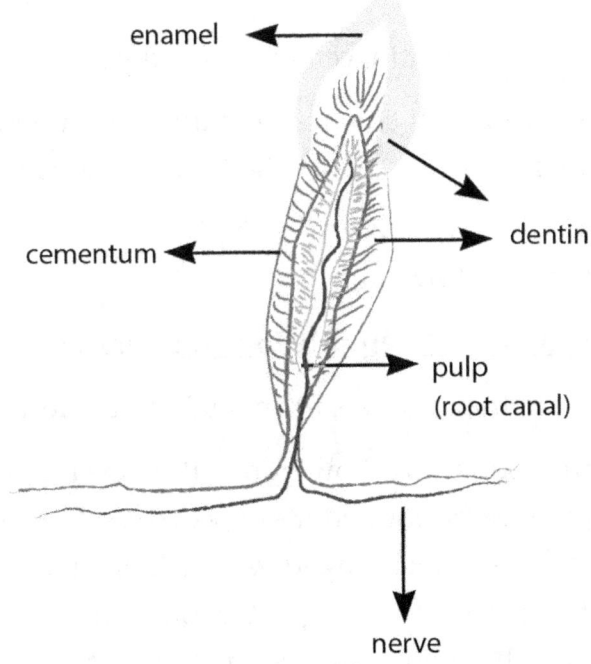

The outer layer of your tooth is called 'enamel'.

Enamel is the toughest part of the human body!

Some people think it is called ivory, but we are not elephants; their tusks, which are really long and gigantic teeth, are made of ivory. Elephants get shot by people who want to steal their tusks. Unless you have tons of golden crowns, there is no chance that this kind of thing will happen to you (I hope).

Enamel, thus, makes up the normal visible part of the tooth. It covers the natural crown. Enamel is one of the four major tissue parts of the tooth.

The other parts are dentin, cementum and pulp.

Enamel is a very tough substance (with high mineral content) which, again, makes this tissue the hardest part in the human body.

On the other hand, however,

Enamel is susceptible to de-mineralization

This means that the minerals in enamel can be destroyed!

It is like your wooden window frame! It seems tough but when it's not properly cared for and it's exposed too long to moisture or maybe accidentally damaged with a sharp tool, cracks will appear in the paint and the protection will disappear. You know what will happen to the wood after that…

Isn't that a pity? Wood is such a tough tissue but it's able to dissolve under certain circumstances. We can say the same about enamel.

There are several causes of demineralization in enamel. Here are a few:

- Frequent use of acids
- Poor dental hygiene
- Infection
- Certain drugs

I will address the most prevalent cause in the following chapter.

It is sugar, babe!

The most important cause of demineralization is the intake of (fermentable) carbohydrates and the attachment to the teeth of the carb-containing plaque.

This carb residue will lead to dental caries which usually (not always) ends up in the development of cavities.

When you have a cavity, you have a hole in your tooth.

This is not a very happy state of tooth-being.

Enamel is strong but it cannot withstand **ACID!**

Tooth cavities are caused when acids dissolve the enamel.

"Ok… now, Doc! Wait a minute here! First you said 'carbohydrates' and now you say 'ACID' is what causes your tooth to fall apart?"

I say, "Well done! You were focused! You paid attention when reading the text!"

Well, it is the combination of the two; it takes these two to tango. A chemical reaction takes place on the surface of your tooth:

---------------------------✂---------------------------

$$Ca_{10}(PO_4)_6(OH_2)(s) + 8H^+(aq) \longrightarrow$$
$$10Ca^{2+}(aq) + 6HPO_4^{2-}(aq) + 2H_2O(l)$$

Enamel + acid ----> a big mess + water
Just to show you there really is something going on ;-))
Don't learn this reaction by heart. Cut it (out) and forget it!

---------------------------✂---------------------------

Sugars from, for instance, candies (the candyman can, and it ain't no music), soft drinks, fruit juices, and cookies play a significant role in the process of demineralization/decay.

The mouth contains tons and tons of <u>bacteria</u>. Some are good (we need them) and some are bad (we need them to take a hike).

The mouth contains a lot of <u>sugar</u> after we have consumed it.

The mouth contains <u>enamel</u>.

Now, let the party get started! But, alas, not a DJ party but a DeCay party.

What? Did you notice that? It's not just two you need to tango, but three? Yes… three. Bacteria also needs to be there.

So the equation on the last page (is it already in your trashcan because you cut it out?) should be slightly different:

$$Ca_{10}(PO_4)_6(OH_2)(s) + 8H^+(aq) \xrightarrow{\text{bacteria}} 10Ca^{2+}(aq) + 6HPO_4^{2-}(aq) + 2H_2O(l)$$

When sucrose, the most common form of sugar, coats your teeth, the <u>bacteria</u> have food, and they interact with it and they produce: **ACID!**

Emotional Alignment Is Easy

Very Schematic - Bacteria Has Its Lunch:

Sugar　　　　　　　　　　　　Acid

Treat or defeat?

You have a cavity; now what?

Do we, as dentists, have to treat this? <u>Yes or no</u>?

"What do you mean Doc, yes or no? I have a cavity so that means you have to drill and fill, right?"

I say: 'No!!! Not ALWAYS'!

Well, that's good news!

As I've already mentioned, for decay to occur you need:

1. Sugar
2. Bacteria
3. Acid

These three are all collected in the sticky yellowish/white deposit on your tooth (you can feel the roughness of it when you haven't brushed for a day). This deposit is called (dental) plaque.

Plaque Is a Plague

Although plaque is harmful, it is a normal process that cannot be prevented.

<u>It is plaque's progression and build-up that leads to oral problems such as gum-disease and jawbone problems!</u>

Hence it is important to remove this mass of bacteria daily! Twice a day preferably. Right after breakfast and just before you go night night.

So how do you remove the plaque? Yes…by brushing and by cleaning in between (!) teeth. Check the instruction video on my website! More about cleaning later.

"Then, when the plaque is removed, the bacteria, sugar and acids are gone, right?" is your question.

My answer is: "Yes"!

"So, Doc….no more caries, right?" I say: "Yes"!

We come closer to the answer of the question

"Treat or defeat?"

First, I need a break to get your attention.

Caries Is A Disease!

Caries is to be cured/stabilized by *yourself* * when it hasn't progressed too far and *by me*, your dentist, when it has unfortunately reached too far into the dentin tissue.

*See chapter 'cleaning'.

Did you know this?

Imagine….no more decay! (No more dental visits! Yeahooooo!) Just kidding! If you didn't go to the dentist, WHO will teach you how to clean? Anyway, decay is by no means the only reason to go to the dentist.

So, I OFTEN do not drill and fill at all;

I always give people instructions on how to clean properly. Patients sometimes find me stern but when they find out that their caries activity has dropped tremendously they know I have a point.

As mentioned, I often do not drill and fill at all. Of course, most of the time I do have to…

Do I mind the drilling? Yes, often I do! You wonder why? "You earn your money with it. It is your job to drill", people will say to me.

The tooth is a <u>living organism</u>; treat it with care and respect! Drilling can mean waste of healthy tissue. This is why I am very restrained in this!

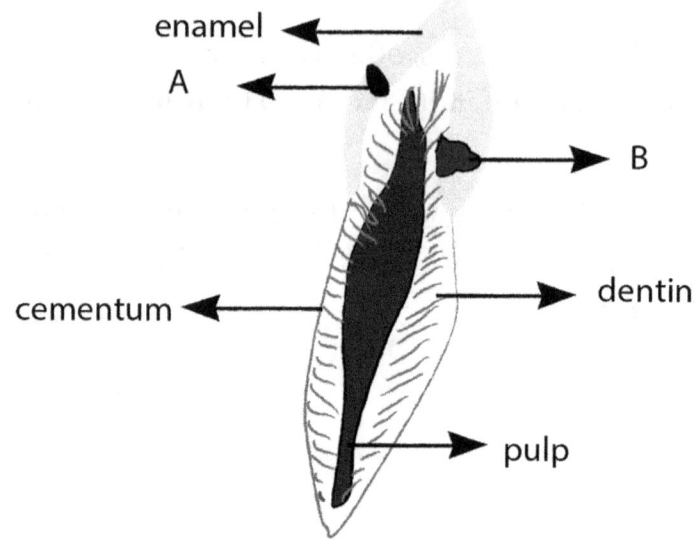

A. Caries in enamel and slightly into the dentin

B. Caries in enamel and dentin; bacteria far into dentin

You can see: caries at B —> bacteria go to the pulp! You do not want that! You might get pain and eventually you will need a root canal treatment or the tooth might have to be pulled. You pick.

The next chapter is about the treatment of caries itself: the drill.

Drill…

Well, there is no doubt: the dental decay (the diseased part of the tooth) has to be removed.

Otherwise the whole tooth might get inflamed and you might end up with a lot of pain.

The worst-case scenario might be losing your tooth.

You know what is going to happen next. We have to use a drill to get the sick part of the tooth out. The drill has to have a high speed and needs to be water-cooled to protect all parts of the tissue, especially the pulp.

Otherwise we will burn tissue! Water-cooling is necessary also to 'wash away' the debris.

There are different kind of burs, fitting in different kinds of hand pieces.

Since enamel is the toughest part of the body, we need a substance that's even harder.! Well… that is **diamond**!

Diamonds may be a girl's best friend but they're certainly not best buddies with your enamel!

Hey! Don't come rob my practice now! I only have a few of those in stock worth a TOTAL of like thirty dollars ($30.00).

The burs have a tiny, tiny, tiny (nanometer thickness) coverage of diamond particles; they will softly glide through the enamel. But because of the sound the drill makes you probably won't notice that.

We need to renew the burs often; sharp tools work best! It works more quickly and the client doesn't feel like they're being pushed through the chair because of dull working tools.

Additionally, using sharp burs will allow for a less painful experience.

So, for treating enamel we use diamond coated burs.

For treating the dentin (which will be soft-ish because of bacterial invasion) we need a steel bur. Or a hand instrument which looks like a small spoon! (I often use this with children or very, very frightened adults.)

A steel bur is to be inserted in a slow-speed hand piece.

To get the soft, demineralized material out of the tooth, you don't need high speed.

It is like cutting rotten wood out of your window frame…

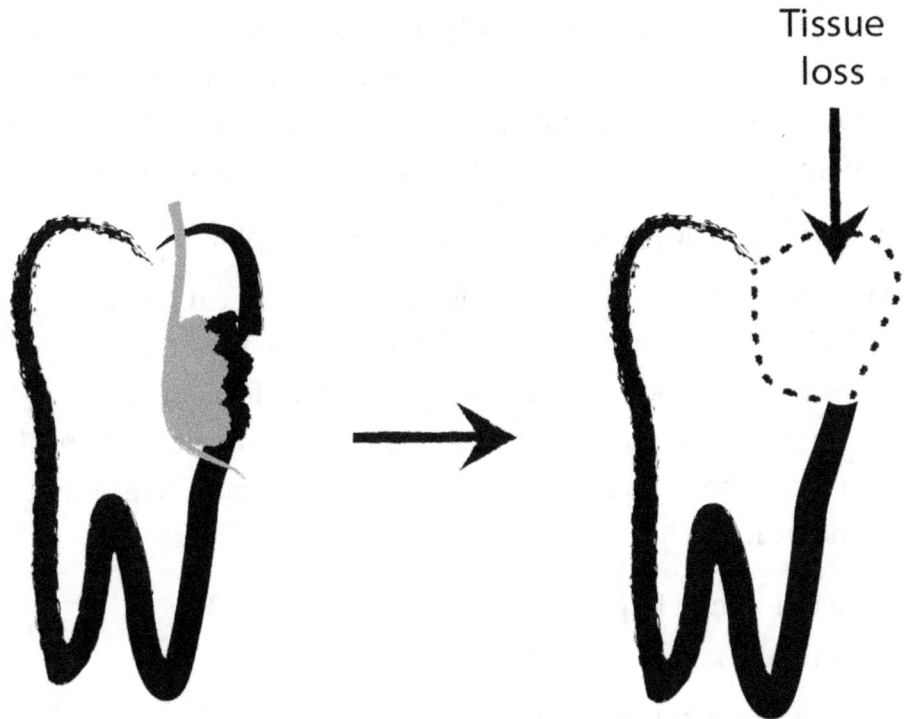

On the left, you see an amazing drawing with a dark spot representing decay; on the right, there's a drawing with a dotted line representing the tissue loss after the drilling procedure. We need access to all the infected tissue to be able to remove it and put in a nice filling.

NOTE: Of course, the missing part will be filled.

The procedure will be described later in this book.

So, don't forget! You need to remember the following very important dental treatment:

ATR — Atraumatic Dental Treatment is the removal of the infected dentin tissue with hand instruments (no burrs). The empty area is filled with mostly a special material that loves a humid environment. I often use this method with children and very frightened people generally. This method is also preferable when caries is located very close to the nerves.

So, drilling is not always necessary! Just sayin'...

Also, very important to know is that not every cavity has to be drilled. I always compare my x-rays with x-rays taken a few years before. When I see no progression in decay activity and the cavity is in stable condition, I absolutely do not drill!! Sometimes bacteria in a cavity can stop its destructive activity because of:

- better dental hygiene
- better food and less sugar
- better functioning of the immune system
- more dental visits and advice

So, in certain situations you might function well with cavities!

Fear!

Fear is an emotion.

Fear is the brain's reaction to a stimulus. Chemicals are released and your heart rate starts to rise quickly.

Phobia is a type of anxiety disorder. It is the persistent fear of an object or a situation. Someone with a phobia will go to great lengths to avoid confronting the thing they fear.

Much of the process of developing a phobia can be attributed to:

Classical Conditioning

The basic facts about classical conditioning (also known as 'Pavlovian' or 'respondent' conditioning) were discovered by *Ivan Pavlov* through his famous experiments with dogs. He was a Russian physiologist who won the Nobel Prize in Physiology or Medicine (1904).

He came up with the theory that new behavior can be learned through the process of association. This means that two stimuli are **linked together** to evoke a new learned response.

Example: a puppy is shown several times to a little child (neutral stimulus). Assume this child is happy to see the little furry animal (otherwise my example sucks).

When the *frequently* showing of that cute puppy goes together with an enormous sound which will startle the child (enormous sound is a natural stimulus and evokes a natural 'fight or flight' reaction), the child will <u>associate</u> that sound with the puppy.

When, at some point, the sound DOES NOT accompany the appearance of the puppy, the child is still likely to startle because it associates it with the sound.

Fear can be introduced this way.

<u>Another factor in the development of phobias can be:</u>

Experience

We fear being hurt because we have been hurt before. It's as simple as that.

Of course: the dentist is a stimulus.

But…

<u>Aren't **you** much **larger** than your thoughts?</u>

Often parents are more nervous for their children than the children themselves when in my office. Parents will sometimes grab the child's hand before I have even done an exam. I understand you want to protect your precious baby however your action confirms to the child that this visit must be scary.

Often I ask the parent to not grab the kid's hand but only when the child asks her mom or dad to. It gives the child the space to experience the visit by itself. Sometimes even the child will push mom or dad away. "I don't need that mom", the child might say.

In some cases, I will tell the kid a little white lie to carry him or her through the treatment. After all The Easter Bunny and Santa Claus are invented to make a kid happy for a while also.

The child's imagination is huge so if I tell them the burr is in fact a brush and let them feel this brush with their fingers they are convinced it will all be ok.

I make up a lot of stories to grab the child's attention to the story and not to my dental instruments.

Almost all of my little clients undergo dental treatment well.

Jim

Microscopic view from Jim, or Innocence is bliss?

'Jim' (not his real name but because of privacy concerns, let's choose that name) is a 9-year-old 'autistic*' boy. I do not like classification but obviously, it is a description of his state-of-being. Actually, in other words; he is happy!

*I am convinced that people 'choose' a state-of-being before birth. The purpose, I think, is to emphasize the variety of people living on this planet (and maybe somewhere else too) and thus stimulate co-creation and people learning to love various kinds of people with their various kinds of consciousness.

Anyway, Jim, besides earning his bouncing ball, **is a** bouncing ball.

Jim is special because he evokes communication.

It's a special kind of communication because he understands every word *literally*.

This is so much fun to deal with!

A conversation with Jim goes like this:

'Jim; I have to scrape some tartar off your bottom tooth'. (I am Dutch; in Holland, we actually call it *'tooth-stone'*. It happens when plaque builds up and, as you already know, becomes harmful. It turns into a stone-like material).

Just before I could explain what this so-called 'tooth-stone' was (I *knew* he would want to know), he asked me, "Is it like the stone the walls are made of?"

"No, Jim, but that was a good question! Tooth-stone happens when there is food left for a long time. In this dirt there are bacteria. Do you know what they are?"

"Yes, yes, yes! I know they are little animals which are bad for you", Jim answered.

"How clever of you to know this about bacteria, Jim! Actually, they are not all bad."

"Ok... but you can only see them with a microscope, right Leslie? Or can you see the animals now?"

"No, Jim, I cannot."

He seemed relieved...

"You are smart Jim to know about a microscope!"

"I have one at home!" he said.

"Hey, would you like to take the tooth-stone home and check it under the scope?" I had it on my instrument... so why not give it to him in a sealed bag to bring home?

"Wow, wow, yes! Daddy can I take it with me?"

"Of course, Jim", his dad answered.

We sent Jim home with his father and the sealed bag containing the instrument with his tartar, to have it meticulously examined...

Well he must have had police escort while driving home because within ten minutes I received an email from Jim!

In the attachment file, I found a picture of the instrument under the lens... The bacteria were having a ball, just like Jim.

Jim is innocent... Jim has no fear.

He wrote: hi.leslie.here.the.picure.bye.jim

He made my day!

Bliss?

Ignorance is bliss? Innocence is bliss? Does that keep you from fear? How do you attack fear? Or do you just not attack?

Fear is an emotion. In prehistoric times, people really needed this emotion to stay alive! Men had to hunt for their food. No hunt, no food. Your fear arouses certain chemicals in your brain which make your body ready to 'fight or flight'.

Well, if you had the choice to have lunch *without* a grizzly bear or *be* his lunch, what would it be?

I think I would kinda sneak away…

Nowadays we find our food mostly in the supermarket.

Of course, fear exists, but is it really always about saving our lives? NO! Most of the time it is not.

Will that tiny little spider (you'd have to almost get Jim's microscope to spot it) kill you? Will the baby mouse?

Will the 'big boss' at work really kill you while he shouts at you? Will the crow up in that tree kill you? I mean Hitchcock's birds didn't even do that!

Should we just ignore things so we won't have to face fear or should we stay innocent? But does staying innocent mean we prefer to stay uneducated?

A lot of questions.

Jim is innocent: a lot of adults are NOT.

How can they lose their fear?

Cry if you want to

Gain your own power, or, the dentist can help you overcome your fear.

Please read the title of this chapter again…

Dentistry is a co-creative business. We are a team!

The *arrows* on the next page represent attention.

Co-creation and co-operation will more likely happen according to the top model than the model shown on the bottom.

Top drawing: all team members pay attention to one other, and the dentist is an empath! There is respect for every person

Bottom drawing: I call this the arro_w_gance formation. You'd better run!

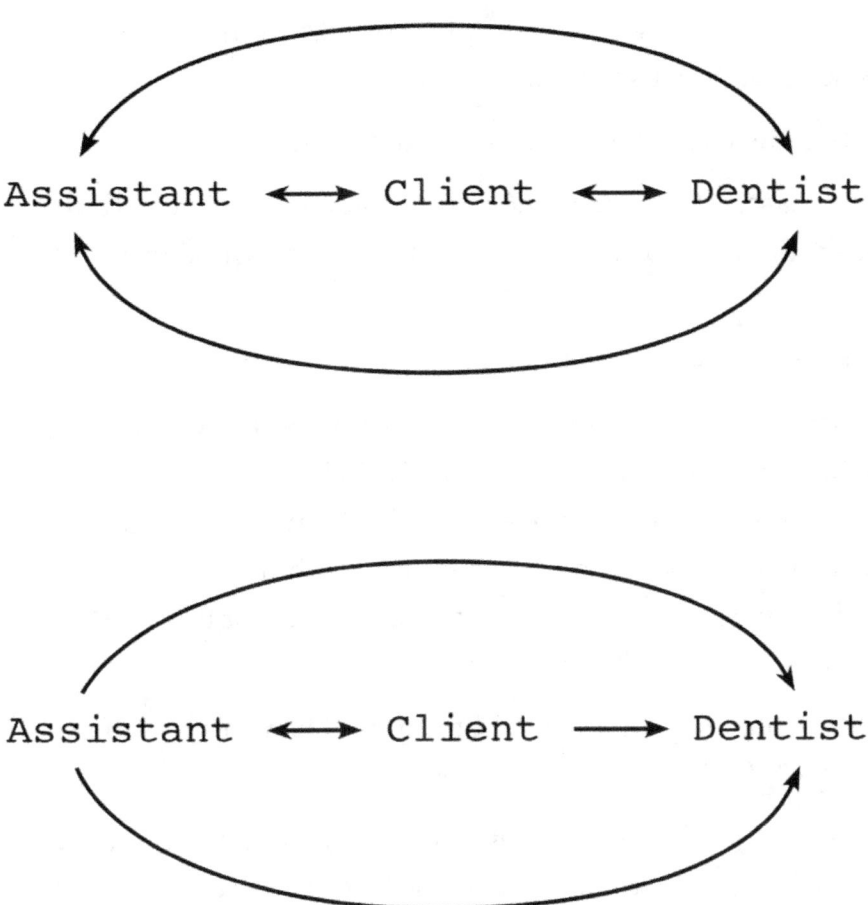

Occasionally, we do emergency shifts. Doing this means we get to meet clients from other dentists. They are in pain and clearly need help.

One patient was 'Fay', a 37-year-old woman. She was nervously pacing around in my waiting room. She told Carolien, my assistant, she was not in pain but had a burning question.

These emergency sessions, however, are not meant for questions only (as Carolien told her nicely).

However, I sensed something else was going on so I said I would see her if she could wait a while.

It became clear she did not have a dentist.

The reason she came to me was to ask whether she had to go to see a dentist ASAP because of a cavity or whether she could wait.

I mean… this is what fear does…

I answered all her questions; it took about twenty minutes. When I saw her tears coming up I told her to go ahead and cry! When people are this close to tears I always say: "You may cry. In fact, you should cry! It releases the build-up of stress." It indeed was clear to me she was less scared of the shark in the movie *Jaws* than she was of dentists, including me.

She asked me if she could become a client in my office. "Of course", I said. "You are welcome."

She did show up for the appointment; I complimented her and did the oral exam. It became clear there were several subsequent appointments that needed to be made. I acted as described in my chapter, 'Communication'.

I made sure to emphasize that she was the boss; I was merely a guide.

I gave her so much room and power back that during the latest visit she even laughed in the chair and was able to indicate the treatment she wanted to have done.

What we accomplished together was alleviation of her fear.

This is the way to go, don't you agree?

The dental exam

What do I actually do when I examine your teeth?

Well, I check whether your mouth is healthy. And indirectly, your body!

I do not *search* for caries.

<u>I also do cancer screening</u>!

Having healthy teeth means:

- no gum inflammation
- no active caries
- no jawbone inflammation
- no pain

I use special tools:

We use the *dental mirror* because it saves our backs; we don't have to bend upside down and backwards to check the upper left molar at the outside. To have the patient do a handstand might also not be too convenient.

The *probe*: a lot of people hate this thing and I understand why!

Then why do I use it? Because I use it the **<u>right</u>** way!

Wow, pretty bold statement, right? The probe serves as an extension of the finger... it is a feeler. I don't use the TIP of the probe but the *side* of the probe at the tip.

It is not handy to use a finger; they are too thick.

Does everything feel smooth? That's what I check. If the answer is no, then I need to find out why not? It might be a cavity, it might be a huge layer of plaque, it might be a broken tooth, it could be a dissolved root….

The probe is meant to be used only as a *whisker!*

It is not made to be used as a *drill.*

Don't poke around with it, dear dentists, and have a victory dance you found caries!

You might actually just have destroyed a demineralized spot which was in a perfect balanced condition (treatment not needed yet, see chapter 'treat or defeat').

Also, this poking around can hurt severely at some places. As I wouldn't want that to happen in my mouth, I won't do it to yours.

Remember Confucius' quote?

"Don't do unto others what you don't want others to do unto you."

A diagnosis follows (maybe in combination with X-Ray or hot/cold tests, for example) the examination.

A treatment plan follows the diagnosis.

In the treatment plan I always ask myself the question:

"What would happen if I didn't apply any treatment?"

A part of the plan can be: do not do anything.

Good 'monitoring' (follow-up) can be the best option in some cases.

The dentist can help you overcome your fear

Before leading you into the most important part of your mouth (and body), the *gums*, I have to explain the often-misunderstood difference between inflammation and infection.

Inflammation is not a synonym for infection. These terms are often used in the wrong way by patients (and sometimes dentists themselves).

Inflammation: (Latin; *inflammatio*) *is a complex biological response of body tissue to harmful stimuli, like a virus, bacteria, fungus or irritation.*

Infection: *is the invasion of body tissue by disease-causing agents, their multiplication and the reaction of host tissue to these agents and their toxins.*

So, inflammation refers to self-**protection**. The body starts a healing process! **(Isn't that wonderful?)**

Our infections, wounds, and any damaged tissue would never heal without **inflammation**!

Often people frantically ask me after having had a surgical procedure like pulling a tooth, tooth cleaning, or for instance a deep cavity treatment, "Do I now have inflammation?"

I joyfully answer: "Yes! You are lucky!" or: "I hope so."

At first, they don't understand. They thought they were in fact asking: "Do I now have an infection?" Then I would have answered: "I hope not."

The inflamed tissue **can** get infected, of course, but the infected tissue **will get** inflamed (at least when your immune system works well; hey, this a must) in order to heal.

Hope the distinction is clear for you now.

The gums can be inflamed, as can the jawbone as well as the tooth itself. More on that and the treatment of it later in this book.

The gum: SOUL of the mouth!

The soul can be defined in many ways.

Here are a few:

<u>'The essential or most important part of something'</u>
<u>'The spiritual part of a person believed to give life to the body'</u>
<u>'The person's moral and emotional nature'</u>
<u>'The central or integral part, the vital core'</u>

You are a **spiritual** being living in a body.

Obviously while we are on earth, our **bodies** transport us. Its action is steered by the **brain**.

The <u>real</u> person inside us is our spirit, I think.

We are a soul experiencing a life in a body on earth.

Our soul encompasses our emotions, will and mind.

The gums represent your inner body!

The gums or *'gingiva'*, consist of the *'mucosal'* tissue that lies over the upper and lower jaw. *'Mucosal'* means a biological layer.

Gums can have different colors:

Pink, red, black, and blue

Meaning of the colors:

Pink: healthy

Red: sign of inflammation, pathology[4]

---

[4] Pathology can have its origin in the gum or can be expressed *through* it.

Blue: inflammation of gum and jawbone, pathology

Black: racial pigmentation, pathology

<u>Diseases</u> which can <u>express</u> themselves include, *for instance*:

Crohn's disease, AIDS, some cancer types, Non-Hodgkin,

Diabetes Mellitus. Kidney disease, Anemia

Mind related!

Stress, fatigue, lack of self –love/esteem/respect

Stress induces an increase of cortisol which has an effect on the blood vessels. Stress can induce a dry mouth.

Also, stress and fatigue can cause people to not brush at all. They don't have the energy for it…

<u>Diseases</u> which have their <u>origin</u> in the gum are for instance:

Squamous Cell carcinoma, Herpetic stomatitis

Mind related!

Gingivitis, Parodontitis

<u>As the above is true, the below is also true.</u>

Gingivitis (inflammation of the gums) and Parodontitis (inflammation of the jaw bone) can cause:

Heart disease, premature birth, increased risk of diabetes, stroke, low birth weight.

More on pathology in relation to dentistry later.

The dentist saved my life

<u>I am sharing this office story to give you an impression about how I experience the body/mouth connection as a dentist.</u>

I'm so proud of my client, a 59-year-old woman who showed up in my office. She had lived on the streets for years and had climbed out of that situation and into a nice home. This woman is such a positive, joyous soul! How lovely.

She needed dental care.

During the dental exam it appeared obvious she needed all her teeth to be removed.

We decided to make not just the best of it but the greatest of it.

We had a lot of appointments; they went very well.

The color and the shape of the teeth in her dentures were properly chosen; I wanted them to fit her face!

Her last session was here: anesthesia, pulling of her front upper and lower teeth. She was ready for her dentures.

They looked great on her. I asked her to come the next day so I could make sure she was doing ok.

Getting dentures is a hugely significant procedure, mostly mentally. I need to really guide clients through this process. The next day she came and was happy.

However, she called me a couple of weeks later. She was in pain! This was strange because the type of pain in her gums she described to me didn't fit that which might be expected. In fact, I didn't expect that she would have pain at all.

Emotional Alignment Is Easy

I decided to see her in my office. I could not, however find anything to worry about.

The patient is always right about their sensation!

So I knew I had to investigate further.

Even though it was against the 'rules', I decided to take an X-ray. Always follow your intuition as a dentist.

But there was no sign of the cause of the pain she had. I felt kind of strange. It didn't add up.

The only thing left to do was to ask her to come back in two weeks if the pain was still there. She agreed. "If it was something to be very worried about, I would have been able to detect that today" … IF it was at all dental related!

I always keep that in mind!

Two weeks later she showed up again, still in pain.

I decided to send her to the oral surgeon for an opinion. I asked her to contact me after that visit. She said she would, and she did.

The comment of the surgeon was: "Everything still needs to heal in your mouth. Don't worry, it will pass."

Well, this was not what I wanted to hear; her gums were hurting. I asked her to contact me in one week at the most because I had a gut feeling something wasn't right.

A week later, she called me again. I decided to see the oral surgeon and communicated my concern.

He saw her that day and took a biopsy.

Diagnosis: *Non-Hodgkin Lymphoma!*

Long story short, she is grateful that I was stubborn enough to continue pushing for a diagnosis from the surgeon. All cancer treatments worked out fine: she is healthy now!!

She brings us chocolate every time she comes in!

Wrong tooth pulled

<u>Again an office story. This time about how cancer can reveal itself through a tooth ache.</u>

Mr. K., a 55-year-old man, showed up at my front office desk. He was crying and in severe pain.

I didn't know the man. Luckily, I was going to have a lunch break in a few minutes so I would be able to check on him.

The *anamnesis*[5] revealed the story of me being the fourth dentist in a row he had visited.

He had been given several treatments for the pain but nothing had worked.

Dentist #1: prescribed antibiotics

Dentist #2: filled a molar

Dentist #3: pulled a different molar

Again, all with no results.

The facts in the anamnesis didn't add up... The pieces of the puzzle didn't fit together.

Time for the examination:

It did not show any signs that worried me. All the tests were negative... it was weird. However, the gums showed a slightly different color than I expected. Red/light blue-ish; it's difficult to explain.

---

[5] Anamnesis: see next chapter

I took an X-Ray: no signs of an abnormality.

Mr. K. was still in severe pain. When the diagnosis is hard to make, you can use anesthetics: you locally anesthetize the tooth you suspect of being the villain, and when the pain is gone you *know* 'this' tooth must be treated!

I anesthetized a lower-left molar and… the pain was gone.

But still it 'felt' strange because the facts from the anamnesis and the treatment to be started didn't coincide.

I knew I had to start a root-canal treatment. I was sure of that, *but* I did not know *why!?*

The treatment went well, the patient went home, and I expected him to be completely pain-free as soon as the sedation wore off. I asked him to please call me the next day with an update.

Well, he didn't call me. He, again, unexpectedly showed up at my office… in severe pain!

This was the strangest thing! I felt just like the day before, when I was uncertain of the 'why'.

I invited him back to the chair. I couldn't figure out what was going on.

Although I'd taken one the day before, I decided to take one more X-Ray. Ridiculous! I mean, nothing could have changed overnight in his jaw, could it?

Trust you gut feeling, inner self, inspiration

And there it was…

The X-Ray showed some abnormality in the bone structure, something called 'sun-ray appearance'. I was in shock... This means trouble... it is usually related to some type of cancer! Why didn't I see this the day before?

I checked the X-Ray from the day before: again, no abnormality.

How could this be possible?

What (luckily) happened was: I took the more recent X-Ray under a slightly different *angle* so the structure became clearer and easier to see.

Now I knew why I didn't know *'why'*!

So, I suspected a terrible diagnosis for him.

I have to be careful about what I say when suspecting something like this because there are a lot of tests necessary for confirmation of the condition.

The thing to do is to refer the patient, diplomatically, to an oral surgeon to have it checked. You cannot say: 'Mr. K. I think you have some kind of cancer!'

Diagnosis: giant B-cell lymphoma (non-Hodgkin type)

Patient was kept in the hospital right away for treatment.

He was about to leave for vacation; they wouldn't let him go.

No worries! He is now totally cured! The root canal treatment I started was also a good decision. The oral surgeon asked me to finish it.

What would have happened if I had not taken the second X-Ray?

I would have sent Mr. K. to the surgeon that day anyway.

Because being in such pain after that initial treatment didn't seem ok to me.

All's well that ends well!

Anamnesis

According to the Oxford English Dictionary:
Anamnesis is 'the patient's account of their medical history'.

This is revealed in the conversation you have with each patient mainly on their first visit, in which you ask questions about their general and dental health, the reason for their visit, about specific problems or questions, about what has been done (or not) about it in the past, and about why they chose you and left the 'other' dentist, as well.

There are a lot of 'dental anamnesis lists' to be found on the internet; hence, I will not bother you with summing up all the possible questions here.

Role of the anamnesis:

- Assessment of the general and dental health of the patient
- Establishment of a successful dental-patient relationship
- Collection of necessary information for a correct diagnosis

One reason why the dentist needs to ask general health questions is because dental treatment <u>can interfere with some bodily diseases and medications.</u>

Please:

CEASE TO SEE THE MOUTH AND TEETH AS SEPARATE FROM THE REST OF THE BODY.

Oral health indeed affects general health (and as you now know, vice versa). Oral health also has an effect on chronic diseases.

Anamnesis right? = Diagnosis in sight!

Don't hesitate to spend at least twenty or thirty minutes on this first contact with your client.

This might seem like wasted time but it is not.

Patients will appreciate that you are willing to take the time to listen to them, and they will be more willing to tell you everything.

Dear dentists:

Do *inter*-act. Be a guide in this conversation.

Dare also to ask why they left the other dentist. What did the client expect? What do they expect from you?

Please avoid the fatal/vital question if you haven't seen a client in a while: 'What took you so long to visit me'? This will embarrass people. There is always a reason and it is none of your business (unless it is health related, of course)!

Rather be gentle and just say: "It is nice to see you again. I hope you are doing well."

I have often heard comments like:

- the dentist was mad when I showed up after x many years
- the dentist didn't take enough time to listen to my story
- the dentist was not even looking at me while talking

Dare to ask yourself as a dentist:

- Did I spend enough time on getting the medical history?
- Did I make EYE contact?

- Was I aware of the ethical (and legal) aspects?
- Did I dare to ask all the questions necessary?
- Did I explain the importance of that specific question?

Very important during this interview are non-verbal aspects:

- Your tone of voice
- Your position regarding the client
- Eye contact
- Quiet room

Be sure there are no obstacles (for example, computer screen or table) between the two of you. Sit, preferably, at the same eye height as your patient, if not a *little* lower.

This reduces the feeling of be interrogated by someone looking down on you. You, preferably, do not want to be 'looked-up to', right? Rather, you want a *co-creation* with your client with the aim of dental health.

Usually my client will sit upright in the dental chair, *or* they will sit **upright** in the middle of the chair with their legs turned towards me.

I will then sit in a regular chair facing them.

Or, they will lean against the back of the chair and I raise the chair so I will face them while standing.

When people are very, very scared, *I* will sit in the middle of the dental chair facing them sitting in a regular chair facing me.

People will leave your office as quickly as they came when they feel hurt rather than heard.

Your teeth are *living* body parts

Your teeth have blood vessels and nerves and a lymphatic system

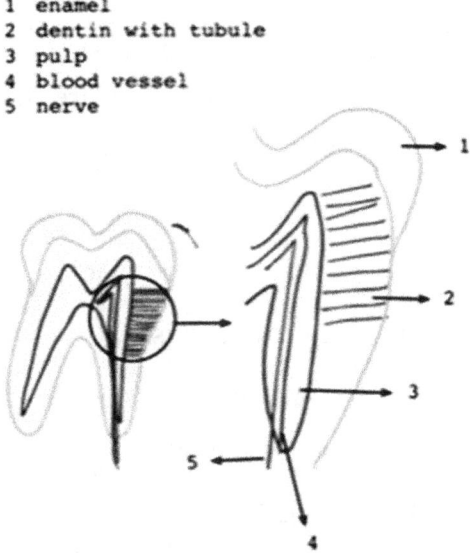

1 enamel
2 dentin with tubule
3 pulp
4 blood vessel
5 nerve

"So", you will ask "a tooth is alive? It has nerves?"

Actually, you already knew this. Think about it. What do we do in a root canal treatment? We take the nerves and blood vessels out of the canal.

The tooth cannot develop in a lifeless environment, and it cannot develop by itself if it is not inside a living body. Heck yes, the tooth is alive!

The blood flow helps the tooth grow and mature *before* it emerges in the mouth.

The formation of all teeth usually begins around the sixth week of embryo development! (Awwww, cute.)

The hard tissue covering the tooth, the enamel (the white or 'off-white' part, or natural crown, which shows when you smile) is made of crystals of calcium phosphate (hydroxyapatite). As you already know from the chapter **'Tooth',** enamel is the *hardest* part of the body.

Dentin is located beneath the enamel. While it is also a hard tissue, it's weaker than enamel. It has more organic matter.

Enamel does *not* have any living cells. Hence it cannot regenerate itself.

Dentin can regenerate with limited capacity.

This is why they invented the dentist...

The pulp is the central part of the tooth. It is here where the nerves and blood vessels are housed.

The lymphatic system of the pulp, the larger conducting lymphatic vessels, accompany the blood vessels and nerves in their course through the pulp.

The nerves are there to help you! You wouldn't think so, would you?

Maybe you've even wanted to ask a dentist, "Can't you take out all my nerves, so I don't have to come see you anymore?"

The nerves serve you when they cause pain - it is a warning function. It warns you of the presence of danger: for instance a cavity or an infection.

It's true, however, that when a tooth has completed its development and reached its final position in the jaw, it no longer needs its nerves and blood vessels to remain functional.

That is why the nerves can be removed in a root canal treatment and the tooth can remain in the patient's mouth for a lifetime.

It can still take part in life functions such as:

- Laughing
- Eating
- Chewing
- Speaking

Isn't that wonderful?

So the tooth is alive (and sometimes kicking) with its blood vessels and nerves.

After the root canal treatment, the tooth is considered dead (R.I.P.) but, again, it can remain functional in the mouth.

Your tooth is connected to the body through the blood vessels and nerves.

The blood which runs through your veins run through your teeth.

The nerves are connected to the larger nerves in your jaws and head.

The lymphatic vessels are connected to your entire immune system.

So, now you (can learn to) understand the _why_ of for instance:

- The question of general health in the anamnesis
- Dis-eases elsewhere in the body can show in the gums
- The impact medication can have on your teeth
- Mental dis-eases can reveal themselves in your mouth

To the bone

As described in the chapter 'Anamnesis' and in the last chapter 'Your teeth are living body parts', we learned that there is a connection between dis-eases and the gums, teeth, and mouth.

The teeth are connected to the jaw-bone, the jaw-bone is connected to the neck-bone, the neck-bone is connected to the head bone… Hey, this sounds familiar.

Wait a minute. Isn't that?

Yes! That is from the song called: **Dem Bones/Dry Bones by James W. Johnson**

Performed for instance by Delta Rhythm Boys:

"Dem Bones Dem Bones Dem Dry Bones"

To me the most *goose bumpy* performance of this song!

Watch it online:
https://m.youtube.com/watch?v=mVoPG9HtYF8

Leslie van Oostenbrugge

Lyrics:
Ezekiel connected dem dry bones,
Ezekiel connected dem dry bones,
Ezekiel in the Valley of Dry Bones,
Now hear the word of the Lord.

Toe bone connected to the foot bone
Foot bone connected to the heel bone
Heel bone connected to the ankle bone
Ankle bone connected to the shin bone
Shin bone connected to the knee bone
Knee bone connected to the thigh bone
Thigh bone connected to the hip bone
Hip bone connected to the back bone
Back bone connected to the shoulder bone
Shoulder bone connected to the neck bone
Neck bone connected to the head bone
Now hear the word of the Lord.

Chorus
Dem bones, dem bones gonna walk around.
Dem bones, dem bones gonna walk around.
Dem bones, dem bones gonna walk around.
Now hear the word of the Lord.

Ezekiel disconnected dem dry bones,
Ezekiel disconnected dem dry bones,
Ezekiel in the Valley of Dry Bones,
Now hear the word of the Lord.

Head bone connected from the neck bone
Neck bone connected from the shoulder bone
Shoulder bone connected from the back bone
Back bone connected from the hip bone
Hip bone connected from the thigh bone
Thigh bone connected from the knee bone
Knee bone connected from the shin bone
Shin bone connected from the ankle bone
Ankle bone connected from the heel bone
Heel bone connected from the foot bone
Foot bone connected from the toe bone
Now hear the word of the Lord.

Chorus
Dem bones, dem bones gonna rise again.
Dem bones, dem bones gonna rise again.
Dem bones, dem bones gonna rise again.
Now hear the word of the Lord.

Finale
Dem bones, dem bones, dem dry bones.
Dem bones, dem bones, dem dry bones.
Dem bones, dem bones, dem dry bones.
Now hear the word of the Lord.

This well-known spiritual song's lyrics are inspired by Ezekiel 37:1-14, where the Prophet visits the "Valley of Dry Bones" and declares a prophecy that they will one day be resurrected at God's command, picturing the national realization of the New Jerusalem.

The book of Ezekiel is a prophetic book in the Old Testament. Its theme includes the concepts of the presence of God and purity.

God transported Ezekiel (probably not literally, but in a vision) to a valley full of dry bones and directed him to speak to the bones. Ezekiel was to tell the bones that God would make breath enter them and they would come to life, just as in the creation of man when He breathed life into Adam. Ezekiel obeyed, the bones came together, flesh developed, skin covered the flesh, breath entered the bodies and they stood up in a vast army.

This vision symbolized the whole house of Israel that was then in captivity.

Like unburied skeletons, the people of Israel were in a state of living death, pining away with no end to their judgment in sight.

Translated to the now: people are very judgmental. It is always the other's fault. People are not happy; overlooking their own power and giving it away, clogging their own pipes.

Well, I am not 'biblical', but the text on the former pages regarding Ezekiel resonates with me. Different 'biblical' people will tell you different 'biblical' truths, which is fine with me; your truth is your truth and you seem to live well by it. Your truth cannot be false! Neither can mine… because we live happily with it, right? Just like one's feelings. *Your* feelings are *your* truth, and *my* feelings are *my* truth.

Or, are you not happy? Then you might want to change your 'truth'…

I have a personal belief in a supernatural realm. I have a quest for sacred meaning and also a strong belief in the wonders of the Universe.

I think that the concept 'Lord' can also mean 'inner being'.

We are all spiritual beings!

This is our truth. This is our true nature. It is the core of our being

We Cannot Not Be Spiritual

As a matter of fact, I hardly ever use the word 'spiritual' because I believe it makes some people think of something they're not able to attain. "He/she is very spiritual" might be something you will hear. Well, *you are,* ***too!*** Being 'spiritual' often sounds like something out of reach, out of sight or out of mind.

The truth is, though, that it is within your reach, within sight and surely within your mind.

I like to say:

"We are personally empowered."

I am not at all a judgmental person (saves a lot of energy, I can tell you that).

One of the biggest compliments I have received in my life was:

"You are brilliant at accepting everybody as they are."

Chemistry of stress

We all know that 'good stress' is sometimes beneficial because it can provide a temporary extra boost of energy or alertness which increases performance.

It is a short, intense burst of energy/tension/anxiety that is felt before events like exams, job interviews, going somewhere new or riding a roller coaster.

But cortisol, the major stress hormone, has negative effects. Over the long-term, it can cause chronic stress which can be detrimental to mental and physical health.

Cortisol is produced by the adrenal glands, located on top of the kidneys.

Cortisol is a steroid hormone. Its primary function is to redistribute energy (glucose) to regions of the body that needs it the most, <u>primarily to reduce inflammation.</u>

Stress was needed in prehistoric times, remember? When we had to hunt for food and duck for cover from life threatening animals. Our body prepared us for <u>*Flight-or-Fight*;</u> the brain and muscles were needed.

Run-and-Hide or Stay-and-Fight!

An example of the *flight-or-fight* response in everyday life now could be getting startled by a loud noise.

As a part of the body's fight-or-flight response, cortisol also acts to suppress the body's immune system!

Stress suppresses your immune system!

Your immune system is your defense system. It defends the body against influences (bacteria and viruses, for instance) from the outside which can make us sick.

The immune system is the total of organs, tissues, cells and cell products that all work together to fight the intruders.

Now, remembering the fact that the function of cortisol is regulation of inflammation, remember inflammation is natural!

Mechanism:

<u>Chronic stress -> Cortisol long present -> Body gets resistant to cortisol -> Inflammation decreases! -> More vulnerable for diseases!</u>

Chronic stress can cause people to develop anxiety, sleep problems, depression, high blood pressure, heart disease and digestive problems. Stress can affect you mentally as well as physically; the dentist can recognize these problems!

The lymphatic system

Most people think of the white blood cells and antioxidants as the main parts of the immune system, but the _lymphatic tissue_ also plays an important role in keeping us healthy.

The lymphatic system helps us fight germs, bacteria, viruses and fungi by distributing immune cells. For dental health, the lymphatic system helps to fight infections so that the gums and teeth will stay healthy and strong.

Most people are not aware that this beautiful system runs through your teeth.

Immune system cells

Neutrophil	Eosinophil	Basophil	Monocyte
T Cell	B Cell	Natural killer	Macrophage

Every single cell has either its own or a combined function. Target: attack all foreign bodies in the body. Isn't it amazing how your own body helps you to stay healthy? Your body is designed to keep you healthy...

Many dental procedures, sometimes even the tiniest dental cleaning and, of course, surgical treatments, can cause bacteria to infiltrate your body.

Some clients of mine need antibiotics before every single treatment in which it's possible that this could happen. Bacteria can even infiltrate after I have, for example, put a mold around your molar when doing a filling. This can happen no matter how careful I am.

Bacteria can infiltrate the body even when you brush your teeth. Don't worry, though: most people have brilliant immune systems.

When a tooth is infected, its contents drain via the lymphatic system through your entire body.

A lot of health problems can therefore arise in people with a depressed immune system after dental procedures!

There can be:

- Toxins from root canal treatments,
- Mercury residue when removing old fillings
- Bacteria infiltration through procedures

The lymphatic veins need us to 'pump up the volume' because they have no pumps of their own (valves). They need us to exercise enough so the muscles work as a pump to keep the lymphatic fluid going. So while in the gym remember: *'I am keeping my teeth healthy'*

So, are some treatments still safe? Should we dentists still carry them out?

Love your K9's!

At least 90% of the adults in my practice do NOT like their teeth!

Especially NOT their cuspids.

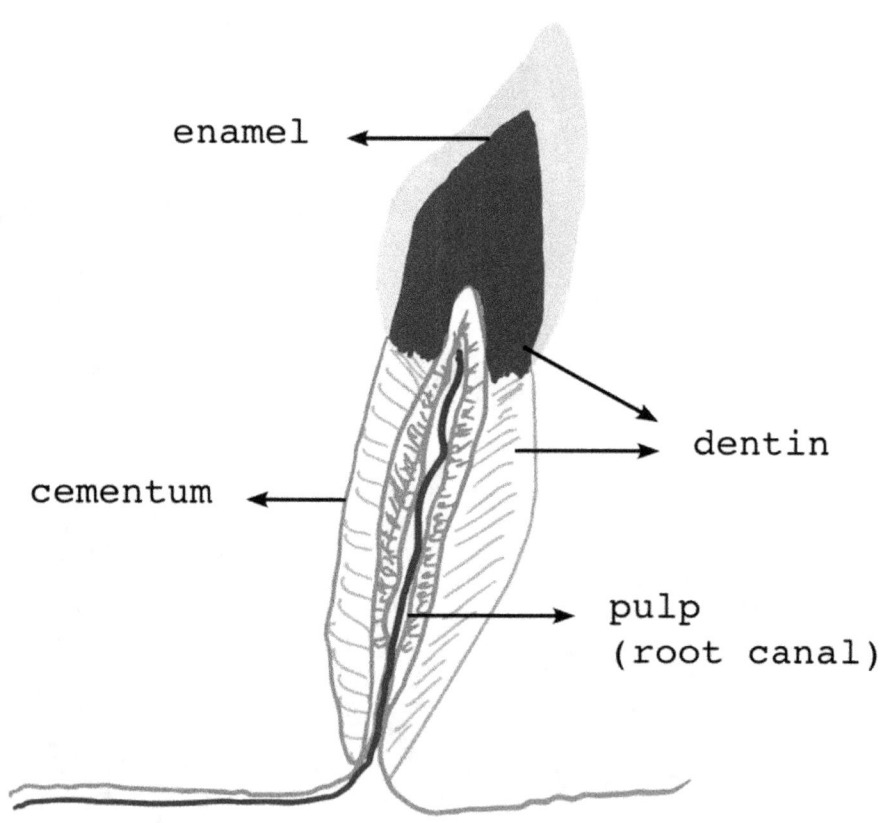

Why the cuspids? Because you tend to find them too yellow.

Well, they indeed tend to be (are) more yellow (*-ish)* than their neighbors (front teeth and premolars).

This is because the dentin tissue in your cuspid is much thicker than the dentin tissue in your adjacent teeth. The color of dentin is dark yellow-brown-*ish.* Because of the thickness of the cuspid-dentin, the 'yellow' will shine through the white enamel covering the dentin.

People can have thick dentin and thin layers of enamel; the yellow will show even more.

One other reason (which I do not like to mention) is *age*.

Although the cells of your body constantly renew themselves, the cells of the enamel and the dentin do **not.**

The dentin grows thicker during life so the yellow will shine through the translucent glass-like enamel.

So that's why tooth color changes.

There are other factors that can cause the teeth to darken. The first and most significant is poor oral hygiene. (A chapter will follow about cleaning) Additionally, specific foods and/or drinks can accelerate stain formation between cleanings; the tannins from teas and wines are recognized for their stain-forming ability. Also, medications taken during the formation of teeth (most notably tetracycline antibiotic) and dental trauma can lead to tooth discoloration.

You can change your attitude to your teeth; be thankful and show love for them. I know, this is tough sometimes!

How do you do this? It takes practice.

That is the mental part.

The physical part is the one in which the dentist comes in handy!

We are able to give you good cleaning instructions, and maybe put in a new fresh filling or bleach your teeth.

After this correction, it might be easier to love and be grateful for your teeth.

Loving your teeth is a part of loving yourself.

Don't we have an issue here? Maybe **the** issue of most people's lives: we do not love ourselves (enough)!

You can only experience two things in life:

Love, or the absence of love...

That's it, that's all.

Once you know this, all else is easy. Actually, you know this on a deeper level - your spiritual level.

Many complaints are being heard by me about teeth, weight and diets for instance.

Sometimes I can help as a dentist; sometimes I **won't**...

A patient of mine was very unhappy with the color of her teeth. She wanted all her healthy teeth pulled out at the age of 54. I had given her so many options on how to save her teeth. She didn't agree with any of them. She begged me to give her dentures. I declined her wish...

She went to a different dentist who pulled 28 teeth.

GPS

As a dentist, I see myself as *your guide.*

You come into my office for a check-up, which means you want to have my advice, right?

My advice regarding:

- your cleaning
- your dental health
- the options and treatment plans when something is wrong
- your gums
- your jawbone
- your joints
- your children's dental health
- your dental costs
- and so on

Of course, I know you come to the office when you actually don't want to. That's okay!

I will do my best to make you as comfy as possible at the dentist. I will be as polite as I can. I will be as helpful as I can. I will be as gentle as I can. I will address your problem as professionally as I can. I will give you advice as honestly as I can. I will not be ashamed to say, 'I don't know'. I will refer to colleagues when it is necessary for your dental well-being. I will not do any over-treatment. I will remember that the tooth is a part of your body and your whole being. I will play a role in prevention against (dental) sickness. I am honored to be able to have *your* mouth as *my field of* work.

Sounds like part of the *Oath of Hippocrates,* right?

The Hippocratic Oath is an oath historically taken by physicians. It is one of the most widely known of Greek medical texts. In its original form, it requires a new physician to swear to uphold specific ethical standards, to treat the ill to the best of one's ability, to preserve a patient's privacy, to teach the secrets of medicine to the next generation, and so on.

I always act in accordance with this oath. Yet, on occasion I sense some distrust from patients about my advice and proposals for treatment.

The reason for this is usually quite simple: money.

Please be assured that I am not here to pick your pocket.

Of course, I understand visiting the dentist costs money, just like it does when you have your car fixed, eat in your favorite restaurant or buy the beautiful clothes you wear.

You couldn't do any of those things with a huge tooth-ache, could you?

I advise clients to have their teeth (and especially the gums) checked regularly, like twice a year - just like having your car checked.

I am a guide, not a judge.

This is especially applicable in cases of aesthetics/cosmetic dentistry.

Cosmetic dentistry is dental work that improves the appearance of a person's teeth, gums and/or bite.

It improves the appearance, not necessarily the *function*.

Who am I to tell you your teeth are ugly? Who am I to tell you that you have to fix the color or position or form of a tooth?

Who am I to...?

Shopping cart

We want to create a beautiful, gorgeously aesthetic filling.

Have you ever wondered *how* and *where* we obtain our filling materials, burs, hand pieces, finishing materials, primer, bonding, tissues, napkins, cups, glasses, X-Ray machines, curing lamps, brushes, and instruments?

Well, we go to our dental shops. We shop online or in-person at the dental depots, or we have the account managers come to our offices. We get magazines or flyers just like you do at home.

Shops are very competitive and have a lot of attractive price promotions.

So it is very worthwhile to compare prices!

We can get discount coupons, bonus materials, kitchen knife sets, and free visits to the Spa, and even win trips to the Bermuda Triangle.

Luckily, I have the best assistants on earth who are like Scrooge McDuck browsing the flyers for discounts. Why pay *four* times the amount just because retailers are able to put the word 'dental' in front of the product name? 'Dental' plastic rinsing cup? For me, it is the same as a 'regular' plastic rinsing cup.

We, of course, order them in a specific color:

Orange. It matches the interior of the office.

So, Carolien and Jose, my assistants, shop until they drop… tissues, brushes, wedges, burs, dental cups, filling materials…

Wait! I have something very important to tell you! Hang on!

There is one BIG item at the top of my Dental-Market list: 'quality'. I buy quality stuff! Of course, a cup is a cup, wake-up, wake-up…

But filling materials on sale? Primers and bondings? Don't mess with them!

How can we judge the quality of a filling material? How do we judge the quality of the primer? What about the bonding? (Primer and bonding precede the application of the filling in the cavity.)

I judge it by checking the results of testing, which you can read about in dental scientific magazines or learn from colleagues, courses, or lectures.

Don't worry. I don't just throw random stuff into my shopping cart and use it on your teeth, hoping everything will be okay in a few months!

In some cases, there are way too many options on the market.

It is like buying matches; they all work but which matches should you buy?

A little-known aspect for the customer (you) is the reality of the *costs* of these materials…

High quality materials <u>are</u> expensive. By high quality I mean, for instance, tough enough to resist your chewing activity, slow wear, relatively easy to apply, and low shrinking percentage.

Q: This also means there are cheap materials, right? Why would a dentist buy them?

A: Because they save the dentist money.

Q: Is it smart?

A: *No!*

Q: Why not?

A: *Clients might experience* **pain** *afterwards* because of the chemical characteristics of the material.

Like every other market, there is rubbish for sale on the dental market.

Amalgam: filling material that is an alloy of metals, including *liquid mercury, zinc, silver, tin, copper.* It is cheap to buy.

Pros and Cons for the dentist:

Pro:

- Cheap for sale
- Fast to apply

Con:

- Mercury might run through your veins! It is poison....

Prior to applying the composite filling, a primer and subsequently the bonding ('glue') is applied.

(See next chapter: '... **and fill**')

Some primer and bonding systems are very cheap and very easy to apply.

A bit like the many hair 2-in-1 shampoo with conditioner systems we've all seen, there are primer and bonding systems: *2-in-1 primer and bonding in one application.*

Pros and Cons for the dentist:

Pro:

- Often cheaper than the separate system
- Saves time instead of using the separate system

Con:

- The 'glue' in some '2-in-1' systems have poor adhesion!

Now, would you want your filling to fall out?

I also prefer to buy tools which are comfy to work with, easy to handle, 'patient friendly', nicely designed (my eyes like nice looking things) and last but certainly not at all least, easy to clean and disinfect.

What we need for a filling:

- 'Mold'
- Primer and bonding
- Cotton roll
- Wedges
- Brushes
- Curing lamp
- Filling material in applicator
- Filling material
- Modeling instruments
- Tray paper
- Tray
- Counter top

'...and Fill'

Now, finally, I am going to tell you something about filling and filling materials.

As promised earlier in this book, I am not going into chemicals, procedures, and dental science and know-how too deeply. There is so much on the Internet that you can explore. If you're interested, just *Google*; *filling, dentist, anesthetic, fear, amalgam, composite, veneers, crown, bridge, implants, drills, endodontics, glassionomeres and more.* Let yourself be guided and informed.

If you do not get an answer to your question you can always email me;

leslie@theawakeningdentist.com

I am happy to assist you!

You can divide the restorations into two main categories: d*irect* and *indirect.*

Direct restorations: involve placing a filling into a prepared (by burs usually) tooth cavity *immediately.*

They are placed in your tooth layer after layer and light-cured in between.

A variety of filling materials are available: for instance, *glass-monomers, amalgam ('silver' filling)* and ('plastic') *composite.* Amalgam will harden once placed in the tooth directly after preparation. Composite or glass-monomers will harden because of the light-curing lamp or because they contain two component chemicals substances so they harden by themselves.

The procedure for *'preparing the tooth for the filling'* (dentist talk: *'preparation'*) will depend on whether it is an amalgam filling and a composite filling.

See the picture below:

A: Composite/plastic fillings

B: Amalgam fillings

Usually with the amalgam fillings more of your precious tissue has to be sacrificed.

A: preparation can be cup-shaped because of the bond/glue; it will stick

B: preparaction needs to 'undercut' the enamel otherwise sticky food will pull our filling out.
It also coms in handy for gymnastics; when doing a handstand the filling will stay in place.

Indirect restorations: involve customized tooth replacements in the form of *crowns, bridges, inlays* or *onlays and veneers*. These generally have to be made by the lab after dental impressions have been made, or after computer scanning. This is why indirect restorations are usually achieved in two visits. Examples of materials are porcelain and gold.

New techniques, however, make it possible for you to get a crown the same day. This is CAD/CAM Dentistry. So you might get the question; 'do you have any errands to run?' from your dentist so they can fix the crown in that time.

Check the next drawing to find out wat part of your tooth/ filling has to be removed in order to place a crown, bridge, inlay, onlay or veneers. Veneers are mostly only for a front tooth or cuspid.

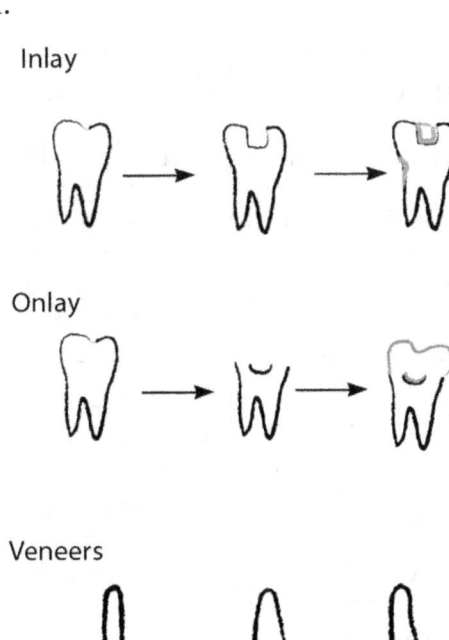

The restoration 'vs's':

Indirect	Direct
Huge tissue loss by preparation	Minimum tissue loss
Expensive treatment	Way cheaper than indirect
More visits/longer office stay	One visit
Dental impressions/CAD-CAM	Application of filling
Insurance covers poorly usually	Insurance covering 75-80%
Need a skilled dentist	Need an **_artistic_** dentist

Technician needed	No technician needed
Can still chip off porcelain	Can break/chip/loosen
Repair: not porcelain or gold	Easy to repair
Sometimes root canal treatment	Less needed
Retention sometimes tough	Retention easy through bonding
Allergic reaction possible	Allergic reaction possible
Dental cement needed	Dental primer and bonding
Tough to take off without damage	Easy to take out

Every dentist has his/her own preference with regard to which type of restoration to use. So, often the decision the dentist makes does _not_ depend on the amount/form of the tooth to be restored but rather the dentist's personal preference! This is something you need to keep in mind when looking for a dentist.

You might encounter a dentist nearby who favors the composite or even amalgam filling, but the next dentist around the corner might think you need a crown. And then a different dentist might advise you to have the tooth pulled...

Filling materials.

I am the dentist who very, very much favors **_direct_** restorations. Yes, because of all the facts mentioned in the 'vs' chart.

You have been blessed with the precious gifts of beautiful enamel and dentin, blood vessels, roots, nerves, lymphatic system, all wrapped up as beautiful teeth.

Who am I to destroy this delicate, well-balanced system?

"What do you mean, *destroy*, Doc?"

"Well, I mean I don't want to drill away more tissue than necessary."

The drilling procedure was invented to carefully scoop away (doesn't sound like it, I know) the infected part of the tooth, the part in which caries is settled. The drill was not invented to wreck the tissue which is left just to be able to place a crown.

I love that 'they' invented composite filling material. It is a 'clay'-like material that comes in many, many tooth colors.

After the drilling process is over (and you are relieved), I start the filling procedure.

It is like putting clay in a mold; I push it gently in the mold without squeezing in air bubbles. I will use special composite modelling instruments, shape it, and let it harden. Take it of the mold and shape it again with a burr. Voila!

Here I go. I:
1. Place the mold
2. Place the dry cotton roll
3. Place wedge in between mold and neighboring teeth

4. Rinse and blow-dry cavity
5. Apply primer
6. Apply bonding (glue)
7. Cure-light it (it hardens)
8. Place first part of filling
9. Gently press it in the cavity with instrument
10. Cure-light it
11. Place next part of filling
12. Gently press it in the cavity with instrument
13. Cure-light it
14. Place next part of filling (if needed)
15. Take out the wedge and the mold
16. Model this composite clump of composite w/ a bur
17. Check 'the bite'

There are a few kinds of filling material. I will address these three:

- Composite (white)
- Amalgam (dark-grey)
- Glass-ionomer (white)

Because composite glues onto your teeth, it is not necessary to take away any more healthy tissue than needed when filling with amalgam. Amalgam *doesn't stick* to your tooth. It is also soft when applied; it hardens by itself, with no curing light needed.

Other facts:

Amalgam is a combination of metals: *silver, mercury (!), zinc, tin and copper.* It is silverish grey in color. I need an **amalgam separator in my unit but it is allowed to put it in your mouth**.

Anyway, *I* wouldn't want mercury running through my veins, would you? Let it stay in thermometers, please. People can be allergic to it.

Composite also contains monomers, Bis-GMA, silica, and photoinitiators that people can be allergic to. It can shrink.

Glass-ionomer contains silicate glass powder and a specific acid. It is white but not as smoothly polishable as composite.

Because of their characteristics, different direct restoration materials are sometimes used in different areas of the teeth: on top, near the roots, beneath the gum.

Many studies have compared the longevity of composite restoration to that of the amalgam restorations.

Depending on the skills of the dentist, patient characteristics (allergic?), and the type and location of the damage (near/under the gums?), composite can have similar longevity to amalgam restorations.

The aesthetics of composite material, of course, are far superior to those of amalgam.

So the more than often heard excuse dentists make when they say: "You'd better take amalgam because the composite fillings are weak"- is outdated.

It takes more time for the dentist to apply a white filling than a silver one, but this should never, ever be an excuse to avoid restoring teeth like new!

One of the things I love the best about composite is the fact that I can restore your teeth like new, modelling the cusps and the fissures (highs and lows in your molars) in their original colors and places

It is important to use quality material.

Studies have shown:

- Cheap primer/bonding systems do not adhere well
- Filling materials might cause dental pain
- Cheap composite might wear fast
- Instruments might break in your tooth

It is important to fill composite in thin layers.

Studies have shown:

- Because of the shrinkage you have to fill in layers

New patients often ask me whether they really should receive a white filling because they have experienced pain in the past when they'd had a tooth restored with composite.

To me this seems to be the result (exclude the factor of drilling too close to the pulp with its nerve) of applying the wrong type of bonding and too much of a bulk of composite at once (not in layers). It shrinks too much off the walls of the tooth, and this overloads the nerve!

Of course, I sometimes place a crown, but this is only when I think a composite crown will not achieve the same aesthetic and/or functional result. This, for *me*, sometimes occurs with the front teeth.

I hardly ever place a bridge because often you have to sacrifice the next-door neighbors. An implant then *might* be the best thing to do. The costs of an implant plus crown are about the same as a bridge.

®

Pain is the second most common reason for consulting a dentist. The first reason is the half-yearly check up!

Pain in dentistry can be caused by: trauma, a huge cavity, pulp irritation, bad cleaning, *your dentist*, braces, bone disease, and more.

But, isn't it ironic? You are in pain, but you don't want to call the dentist because you *believe you will* experience pain.

Too many people will put up with pain until it becomes severe, at which point they'll finally see the dentist. Remember that pain could be a symptom of something more serious for which you need treatment.

Pain is an amazing incredibly fantastic warning system: 'hey, you!! Something is out of balance somewhere in here', your body screams.

Guess what? We dentists can reduce the pain by using anesthetic (or teeth sleeping water as I call it with kids).

Awwww, yes. I forgot. You are afraid of the needle.

I know, dear people, I know…

I am <u>not</u> saying: "There is nothing to be afraid of." I know you *have* experienced the needle many, many, times and it hurt, right? Right?

You got programmed/conditioned according to the following equation:

NEEDLE = PAIN

Emotional Alignment Is Easy

This is absolutely understandable.

Luckily, there are things that we can do to help reduce or eliminate your pain:

- *The Wand®:* is a CCLAD (Computer-controlled Local Anesthesia Device)
  It delivers anesthetics painlessly and effortlessly.

- *N2O:* nitrous oxide or laughing gas :-)
  Not to be confused with "NO" from the **'chemistry of pleasure' chapter**, although that molecule might make you smile at the end, too!

- *Narcosis:* State of unconsciousness
  Induced by a narcotic drug in operating room!

The above-mentioned options are terrific options.

However, they are <u>more expensive</u> than regular dental anesthetic (dentist with needle) and more time-consuming for the patient as well as for the dentist.

Fortunately, I have my invention: Patien*t*ce ®

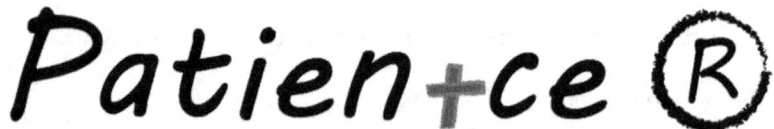

Benefits of this system have proven to be huge!

Clients are absolutely wild about this and very thankful.

I keep my office costs low. When I buy an expensive machine I cannot ask a higher dental fee. In the Netherlands we have fixed dental fees.

So time, expensive materials, and so on cannot always be included in the fee.

First some chit chat about 'the' needle.

The needle is designed *not to hurt*; it is bevel- shaped at the tip.

Sharp part of needle to go into gums/flesh <--- = direction of fluid/anesthetics

Dental needle with beveled edge on the left -> which enters the gum. The other part of the needle goes inside the ampoule with anesthetic on the right.

Now, mind this: *only half of the needle will punch your flesh....*

Q: 'Then *why* does it hurt, Doc?"

A: Because the needle is inserted by a dentist *not using the Patientce®.*

Patientce® is *the* way to get <u>painless</u> anesthetics;

The invention is simple: patience with the patient! Giving painless anesthetics is *no more than* taking time to deliver the drug. Really; take at least one whole minute to give one ampoule. That's all, folks!

Just before I enter your gums, I sprinkle a few drops of the anesthetic liquid on your delicate flesh, then I punch with the beveled side of the needle through the tissue and gently and very, very slowly apply the fluid. I watch your face and eyes (out of the corner of my eye) to make sure you are ok, then I gently move the needle forward, continually releasing the fluid.

After 1-2 minutes I am finished. I always tell you that it takes quite a bit of time for me to administer the anesthetic (1-2 minutes might seem like a lot when somebody is 'doing something' in your mouth and you don't know *what*). At first you are surprised (*that long?*), but then you understand.

Physical Pain, Mental Pain

According to the Oxford English Dictionary pain is a: "Highly unpleasant physical sensation caused by illness or injury." Stubbing a toe, delivering a baby, burning a finger, losing a loved one, falling off a bike, getting divorced (mostly), being bullied are pain causing issues.

The world would be overpopulated if the wish of so many female patients was granted; "I would rather give birth to a baby than go to the dentist" is a well-known declaration in the dental chair.

The above-mentioned incidents all cause pain, either physically or mentally. Pain motivates the individual to withdraw from the environment which harms them so the body or mind can heal. We learn to avoid such stimuli in the future.

The definition of 'pain' is tough to give because it is a complex, *subjective* phenomenon.

The definition of pain according to the

International Association for the Study of Pain:

"Pain in an unpleasant sensory and *emotional experience associated with actual or potential tissue damage, or described in terms of such damage."*

In medical diagnosis, pain is *a symptom.*

In the dental office, we are confronted with dental pain, or toothache. This is pain in the teeth and/or their supporting structures, caused by dental diseases or pain referred to the teeth by non-dental disease.

Common causes include:

- Inflammation of the pulp (result of decay/trauma)
- Dentin hypersensitivity (exposed root)
- Apical periodontitis (inflammation of the bone and ligaments, around root apex)
- Dental abscess (localized collection of pus)
- Gingivitis (inflammation of the gum)
- Pulpitis (inflammation of the tooth nerve)

These will all be addressed later on.

When people come in my office, a standard question of mine is: "Do you have dental complaints or pain in your teeth?" When you say no and I tell you I have to make X-rays, you can sometimes be somewhat distrustful saying: "*Why? I do not have any pain, so I do not think anything is wrong!*"

Unfortunately, I have to tell you, you are 'wrong'…

Enamel is non-vital tissue, as you know by now, right?

It doesn't have blood vessels, nerves (the *inside of the tooth does, but not the enamel*), and living cells.

Therefore: *Pathological processes involving **only** the **enamel** tend to be painless.*

Pain mechanisms and pathways:

How does pain arise?

How does pain reach your brain?

What is needed to experience pain?

Of course: stimuli, either physical or mental are needed.

Why do *mental* stimuli hurt? Have you ever thought of that?

Even *thinking of the dentist hurts...*

Well, I would never have guessed, while studying dentistry, most of you would have to *drag* your bodies into my future office... Even clients of mine who encounter me around town, at the bakery, in the restaurant, on my bike, or in the gym, are usually not happily surprised.

But... that is *your* monkey, right?

So, what about the mental PAIN?

How does that reach your brain?

How does *emotion* cause pain in the body?

Well, it appears that: **emotions can cause activation of the same areas of the brain as when people feel physical pain.**

Isn't that something? So, physical and emotional pain have similar neural signatures: the same nerves are responsible to guide these stimuli to the brain where you will become 'aware' of the intensity, form, and duration of the pain.

The brain is massively interconnected with all the cells of your body.

Physical pain: there is an obvious clear link between hitting your cute small toe against the post of the couch and the awareness in your brain *of the location of that physical injury*. Route: nerve endings-synapses-nerves-spinal cord.

Emotional pain: *must then* have a physical location in the body because their stimulus end at the same spot, right?

Emotional Alignment Is Easy

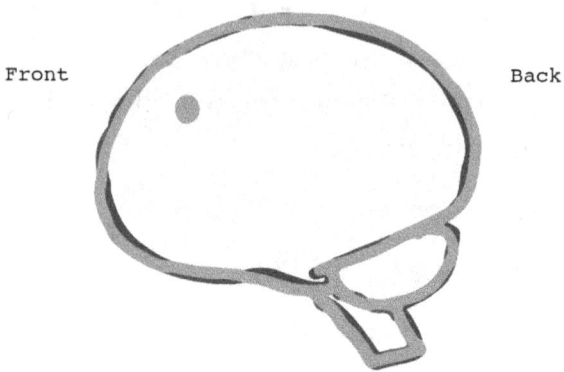

See the drawing above of the anterior insula.

Then in what way might emotions be *embodied?*

Your *heart* can be broken, somebody is a pain in the neck, you are sick to your stomach...

All emotions have a motor (muscle) component!

Even if you try to hide your feelings, there will be a micro-momentary muscular activation. Instead of crying in the dental chair due to fear you might still have residual muscle tension in your neck.

Sometimes you try to hide feelings at my office: your anger (I'm here again! 6 cavities because you didn't take the time to properly clean your teeth), your despair (will she be careful?), or your worries about your child (you envision the child experiencing the same anxiety you have).

Often you do not succeed in hiding your feelings. I will sometimes tell you that it is ok to cry (I've already said this, haven't I?), as it releases and relieves emotion.

I am trying to create an environment in which you might start to feel comfortable... eventually...

Most established clients of my practice are pretty comfy.

New clients? We will hopefully help them to reach their comfort zone.

We really do our best to keep you out of the vicious dental merry go round.

That is our contribution; you do the 'rest', ok?

Emotional Alignment Is Easy

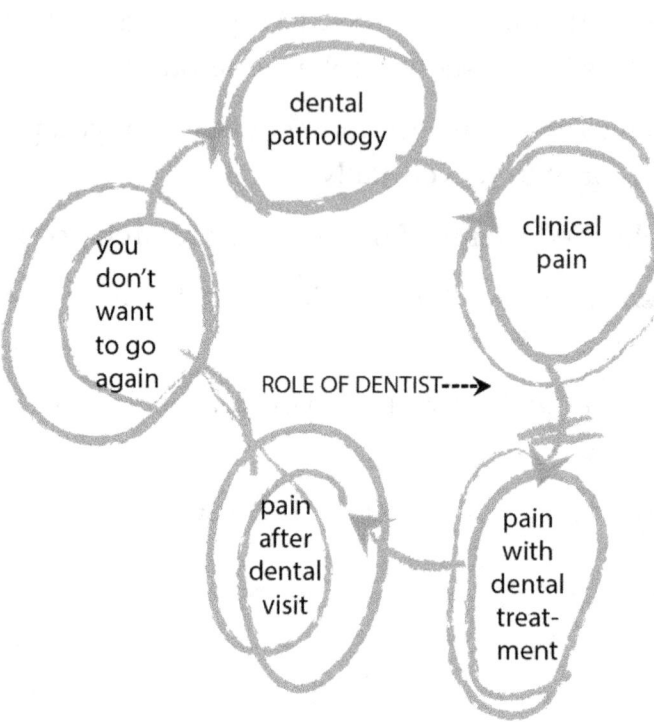

The role of the dentist is to cut the connection between 'clinical pain' and 'pain with dental treatment' that occurs as a result of fear.

House of teeth

The role of the dentist is to help the patient through a treatment, which is hopefully as painless as possible. Another part of the dentist's role might be creating an environment that is **low** in stimuli which might reduce extra fear.

I, for instance, decided to use colors in my house of teeth (otherwise called a dental office) different than the regular blue or apple green. While there are certainly beautiful offices decorated in these colors, I decided to step outside my comfort zone to use orange and red, instead.

Red is the color of energy, passion and strength.

Orange symbolizes health, attraction and happiness.

I make sure as many of my accessories as possible are red and orange including, for example, cups, face masks, mirrors, coffee mugs, and suction tips. Red and orange instruments like composite modeling instruments and dental mirrors with red handles and orange frames are my favorites. Our uniforms consist of orange shirts and orange/red shoes and even orange socks! Sometimes I encourage patients to play a game where they spot as many red and orange things they can!

It is a 'non-hospital, sporty look'. All of my patients love it. The adults appreciate the cheerful colors, and the kids think the look makes us cool. They even comment on the socks!

They all like the poster I have on the ceiling; it's something they can look at instead of my face (lol). I prefer a poster to a television screen. TV overload is everywhere, and it inhibits communication. Plus, imagine if I had to duck so you could see your favorite show.

When I started my practice, I did not realize how much of an impact the colors and design I chose would have on my patients. I'm glad I trusted my intuition.

'House' with teeth

In my view, another of the dentist's most important duties is allowing clients to be 'themselves'.

(The **big** question, however, is what is 'being yourself'? I discovered the answer… you can read about that later in this book, in Part II.)

We can encourage patients to be themselves by:

- Communicating well
- Working from the heart
- Providing access to clients' favorite music
- Being gentle while working

Never rush through things (for example, because you're running late or the next client is waiting) to fill all six cavities *today*. The client will invariably sense it and feel uncomfortable, and you'll experience more stress than necessary.

When I cannot finish 'the work' I am supposed to do *today*, I will inform the client: "John, I know you'll probably be very disappointed but I have to tell you that I do not have the time to finish ('you off' might be the joke afterwards) my work today… I know you hate to come back. I am sorry but I need to be able to take the time necessary to do a good job." People usually understand.

Sometimes we dentists run into unexpected things such as cavities being bigger than is apparent on X-rays, roots being more crooked than can be seen on X-rays, or clients being more nervous than expected. All these things demand more time.

I said to a client once: "Dear X, I am really tired now, actually. I do think it would be in our shared interest to make a new appointment. I have to get some rest." (I had to fix a molar which was broken to the gum-level.)

Well, the client very much appreciated my honesty.

Dare to be vulnerable, dear dentists. After all, we are human…

My heart tells me also to have 'room' for all of your feelings (including the bad mood you'll probably be in because you're visiting me). If I do not leave space for you to express that, you will be more nervous and less likely to trust me. Allowing you to release the tension you feel will make you more open to whatever procedure needs to be done.

This kind of approach is my natural state of dentist-being. However, I know many other dentists have a different kind of attitude and that at other offices you probably haven't had the chance to get a sentence out before the needle is in your mouth! Unfortunately, it's a kind of a 'shut your mouth but keep it open'-thing.

I will even tell you to bring your own music on an iPod or smartphone, if you'd like. Alternatively, you could just listen to *my* radio blasting through throughout the office; I don't care. As long as it will raise your vibration it is fine with me.

My working field is *in* your body while you are lying backwards… it is a vulnerable position. You think that I have power over you.

Do NOT Give your POWER away. Never, ever, ever.

I will guide you during the surgery or other procedure. I describe all the steps involved (that is, if you want to know).

For example, first the mold… now primer… now bonding… now first layer of composite then the curing light… now the second layer… and so on. It gives you an assured feeling.

I will use my mirror and probe (whisker) very carefully, remember? I won't poke around. Hey! It is not a hokey pokey clinic!

Once I have done my part of the teamwork, what is yours, dear patient?

Despite all my efforts as a dentist, some of you are still very grumpy. You might be worried and blame me. Perhaps you have tears in your eyes and make nasty remarks while taking *da* seat. You've been so afraid that you didn't sleep.

Maybe you've hardly slept for a week because of your worry about a 15-minute procedure.

Stop and think: is there anything you could do to alleviate this fear in advance?

Metaphysical meaning of pain

So, we know pain is a symptom, right? Pain has a profound meaning. It means tissue damage and it wants to 'tell' you something. How do we recognize pain as a symptom? As a symptom for what? And what is *the cause?*

The following might be very unexpected and tough to chew on. Bear with me; it's worth reading.

We <u>**ALL**</u> know there are *more* things in heaven and earth, don't we? Of course! You recognize the feeling when you meet someone and it seems *'like you have met years before'*, or when you enter a room and think to yourself, *'this doesn't feel right'*.

There are things that exist that you cannot see.

But… *WHAT* is out there*?*

'Meta' is a word-forming element meaning;

- 'After, behind'
- 'Changed, altered'
- 'Higher, beyond'

Metaphysics, according to the Oxford English Dictionaryis a:

"Branch of speculation which deals with the <u>first principles</u> of things, including abstract concepts such as beings, knowing, identity, time and space."

This is, in turn, from Greek *'ta meta ta physica'*, meaning: *'after the* Physics'.

This name was given to the works of Aristotle by Andronicus of Rhodes, a Greek philosopher. Andronicus was most famous for publishing editions of the works of Aristotle, Greek philosopher and scientist (384-322 B.C.). History tells that while Andronicus was arranging the works of Aristotle in the library of the Philosophical School of Alexandria, he placed the work after the ones on Physics and named it:

'After the Physics'-> *'ta meta ta physica'*

Aristotle himself named his own work 'First Philosophy'.

So there is a kind of misunderstanding there in the name giving. Andronicus placed the work of Aristotle in the library just behind the branch 'Physics' and named it 'metaphysics'. Aristotle didn't like this but it could not be renamed.

Metaphysics is the crucial, rational and systematic study of existence. It is a critical inquiry into the origin, nature and destiny of human existence and our place in the cosmos. It is an investigation of reality.

Aristotelian 'physics' is different from what we call 'physics' today. He was referring to *'philosophy'* instead of modern *'physics'*.

The chief purpose of Aristotle's work was to discover the first principles and causes of change, movement, and motion, especially that of natural wholes.

So it is a philosophical study of nature and the physical Universe! (From particle to the Parallel Universe?) It was dominant before the development of modern science.

Science is based entirely on knowledge that is testable, with which we can make predictions about the Universe.

Metaphysics, on the other hand, is a traditional branch of philosophy concerned with explaining the fundamental nature of *being* and the *world* that encompasses it. It attempts to answer two basic questions in the broadest and simplest terms: *Ultimately, what* is there? And *what* is it like?

In current popular literature, the term 'metaphysics' is often used more loosely, meaning simply the non-physical. Thus, 'metaphysical healing' means healing through remedies that are not physical.

Quite a long story (I know *you* struggled through this; I am proud of you). But it's always worthwhile to discover that deep-rooted words, as well as things, thoughts, habits or beliefs can be built upon facts which appear to be not true or the result of misunderstandings.

Wow... it makes you wonder what is 'true' about history.

I have *always* been the inquiring type. It must have started from the moment I could think my own thoughts. The detective in me wasn't always welcome, especially in college, but I didn't care and still don't. I simply must find the answers.

I could sense people's emotions and speak aloud things I wondered about myself. I was often surprised by my own answers.

At a very early age I told my mother she was egotistical in missing *her* mother! It was kind of a surprise to myself saying something like this. Where would I get this kind of information? Her mother had died about 10 years prior to that moment.

I have always felt that 'dead' is not 'dead', but rather out of sight. I was convinced we could actually talk to her if we wanted and knew how to.

At a later age, I bought many books regarding the afterlife, speaking with the dead, near death experiences, ghosts and so on.

Unfortunately, being too busy with 'down-to-earth-life', I never read them… until many, many years later.

Your body as a manifestation

Everything on the physical plane is a manifestation of something on the metaphysical plane.

The signs and symptoms that are apparent on the physical plane should lead us to inquire more deeply into ourselves as energetic and spiritual beings. What a blessing it would be if everyone all around the world did this.

I would call that a www: worldwide wonder.

We tend not to worry too much about anything if our body seems fine; if there is no pain, if there is no bad disease and all goes well. But… when we **do** get pain, are having troubles or become disabled, we want to know the big *'why'*. Do you want to know the big *'why'*?

Or do you just 'go see the doctor' and have physical problems fixed as they arise? Do you have your neck repeatedly crushed by a chiropractor, have your lower back injected every month by the other doctor, or, lo and behold, have your teeth fixed every half year?

In a later chapter, I'll discuss a study carried out by Ellen Langer PhD, in which a group of elderly men in the 1950s were able to steer the functioning of their bodies with their minds. Their pain disappeared.

What if this could happen to **dental** pain?

When our body is in pain or does not work according to our expectations, it is not broken. It is TELLING us something.

One of the functions of the body is to carry messages from the higher energetic planes to us. In fact, we are translators of energy waves (vibes).

The body is like a river, constantly flowing and changing.

It is like the wind, an empty space containing a swirl of energy.

The body is an idea of the mind… In other words, we are not our bodies.

The mind came first because you decided to come live here in this body, so the latter came second. The millions, even trillion cells of our bodies know what to do, can repair anything that is off and tell the brain what they need.

Our cells obey the natural cycle of rest and activity; they follow the deep understanding of life embedded it our DNA.

We used to think that DNA was a given, a static, stable chemical. Little did we know that DNA is responsive to everything that happens in our lives.

DNA is responsive!

We are responsible!

So, cells are not here to attack us! We are not the victim of our cells.

We use our body's sense organs:

- Eyes with their trillions of beautiful cells (visible light comes in waves; 390-750nm),
- Ears (audible sound comes in waves, frequency; 20-20.000Hz),
- Touch (e.g. feeling texture; your skin vibrates 50-300Hz),

- Nose (smell; receptor gives off an electric signal to the brain in waves),
- Taste (receptors for bitter, sweet, sour, salty and savory give off electric signals to the brain).

All these signals go to the brain. They get translated *there!*

Now, *we do* recognize; we see a bird, we hear a motorcycle, we feel sand, we smell the flowers and we taste the bittersweet.

"Then *what* does that tell us, Doc?"

You just said; *"When our bodies are in pain or do not work according to our expectation, it is NOT broken. It is telling us something (some thing)."*

According to Western wisdom and Western medicine: we feel pain because we have so many receptors and nerves. That's it; that's why!

So, accordingly, the 'Western' approach is to determine where this pain comes from *physically* and then to attack it with painkillers, drugs and/or surgery. The pain receptors get numbed and/or the sick part of your body will be taken out by the surgeon. It is a wonderfully terrific method for repairing that broken ankle or stitching that wound so you won't bleed to death. It's terrific, but often ultimately temporary.

Thanks to all the professionals who pour their energy and passion into treating and curing people!!

Actually, this also sounds like **my** job. I love my job so much. I love to make that beautiful filling so you can go ahead and chew your favorite food again and drink a cold beer. You might ask, "Why on *earth* did you become a dentist." My reply would be, "Assignment of *heaven*…"

Human beings have made amazing strides in understanding science and health. And yet, it unfortunately must be said: the more we know… the more we don't.

We don't know what we don't know…

We, 'patients' have learned that 'someone *else*' can and will take care of *our* health or be in charge of our own illness. In fact, we have been educated and raised that way. We have the doctor's or dentist's number saved securely in our iPhones.

Preferred time to call: *just before your weekend starts.*

BUT there is a trend going on, a shift, actually: people are increasingly encouraged to take responsibility for their *own* health.

It is as much for economic reasons as for reasons of spirit and human development.

I love when I give you instructions about how to properly clean your teeth, and you actually follow them. I love seeing you for your next check-up and seeing that all is well, and that there are no cavities, gum irritation, or any other problems.

You are relieved and you thank **me** very much, but actually it was **you** who did it. I was merely the guide, remember?

No pain, but gain.

Ancient wisdom and ancient medicine says that people are encouraged to take responsibility for their own health/lives. We use our bodies to communicate with ourselves (first!) and with others. We tend to judge our pain and sick body negatively... but according to the ancient Taoists, 'good' and 'bad', 'right' and 'wrong', 'yin' and 'yang' are just different points of view. They are typical human (ego) statements!

Of course, there is such a thing as 'being sick' and 'being healthy'.

The ancient wisdom and all its (whole-istic) holistic[6], meta-physical healers look at different energy levels; healing occurs on one or more of these levels.

The holistic approach is often called 'alternative'; it's a healthcare philosophy in which the entire patient is evaluated and treated.

Did you notice that this sounds like my approach? I do not see teeth as being separate from your body, mind and soul.

Example: a holistic approach to a certain kind of pain in your teeth.

<u>Problem</u>: last week pain in left upper molar, but now pain is slightly gone.

<u>Examination</u>: nothing appears to be *visibly and X-ray-y 'wrong'* (yet) with that molar.

After asking the patient some more (after having had the anamnesis), I was being guided to check the muscles around the TMJ[7] joint. These muscles felt very, very tense.

---

[6] holistic means emphasizing the importance of the <u>whole</u> over the independence of the parts/ concerned with wholes rather than analysis or separation into parts.

[7] TMJ-joint=Temporal-Mandibular-Joint. It attaches your lower jaw to your head.

It appeared that client has been 'clenching' and 'grinding' his teeth. This habit had started three weeks earlier as a result of the divorce he was going through.

In clenching and grinding, he had been pressing his teeth against each other. This 'pressing' happens when you (unconsciously) tighten your jaw muscles. This gives such an enormous overload to the nerve of teeth that it can result in throbbing, aching tooth pain. It is like hitting your elbow against the door over and over again; the nerves in your elbow will protest and eventually will hurt without any stimulus.

Many, many misdiagnoses have been made concerning these kinds of matters. People have been mis-treated; for example, a slightly painful molar might have received a root canal treatment unnecessarily! Instead; the client should have had instructions to relax his jaws and jaw-muscles.

Let's look at a metaphysical approach to dealing with tooth pain from decay caused by irregular brushing or poor diet.

The fact that you haven't been regularly brushing as you should and eating healthfully points to the likelihood that it is hard for you to stick to routine and you refuse to recognize what you need to do to take care of your long-term well-being.

You mistrust authority, including your own.

Allowing your teeth to 'rot' means you have given your power away. It is time to have courage in your life again. Issues might have occurred in a past life, which you have to solve now… for your own sake.

The moral of this toothache story is:

Take your body seriously! Pain is the only way through which the body can say: "Hey, something is not quite well here!"

Not paying attention or, in many cases, totally ignoring your feelings is ignoring your emotional wellbeing.

This can lead to many dis-eases.

Periodontal disease:

This affects the soft tissues (gums for instance) and bone. It is initiated by the increase of a specific bacteria (P. Gingivalis).

It impairs your immune system.

Caries (dental decay):

This affects your enamel at first. It has been causally linked to the bacteria Streptococcus Mutans.

These bacteria love to live in the dental plaque which sticks to your teeth immediately after a meal.

When bacteria that cause tooth decay and gum disease enter your circulatory system, your liver releases C-reactive proteins which have inflammatory effects. Inflammation is a disease-causing force leading to many chronic illnesses.

This is why brushing and cleaning in-between your teeth is life-saving.

Inflamed and diseased gums may increase your risk of fatal heart attack by up to ten times! When people need heart surgery, the cardiologist will refer them to the dentist first!

If there is just one thing that you remember from this book, it should be this:

Bleeding Gums Are Not Ok, Go See A Dentist!

I have had new clients tell me: "I have had bleeding gums all my life." I tell you: this is not the way cells will treat you if you are taking care of your teeth and yourself.

<u>Periodontitis is related to diabetes, coronary diseases, rheumatoid arthritis and low birth weight babies!</u>

Please, do not tell me that you smoke…

Mechanisms of oral pain

How does the physical pain component work? How come you can *feel* the pain? Well, you need nerves, cells and a brain; we have those!

The trigeminal or 5th cranial nerve or CN **V**

(tri=3, -geminus=thrice twined) has three branches.

1 eye branche
2 upper jaw branch
3 lower jaw branch
4 ganglion
5 5th cranial nerve

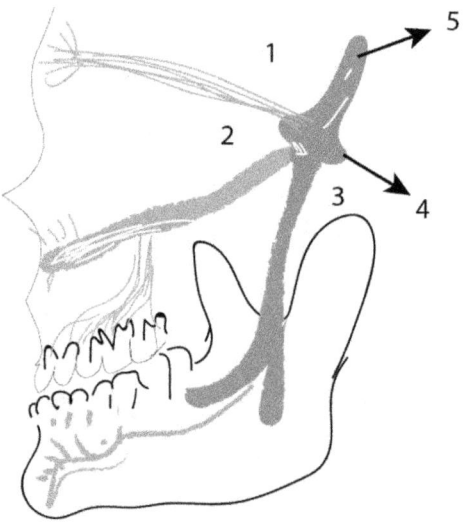

This drawing shows that at number 4, three different branches enter the 'nerve knot'. Can you understand why that means **you** therefore sometimes might NOT be able to determine where your pain comes from? You sometimes think the pain comes from an *upper* molar but… it appears to be a problematic *lower* premolar or your TM joint, or even your ear or your sinuses!

The eye and upper jaw branch are only sensory! This means the branches can only inform your brain about things connected to the senses (no movements).

The lower jaw branch has sensory as well muscular function.

A ganglion is a 'nerve knot'; the CN **V** divides into 3 branches.

I have to show you the next drawing because it is important in explaining how a pain stimulus travels to your brain.

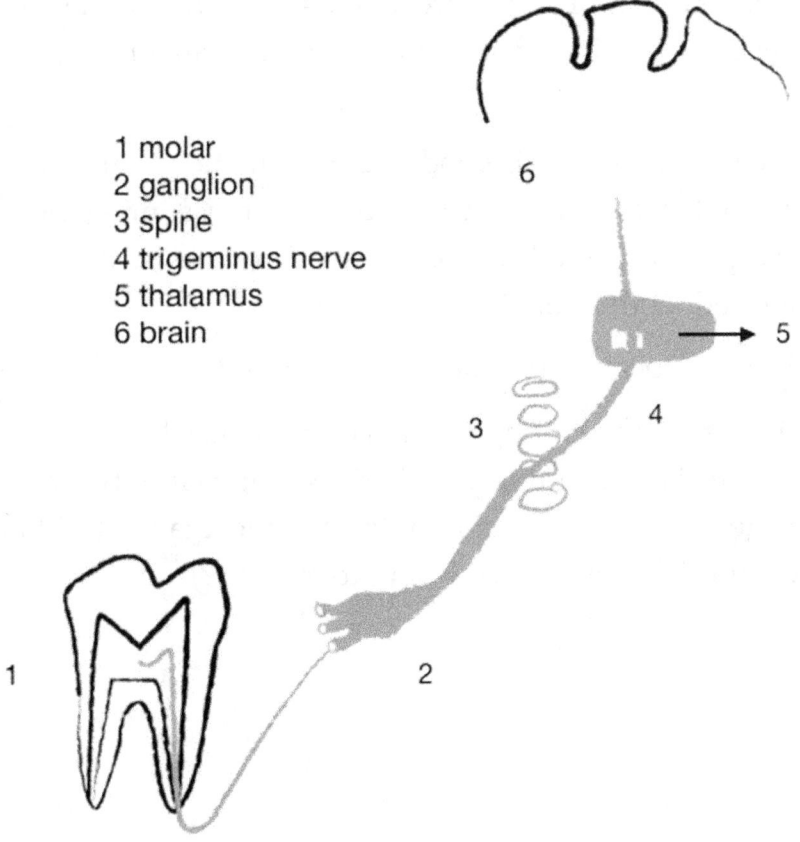

1 molar
2 ganglion
3 spine
4 trigeminus nerve
5 thalamus
6 brain

It is only when the stimulus reaches your brain that you will be _aware_ of either a feeling or a command to move a muscle.

This is the pathway of the stimulus until you say "ouch". The stimulus could be, for example: hot coffee, cold tea, your fingernail, a hair of your toothbrush, the icy wind outside, the dental bur, trauma or even your tongue when pushed against a tooth. This stimulus will travel to your brain.

But when you point your finger to that specific molar, how do we dentists know we will treat the right one?

A lot, and I mean a **lot,** of misdiagnoses have been made and subsequent inappropriate treatments have been done because dentists just followed the finger of the patient and started drilling…

When our anamnesis is good, our examination is great and we still aren't 100% sure which tooth to treat (assuming the cause of the pain is a tooth problem), we _of course must_ numb the suspected tooth locally!

If the pain goes away… the culprit is found!

(Message for my colleagues: it is easy to anesthetize locally in the lower jaw with the Anesthetic Syringe Gun. But be very, very gentle and careful not to damage the ligaments. Nothing new, right? Anyway… who am I to tell you?)

4 x ¼

Upper, lower, left, right. Communicating about teeth is easy! Patients will for instance say, "My upper right… (pointing to their tooth *under the right eye*), is that *your* upper left, Doc, or what?"

Well we always look from the patient's point of view:

Your right tooth is YOUR right tooth

Yes, even if I am standing upside down and looking in the mirror…

So, when I am talking to you on the phone because you have a problem I will ask, "Is it the tooth at your left eye or right eye side?"

In the dental world, with colleagues, I talk about the numbers the teeth are given. The sides of the mouth also have (Latin) names.

That's why you hear us say 16 (one six; not '16'); it is the 6th tooth of the 1st quadrant.

When you have a cavity, you might hear a dentist say "34 disto-occlusal." Or we take a short-cut and say, "34DO."

This means you have a cavity in the rear part of the premolar in the third quadrant. "Oh great, thanks! Wait, what did you say, Doc?"

So, if you complain about the yellow left upper cuspid, which number is that? With your new knowledge, maybe you can figure it out.

So 'your lower left molar' is your lower left molar.

But in dental world we give the teeth and molar numbers while facing to you.

Look at the next picture; imagine it is someone with his mouth wide open in front of you. Now the countdown starts:

Number 1 is the first tooth (incisor) in the second quadrant, so that front tooth is called the "21" (two-one).

Number 2 is the second tooth (incisor) in the second quadrant, so that tooth is called the "22" (two-two).

Number 3 is the third tooth (cuspid) in the second quadrant, so it is called the "23" (two-three).

Number 4, is the fourth tooth (premolar) in the second quadrant, so it is called the "24" (two-four).

Number 5, is the fifth tooth (premolar) in the second quadrant, so it is called the "25" (two-five).

Number 6, is the sixth tooth (molar) in the second quadrant, so it is called the "26" (two-six).

Number 7, is the seventh tooth (molar) in the second quadrant, so it is called the "27" (two-seven).

Number 8, is the eighth tooth (wisdom tooth) in the second quadrant, so it is called the "28" (two-eight).

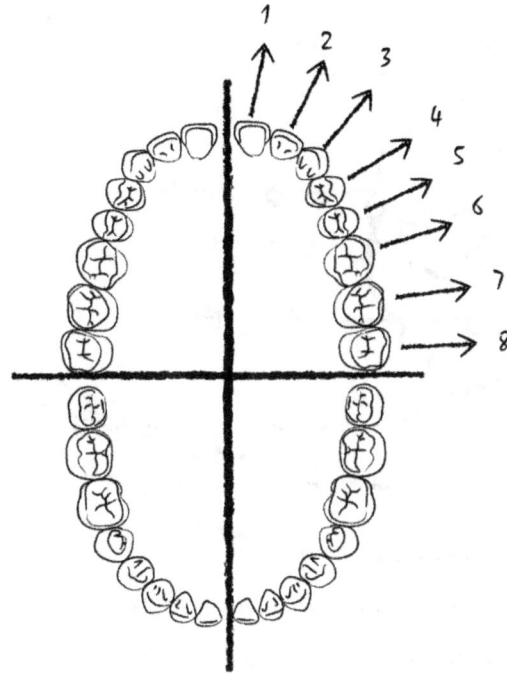

The quadrants: under upper right eye (upper right jaw) is the first quadrant; under upper left eye (as shown in the picture) is the second quadrant; low left jaw is quadrant three, and lower right jaw is quadrant four!

Emotional Alignment Is Easy

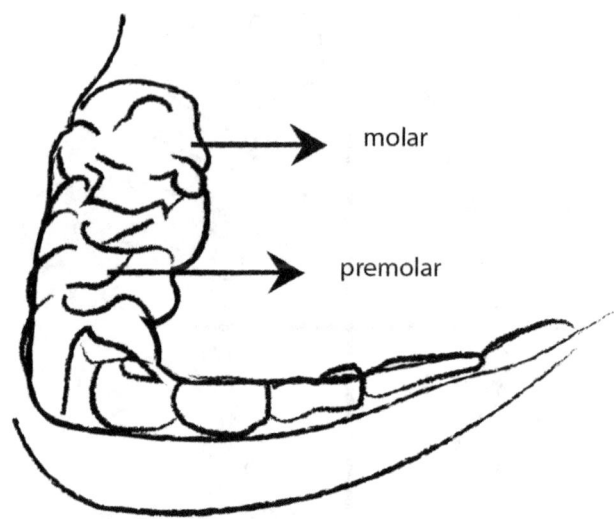

For a different view, check this picture: here the premolars and molars of the right lower jaw are shown.

The numbers of premolar and molar (arrows) are the 47 and the 45.

Tooth development:

All your teeth are present before birth and can be present thousands and thousands of years after you die.

By eight weeks after conception the tooth buds of all primary teeth can be discerned, by twenty weeks the tooth buds of the permanent teeth start to develop.

Tooth eruption times vary from time to time, the ages are averages.

Age 5-6 *months*: the child's first primary teeth appear.

Age 2.5-3 years: most children have their full complement of 20 primary teeth. Ten in the upper jaw and ten in the lower jaw.

The lower teeth tend to appear two months before the upper teeth.

Age 5-6: the first permanent (lower incisors) teeth as well as the four first permanent molars (upper and lower) start to appear in the mouth. These molars erupt at the very back of the mouth *behind the last primary molars*. As no teeth fall out to make way for these new *permanent* molars, it is not unusual for the emergence of the first molars to go unnoticed.

Many parents and kids therefore are surprised when I show them the first 'grown-up' tooth has erupted. This is always a special moment to share.

Over the following six years or so all the primary teeth fall out and are replaced by permanent teeth.

From about 11-12 years the four second molars appear behind the first molars which showed up when you were about 5-6 years old.

The last teeth to appear are the third molars also called the wisdom teeth or M3's.

These can erupt anywhere between the age of 15 to 85.

When you have had dentures for many years and you are experiencing pain all of a sudden, the eruption of a third molar might be the cause.

There is a considerable variation in the development as well as the eruption of that M3. The tooth bud might not have developed at all or you can even have 5-6 M3's. It might erupt horizontally, it might not erupt, think of any variation and it might be true.

Be-cause

As referred to in chapter 'Physical pain, Mental pain', there are many causes of dental dis-eases.

A. Inflammation of the pulp (pulpitis)
B. Dental hypersensitivity
C. Apical periodontitis
D. Dental abscess
E. Gingivitis

'-itis' at the end of a word refers to inflammation.

A: Pulpitis: inflammation of the pulp because of the entrance of bacteria in the pulp/or because of trauma. Cause of pulpitis: caries leading to dental decay! Because of bad cleaning of the teeth, usually!

The reaction of the body to the invasion of bacteria into the pulp causes this pain. Remember, caries is a disease.

Another cause of pulpitis can be: trauma to the teeth!

Trauma is represented by "direction of the stimulus" in the next drawing.

Trauma can be a high impact-short duration force:

A blow to your teeth while fighting, injury while falling from your bike, while in the pub getting your glass elbow-bumped into your front teeth, and so on.

In the worst-case scenario, the nerve and blood vessels can be ripped…

Trauma can also be a low impact-long duration force:

A constant force like pen chewing while studying, teeth clenching or grinding because of stress, or nail chewing!

These forces are similar to the forces that cause RSI's. Repetitive Strain Injuries of your arm, wrist, or thumb, for instance, because of long, intense computer work while having a bad posture.

Because of the constant nagging force, your nerve gets really upset... your tooth will hurt. You are not able to touch it anymore without pain. Brushing even hurts!

It is as if you have bumped your head five times at the same spot...the nerves will overreact at the <u>slightest touch.</u>

Your tooth will react the same way as any limb will react on high short-, or low long impact forces: it can break, it can 'sprain', it can (partially) dislocate! It can bleed inside, it can become discolored, it can heal itself from within or be cured with professional help.

I mentioned the low impact-long duration force of <u>nail biting</u>. I am appalled by the number of children who have this habit! At a very young age I can see enamel loss because of the tear and wear caused by, in most cases, trying to release stress through gnawing. Of course, many grown-ups have this habit, too.

In some cases, it has even led to a root canal treatment!

The nerve of the tooth has had such a blow it cannot recover from that on its own. Sometimes the dentist needs to take out the sick tissue.

Sometimes pulpitis can even be introduced by… your dentist! Leaving a restoration too high can lead to the nerve getting overloaded whenever you simply close your mouth with slight teeth contact. Hence it is very important for the dentist to check the height of the filling and ask the patient to confirm that the right and left sides of the teeth touch at the same time when closing the mouth.

Sometimes though, it is tough to register that because of numbness after anesthetics.

In this case beginning pulpitis can resolve on its own when the stimulus is taken away, which should be as soon as possible.

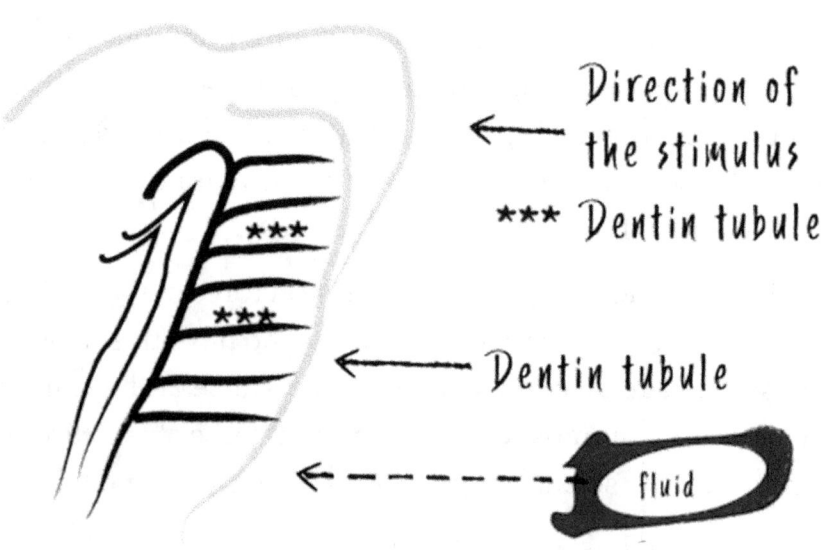

In this picture, you see an enlarged cross section of a molar.

The picture shows the direction of the stimulus. Fluid runs in the dentin tubule. After the stimulus, the fluid runs from the outer part of the molar to the inner part, the pulp. This stimulus gets translated into energy signals that are sent up to the brain. (See earlier picture showing the molar through ganglion to the brain.)

Some processes/stimuli move very *quickly!* Some of these include hot/cold drinks, the touch of your nails, or *one* hair of your toothbrush scraping the dentin. Some processes move slowly; one of these is caries (there are possible exceptions to this) moving into the dentin.

Love at first bite

The importance of food to our oral health is still not very well accepted. Many books have been written on food and the gut. The gut, however, doesn't have to deal with bad foods if you do not put them in your mouth. It is as simple as that!

Teeth's happy state depends not only on your daily cleaning but the food you offer them to chew. Eat, clean, eat, clean, eat clean… repeat. This is, of course, a cycle which shouldn't stop as long as we live.

As stated before, we need to stay away from carbohydrates. Sugar harms our teeth in many ways. Since digestion starts in the mouth, I want to address the impact of foods on your oral cavity:

I call it the P4!

YOUR P4!

- The ph
- The power of muscles
- The pleasure of digestion
- The protection of saliva

P1 pH:

The enamel cannot cure itself that is when the negative influences stay around!.

Millions of microbes live on the surface of your teeth. They are not waiting to attack; in ideal conditions, they want to protect your enamel (we are divine creatures, remember?); they contribute to the constant exchange of minerals and nutrients between your enamel and saliva. <u>*You, however,*</u> cause them to attack your enamel by eating <u>foods which cause your pH to drop.</u>

Some bacteria just love this kind of environment. Even 'good' bacteria go wild in this acid environment, like a kid in a candy store. The enamel is in a constant state of flux: it is continually exchanging minerals and nutrients with your saliva. When eating food, at your first bite your salivary glands add enzymes to your saliva. Here the first part of digestion takes place…

What foods contribute to the bacteria to start panicking and attacking your teeth?

Foods containing sugar: (A lot more foods than you realize fall into this category, so make sure to check the ingredients lists on packages!)

- Processed foods (corned beef, ketchup, microwave meals, for instance)
- Some grains
- Sodas and other sweetened beverages
- Fruit juices!
- Sticky foods (granola bars, licorice and dried fruits, for instance)

Nonfood: certain medications!

When you eat foods containing sugar, not only do the bacteria in your mouth go crazy but your blood sugars will rise.

The tooth is made in such a way it can handle some sugar and a certain amount of acid, but not for days and months at a time.

The bacteria will eventually withdraw calcium from the enamel because they start lacking it. A cavity is eventually born.

Dental caries is an epidemic in the Western world. Our mouths were not designed to eat many of the kinds of foods that occupy such a prominent place in the modern diet… It was the Industrial Revolution that led to a dramatic shift in the types of food we eat. This resulted in an increase in the prevalence of the bacteria Streptococcus Mutans and Lactobacillus Acidofilus. Additionally, the natural diversity of our oral microbes was decimated.

Now! Love at first bite!

P2: The power of muscles

Now chew on this next piece:

All the internal and external muscles around your mouth and your jaws (TMJ-joint) act together in a very organized and subtle way.

You can feel this when you try to keep on talking while chewing; your cheek or tongue are the first ones to know that this isn't possible…

Mushy foods do not invite your muscles to become active. If such foods are a large part of your diet for years, you *will* lose muscle tone! You wouldn't like to have a face hanging on your knees, would you? Some of you might go to the gym to build enormous biceps but perhaps ignore your facial muscles. Except for the grins you make while lifting 180 pounds.

Your biggest jaw muscles are the Masseters (cheek) and Temporalis (side of the head). Now use them!

The strongest muscle of your body is your tongue! It moves around your food in a way that makes it easier to digest.

If for whatever reason your muscles are weak, it can cause your teeth to shift!

No upper lip muscle tone: your teeth might wander in front of you.

No cheek muscle tone: your molars might shift towards your ears.

In a 'normal' situation, there is a balance between oral muscle tone and tongue muscle tone. This is why your lower front teeth are situated nicely.

Eating carrots, raw foods, muesli, oats and so on stimulates the use of your muscles.

The better your teeth stay in place, the better your digestion.

P3: The pleasure of digestion

In the Western world, we have everyday access to refined sugars and white flour. Our addiction to these foods made us forget we eat for a living purpose.

Making them a large part of your diet means that eating and chewing is in many cases not done properly. Because of our busy work schedules, we do not take the time to chew. You need to chew every bite at least 30 times! This causes the food to mingle properly with the saliva and not stick on your teeth. Chewing this much makes you also conscious of the fact that you are eating, which tells your brain you have had enough at some point. In this way, consciously enjoying your food might save your teeth.

I see a lot of people who broke their teeth on '...a quick bite'.

Choose foods that are rich in taste and need time to chew on. Your brain will love that.

P4: The protection of saliva

Saliva protects your enamel because it buffers the pH in the mouth. No saliva? Dental decay is very likely to happen even if you clean well.

The key to good saliva also lies in the quality of your nutrition and the amount of water you consume. Certain medications (including, for example, diuretics, appetite suppressants, and specific antidepressants) may interfere with your saliva production. It goes without saying that smoking is terrible for your saliva (and your teeth)!

Alcohol and lots of coffee can also cause a dehydrated mouth.

I'm continually astonished by the number of people who are on antidepressant meds! I usually advise these people to come into my office every three months to monitor their oral health.

If you experience dry mouth symptoms, please call your dentist or get a consult from me by sending an email to: leslie@theawakeningdentist.com.

Remember I am here to help you.

Exercise

As a former physical therapist, I am quite familiar with the use of muscles. I am also quite familiar with misuse, too.

As already mentioned, when facial and or oral muscles are weak, your teeth can move in unwanted directions. When lip muscle tone is weak it can also affect your breathing. Your lips will not close well; this can result in breathing through the mouth instead of the nose. Breathing through the mouth can result in dry mouth and put you at greater risk of developing decay. Often I see more plaque accumulated on your lower front teeth if this is the case.

Good muscle tone is needed for:

- Facial expression
- Chewing
- Looking good ;-)
- Speaking
- Swallowing
- Breathing
- Feeling good
- Sleeping well

We can exercise the masticatory muscle groups.

Consult me online (www.theawakeningdentist.com) or consult your dentist or an orofacial physical therapist if you have any questions about when and why you might need to strengthen these muscles...

NOTE! Be careful not to exercise the 'mouth closing' muscles with the clenching exercise when this <u>causes</u> you pain.

Clenching is a very common misuse of the jaw muscles. People do not recognize when they clench and very often this overload is overlooked by dentists too. One needs to understand the difference between muscle aches that may reasonably occur as a result of exercise and pain caused by overloaded muscles.

NOTE! Be careful not to overdo the 'open your mouth' exercises if you are familiar with dislocating jaws! Some people's jaws dislocate quite easily.

Many root canal treatments have been done unnecessarily because the dental pain was actually a referred pain from the overloaded jaw muscles. When you are about to have your fourth endodontic treatment in a row, you hopefully remember what I am writing here.

Before doing these exercises make sure you are warmed up.

Warming up: laugh out loud, talk, rub your cheeks or place a warm cloth against your cheeks.

√ Exercise for the masticatory muscles: the masticatory muscles are responsible for opening and closing your mouth (this includes the Masseter muscle and Temporalis muscle, for instance).

1. Press your teeth firmly for 30 seconds. Repeat 6 times.
2. Open your mouth as wide as you can. Use your finger to help stretch the muscle group for 30 seconds. Repeat 6 times.

Do this exercise twice a day.

If you have become stronger or you do not like to press your teeth that hard against each other, you might want to try the Jawzrsize ® created by Brandon Harris (www.kickstarter.com) or use the Myobrace® (www.myobrace.com)

√ Exercise for the masticatory muscles. These are the exercises for the muscles which are responsible for opening the mouth (Digastricus muscle, for instance).

1. Put your hand under your chin and press upwards. With this pressure in place, open your mouth as far as you can without it hurting. Repeat 6 times.
2. Now open your mouth 2 cm more, and increase the pressure against the chin. Do not close your mouth! Hold it steady for 6 seconds. Repeat 6 times. Do this exercise twice a day.

√ Exercise for the masticatory muscles. These are the muscles responsible for the jaw being able to move to the left and right. (For example, Pterygoid muscle).

1. Put your right flat hand against the right side of your chin. Move the lower jaw towards the right while your hand presses against it. Repeat 6 times.
2. Now do the same on your left side. Repeat 6 times.

Do this exercise twice a day.

In many cases, the Masseter muscle might need to be relaxed instead of activated. You activate this muscle very often without knowing this.

√ Stretching exercise for your masseter muscle:

Put two fingers of your <u>right</u> hand against the *inside* of your <u>left</u> cheek.

Now gently push the cheek as far as you can towards the *left*. You can feel the stretch. Maintain this position for 60 seconds. Repeat this 6 times.

Do the same exercise for your right cheek while using two left fingers.

Be aware that the 'wrong' use of your muscles can lead to crooked teeth. I urge you to stop/adjust as soon as possible:

- When children use a pacifier for too long, an 'open bite' can result.
- Nail biting
- Pencil chewing
- Tongue pressing

When teeth are crooked, we are almost always able to get them back in place. We are able to get teeth back in place with braces/brackets or in many cases: the myobrace! It's essential that you unlearn your bad habits as well, or your teeth will move back to the unwanted position.

You should be aware that braces, *the passive solution,* can cause harm: this includes root resorption because of the forces used and dental decay because brushing is difficult (being a teenager even tougher).

The myobrace, *the active solution,* can cause some muscle pain because it is a training device.

Back to clenching: you tend to clench when the going gets tough or even when you think it might get tough.

You need to get aware of this or you might eventually start to experience:

- Toothache
- Headache
- Pain while chewing
- Pain while laying on your side
- Pain while speaking

How to raise the awareness?

Usually when your jaw is relaxed, your upper and lower teeth *do not touch* each other. Try this now for yourself.

So, what did you feel?

Did the upper row of teeth touch the lower?

No? Pretty amazing! Congrats!

Yes? You might need some muscle stretching and relaxation exercises.

When do you tend to clench?

- Driving in traffic
- Surrounded by tired kids
- In a hurry to go somewhere
- When under pressure
- Weightlifting at the gym

I advise clients to hang stick-on notes with this question:

"DO I CLENCH?"

Stick it throughout the whole house, car, office, your spouse's forehead, and yes, even your bike.

Every time you encounter this note, you will be reminded of your jaw position and from this point on you will be able to reverse the situation. You just have to be determined.

My goal is to raise your awareness.

My cell phone is your placebo

'What you think is what you experience.'

A placebo, according to the Oxford English Dictionary is:

"A medicine or procedure prescribed for the psychological benefit to the patient rather than for any physiological effect."

Placebo comes from the Latin word *placebo*, which means: 'I shall please' and from *placeo*: 'I please.'

A placebo may be given to a person in a clinical context in order to *deceive* the recipient into thinking this is an active treatment.

For obvious reasons, it might be ethically problematic for a doctor to try using a placebo with patients.

It is true, though, that the placebo effect has been shown to be clinically powerful. They must be a result of the brain's role in physical and mental health. Brain imaging techniques have indeed shown that placebos can have real measurable effects in the form of real physiological changes in areas such as:

- Heart rate
- Blood pressure
- *Chemical* activity in the brain

MRI studies have revealed that a placebo can reduce pain-related neural activity in the spinal cord, indicating that these effects can extend beyond the brain.

How does this work?

Keywords are: conditioning (see also earlier in this book) and expectations.

A placebo and an actual stimulus are used simultaneously until the placebo is associated with the effect from the actual stimulus.

Conditioning has a longer lasting effect than expectation.

Motivation is another important factor which may contribute to the placebo effect.

It might also link to the meanings we attach to illness and its treatment in the culture in which we live.

Some people see illness as punishment from God or a result of karma or bad luck. Others see it as a sort of warning system, waking us up so we'll make the effort to live a better life and improve as a person.

My own mother saw her sickness as a punishment. "This is my punishment", she said, when we found out she had metastasized oesophageal cancer.

I, on the other hand, saw it as a warning system. She had neglected herself all her life and feared what people might think of her. She had also had an abusive father and lost her mother and brother at a young age.

A placebo would not have worked, that is for sure.

Expectation: the bigger the expectation, the better the result. Studies have found out that the color and the size of the pill is important. "Hot-colored" pills worked better as stimulants and "cool-colored" pills as depressants. Capsules seem to be more effective than tablets. It might even be that the bigger the pill, the better the effect. I can imagine that more expensive pills work better, too.

In my dental office, I do not offer placebo-pills. I offered my cell phone number.

In explaining the entire treatment from A-Z and what people can _expect,_ clients are a lot less scared of pain.

I offer my clients the possibility to call me after I have done a treatment, even after office hours.

Guess what will happen? Hardly anybody calls me…

I very much believe that when caretakers really take care of their clients, and are interested in their lives and their ongoing issues, clients will feel at home and feel heard instead of hurt!

Dare to care!

A bitter pill to swallow

In the former chapter 'Love at first bite', I mentioned the influence of medication. Many medications and some vitamins, minerals, and herbal preparations can have negative effects on your oral health.

Below you find the triangle disease/medication/effect oral health.

Abnormal bleeding:

<u>Medication</u>: Aspirins and anticoagulants.

(Helps for the blood not to clot – Heparin for example.)

<u>Dis-ease:</u> Stroke, heart disease.

They can cause abnormal bleeding with cleaning sessions or oral surgery. I had a client who almost died in the hospital because of the extraction of a tooth by the oral surgeon. Abnormal bleeding caused him to be black and blue all over his face and breast.

Oral sores, inflammation or discoloration of the soft oral tissues:

<u>Medication:</u> Blood pressure regulators, (beta-blockers) chemotherapeutic agents as well as immunosuppressive agents.

<u>Dis-ease:</u> Cancer, autoimmune disease, organ transplant patients.

They can cause a very dry mouth (Xerostomia, because the medicines contain substances which grab on to beta receptors*, this decreases the production of saliva), ulcerations of the soft tissues and a very, very sensitive tongue. All sharp edges of teeth or fillings need to be made smooth to prevent the tongue from being damaged. It could bleed and become inflamed otherwise. This is usually because of the lack of saliva!

*More in chapter: 'Saliva, your holy toothwater'

Gum tissues reaction, overgrowth of the gums:

Medication: Anti-seizure meds like Phenytoin and calcium channel blockers.

Dis-ease: Heart failure, epileptic seizures, organ transplant patients and migraine.

These can cause an overgrowth of the gingiva. This will mean that cleaning of the teeth will be very difficult. You need to get under the gums to clean the teeth, otherwise inflammation and infection can occur and decay lurks around the corner.

Taste altering:

Medication: cardiovascular meds, sometimes nicotine skin patches, respiratory inhalers, central nervous system stimulants.

Dis-ease: Heart failure, COPD, lung diseases.

Sometimes altering of the taste can be worsened by the fact you still might have amalgam fillings. Amalgam is an alloy of mercury with another metal. Sometimes medicines which fight anemia can cause this taste (as they contain iron components).

Dental decay:

Medication: Cough meds, respiratory medication, inhalation therapy. Chemotherapy, anti-depressants (beta blockers)

Dis-ease: asthma, COPD, cancer, depression

Children taking syrup based medications (like cough medicines) are left with sweet residue in their mouths...you know what might come next, especially in younger children because they tend to dislike brushing their teeth. Brushing sessions can sometimes feel like a martial art clinic! Please everybody, rinse your mouth directly and thoroughly with water after you have applied this medication. Sugar is frequently part of liquid medications like cough drops, vitamins!, anti- acids, and anti-fungals.

Increasing jaw bone density:

Medication: bisphosphonates (calcium tablets, or in some cases intravenous infusion)

Dis-ease: osteoporosis (poor bone density, you are likely to break a leg easily).

Most drug treatments for osteoporosis work by slowing down the activity of the cells that break down old bone (osteoclasts). Some treatments stimulate cells that build new bone (osteoblasts). The main aim is to decrease the risk of you breaking your bones again. Usually they find out you "have" osteoporosis when you have broken a bone without a legitimate cause.

Now mind this: because of the increasing density of your bones (in your whole body), the density of your jawbone will increase too.

Now, bone is living material, with blood vessels wired all through the bone cells.

When the bone gets denser, the blood vessels can be weakened and have a tough time keeping the blood flowing properly!! Now, you'll remember we learned earlier that teeth contain blood vessels too, right? The vessels run through just a tiny opening which is called the apex of the tooth. As we discussed, when the bone is very tense, the vessel will have difficulty in staying strong. In combination with the fact that it also has to run through the fragile apex, there is a risk of blood loss in your teeth. This will not happen directly but after having taken these drugs for maybe months or years.

Your teeth might start hurting and will die….

Many misdiagnoses have been made here, and root canal treatments done unnecessarily!

As dentists, we have to be careful if we need to extract a tooth. The bone can become inflamed and eventually infected because of the loss of proper blood flow. It's clear that whenever you go to a dentist, you should take your list of medications with you.

Water your teeth. When you use any kind of medication, make sure to rinse your mouth with water frequently and to drink a lot of the liquid, too.

SALIVA, your holy tooth water

Although I know I have mentioned saliva in former chapters I need you to know how freaking important this nourishing, moisturizing, dis-ease fighting liquid is.

Saliva is the cheapest mouthwash!

Saliva is a clear liquid which washes around your teeth. It is made by several salivary glands in your mouth. You can find the biggest glands under your tongue, in the roof of your mouth and in your cheeks (next to your ear). The latter might cause some contraction when you eat something very sour; you might feel a tingle around your ear and your mouth will fill with saliva.

Saliva helps to keep your body healthy because it keeps your teeth healthy. It is mostly made of water but also contains important substances necessary for digestion (enzymes).

Saliva keeps your mouth moist and comfortable so you can chew, taste, speak, smile, start to digest food, and swallow.

Remember: digestion start in the mouth!

Saliva fights germs; it contains immune molecules. It also contains a lot of antibacterial components; it helps to fight bad breath.

The fact that proteins and minerals are present makes your enamel jump for joy. Your gums are in love with your saliva too.

How do you make saliva?

When you chew! The harder you chew, the more saliva you make. Sucking on (refined sugar-free) candy or chewing gum helps you make more saliva, too.

On average, a human being can produce 1.5 liters of saliva per day.

The secretion of saliva is mediated by the autonomic nervous system. A chemical is being released which transmits a signal to the glands: produce saliva.

(Bear with me... I know I know this is tough... I love you.)

The autonomic nervous system is a division of the nervous system that supplies smooth muscles and glands.

Smooth muscles generally form the supporting tissue of blood vessels. They <u>need to contract</u> to make sure the blood gets pumped through your body. They are located in the walls of hollow organs like the uterus, stomach, intestines, urinary bladder, heart, and <u>*salivary glands.*</u> (Thank you for staying with me... you made it).

Smooth muscles are also called 'involuntary muscle' because it is not under voluntary control! This type of muscle keeps us alive without our having to think about it.

Calcium plays a part in their contraction.

Doctors typically turn to beta-blockers when people experience problems such as:

- High blood pressure (stress)
- Irregular heart rhythms
- Migraines

- Anxiety disorders
- Tremors (e.g. Parkinson's disease)
- Drooling (e.g. Parkinson's disease)

Why do they prescribe this?

Because doctors want to relax the involuntary muscles so the organs come to a rest if they are overreacting to things you experience in your life.

Stressed hearts need to relax, and the heart is a muscle.

The beta-blocker blocks the beta receptor on the salivary glands, and the smooth muscle will RELAX…..and here we are: the salivary glands will produce less saliva!

While this therapy is sometimes given with full awareness of its effects on saliva, for example for patients with Parkinson's disease, the impact on saliva production is still mostly a largely unknown side effect!

Dehydration of the mouth can lead to inflammation of the gums, dental decay, sore soft tissues, irritated tongue, difficulty speaking, and weaker appetite. Additionally, people with dentures might find them more likely to come loose. This is because of the lack of a vacuum created by saliva film on the roof of your mouth.

Tongue tied

The tongue is a muscular organ in our mouth. We need this muscle to manipulate the food for mastication. How else would the food be thrown from left to right, so it can get chopped up by our teeth?

Another major function of the tongue is enabling of speech in humans. (And vocalization in other mammals.)

The left and the right side of the tongue are separated by a vertical section of fibrous tissue known as the 'lingual septum'. If you can stick out your tongue very far to the dentist, your tongue is not very much tied to the bottom of your mouth, which is fine. If a baby is unable to do this and has a tongue-tie, they might have difficulty in breastfeeding. It's possible that the septum might need to be cut. This because the infant isn't able to latch on to both the breast and the nipple.

The tongue plays a huge role in tasting.

This pinkish-brownish muscle's upper surface is covered with small bumps called 'papillae' with their taste buds.

The sensation of taste includes five established basic tastes:

- Sweet
- Sour
- Salt
- Bitter
- Savory

Specific taste receptors (protein molecules or ions) on the tongue are responsible for the different tastes.

Out tongue tell us a lot about our health. You will not leave an acupuncturist's office without sticking out your tongue. Have you had a difficult life? Your tongue will tell!

The color of the tongue, the shape, the coating, and the surface itself reveals our state of being. I will mention just a few of the possible colors and characteristics of the tongue that can hint at certain possible conditions or circumstances:

- Pale or pink: blood deficiency
- Swollen: retaining fluids or bloated tummy
- Cracks: low/poor nutrition
- Thick: issues with digestion

Bacteria are also present on your tongue. As a dentist, I often tell clients to also brush their tongue! It keeps it fresh.

Some clients love to have tongue piercings. I'm sure you're already aware that they can harm your teeth.

It's always surprising to find there are people who are scared of the dentist but not of chipping of their teeth.

I have a client who is scared to death of my treatments yet she decided to get a tongue piercing!

Guess what: it will take a huge, huge amount of energy to repair the damage. This client will cry during her whole treatment…

Remember I am a human being with a certain amount of energy. But hey, I will help you through this agony.

OUCH

Have you decided how long you want your ouches to last?

I did not ask: "How long will your ouches last?" but, "How long you want your ouches to last?" I can hear you think: "What do you mean? I have no control over that. They just happen to me. I am the victim."

No, no, no! You are not the victim. You are a victim of your own thoughts... that's all, nothing more and nothing less.

I have shown you that teeth are a vital and brilliant part of your body. If you think they don't look nice, you won't smile and you might hide them behind your hand if you do; if they're causing you pain, you won't eat. Your total body will be affected, and illness might result.

The following might be a revelation for many people:

Illness requires something *from* you which you might not even know (yet). It requires you to take action towards healing. This is on your unconscious level.

Two factors that can lead to the development of illness are:

1. Unconscious guilt
2. A certain type of mental belief system

1: 'If we all would be willing to forgive other people's choices, and our own and let go of our judgements, we would all be free'.

2: The mind must believe certain kinds of beliefs for illness to occur. This might be at the subconscious level.

A belief is a thought we keep on thinking. It gets stored in our subconscious system and our bodies will react accordingly.

Our beliefs get expressed through the:

- Autonomic nerve system (nervous -> toilet)
- Hormonal system (scared -> sweating)
- Stress system (angry -> heartbeat up)
- Acupuncture system (meridians -> energy transporters)

Teeth have a place on the meridians, check the next drawing.

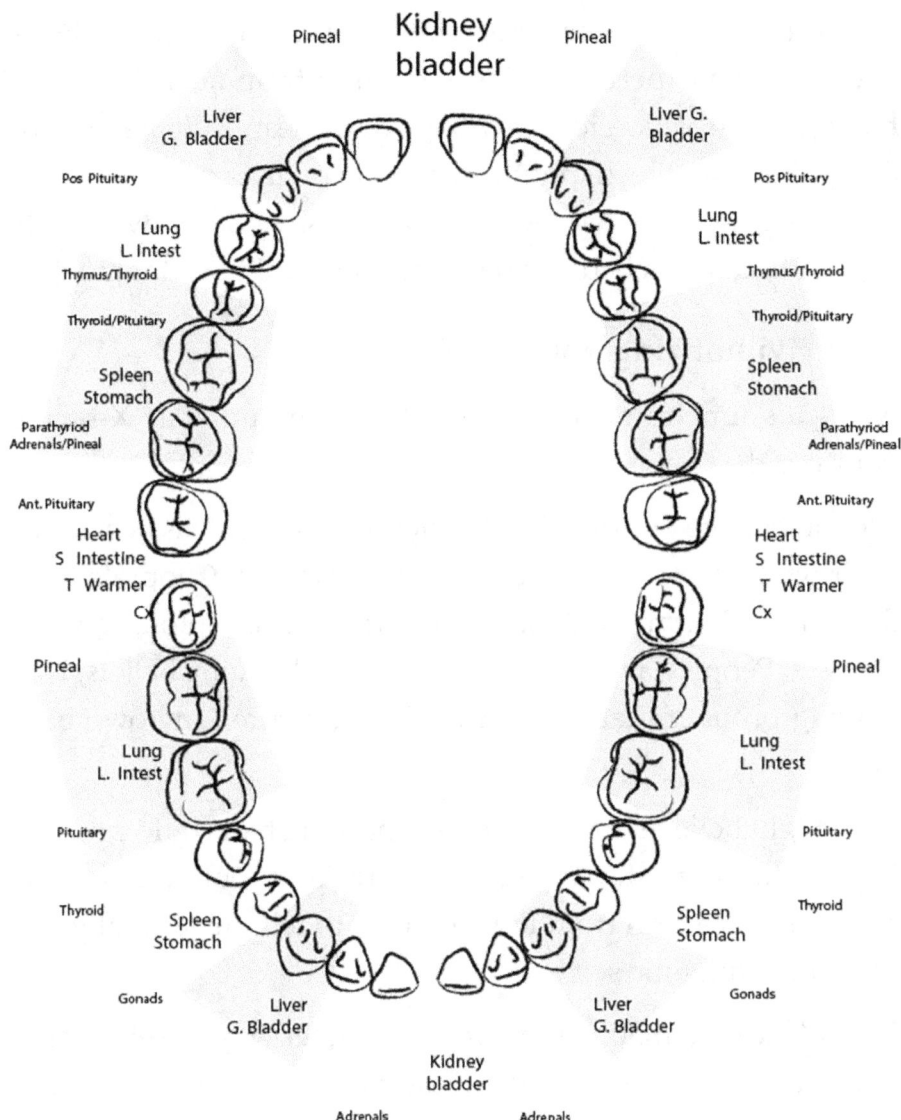

(More on this in part II of the book)

Healing comes from your attitude and belief system, since we are subject to what we hold in the mind!! If you do not believe the latter, try to remember what happens when people are hypnotized. They receive messages on the subconscious level, and they can experience effects ranging from acting goofy to having their allergic reactions disappear. Whatever the assignment is, the hypnotized person will carry it out. The body responds to what the mind believes. So, stop saying "My dad and grandma had periodontitis, so I will have that too!"

Stop Hypnotizing Your 'Self'

Now! It's time to heal your belief system and start X-raying your mind.

We can change our own DNA; enough research has been done to prove that. You may want to check Deepak Chopra's book *Supergenes* (Harmony Books, 2015) and Bruce Lipton's *Enough Illnesses*. People have been cured by their changing beliefs; I am a living proof of that as a human being. I cured my own back pain!

You might believe that as a dentist, nothing bad could possibly happen to my teeth. Wrong! I lost my front tooth a few years ago… it was a sign from the Universe to tell me to finally live up to my authentic self.

I wasn't scared, mad, angry, or in any other way upset because I just knew this message was going to set me free…

Listen to your emotions, to your tears, aches and pains! Accept them and decide to work on them. Part II of this book will reveal how I managed to finally meet the real me, and how you can do the same. In the meantime… just breathe. Oxygen is our life food.

Mind your step:

A practical guide to a new consciousness

Until death do us not part

One last look over my right shoulder affirmed it to me: she was fine. She was lying peacefully in her bed with her pillows stacked behind her. She had to prop herself up a little otherwise she couldn't sleep. She had slept like this for months... Her breathing was calm, so I decided to leave.

Prior to leaving her to go home to my 3, 5 and 7-year-old children, I asked her: "I think I might go home to the kids... is that OK with you? So when you wake up I might not be here. Is that OK with you? Or would you rather have me stay here?"

It was a terrifying decision for me; it felt like I had to choose between my kids and her, a choice which was difficult to bear, but I figured she didn't need me when she was asleep.

The kids were at home and hadn't had my attention all day. I had missed them... I wanted to be with them so much.

But I also wanted to be with her...

"But, honey" I said to her, "When you wake up have them call me and I will be here in a second, ok?"

That was fine with her. She couldn't talk... there was only a very weak nod.

Then my mom was given the injection with sleep medication that we asked for and she immediately fell asleep. I was glad I had asked her the questions. Better safe than sorry, right? I stayed with her for a while until I felt she was at ease... then I left.

The last look over my right shoulder showed my mother sound asleep in a bed which didn't even take up a quarter of the huge, beautifully decorated room in the hospice. I was thankful that she was in so lovely a place.

She had always said that anesthetics, sleeping pills and narcotic drugs didn't work the amount of time they were supposed to. It was because of this that I was afraid that the sleeping medication she had been given wouldn't last all night.

The very split second I stepped outside the room and closed the door I started to frantically wring my hands.

I was shocked: this movement was completely unfamiliar to me. I had never wringed my hands before.

What is this?

"This is not you, Leslie" I was telling myself. "Why are you wringing your hands?" was the question I asked myself. "Why?"

Then I screamed at a nearby nurse I had never met before: "This evening or tonight it will happen! This evening or tonight it will happen, I just know! My mother will die. I am not going home. There is nobody in this world who can keep me away from her! I am just not going!" While it wasn't like *'me'* to shout like this, I felt I was right... I felt the truth...

The nurse who had been with me since the administration of the drug tried to calm me down. We walked together to the hospice's cozy living room area.

She gently asked me to go home, explaining she could see a desperately needed sleep. She suggested I should come back in the morning. "Well, in the morning I have to go to work... I have a busy dental office to run, ma'am!" I replied quite obnoxiously.

I could see that the hospice nurse felt sorry for me, being here all by myself and dealing with this.

'Well, I am used to making decisions by myself and not being comforted or really supported, so that's fine. She doesn't have to feel sorry at all', were my thoughts.

I decided to go back to mom's room and peak in one more time... she still looked very peaceful and at ease in spite of her horrible disease.

I took this as a signal that I should indeed go home. I called my husband to please come pick me up.

She had been transported today to the hospice from an academic hospital.

As I'd gathered all the stuff she had in her hospital room, I'd checked again if the closets and drawers were empty, and they were. Everything had fitted in a duffle bag. I cried so hard seeing her lying on that gurney ready to take her last trip... I remember I walked by my mom's side as she was wheeled down the hospital corridors. The duffle bag was on her gurney. There was more than enough space on that bed, for mom was now only 80 pounds. Her cancer had made half of her body disappear. We walked past her colleague; I was glad he didn't notice us. They had worked together for 25 years at the hospital's purchasing department.

And so, on the present day as my mom slept peacefully in the hospice, I decided to go home and see my kids.

By the time I arrived it was 10 o'clock at night. I rushed up the stairs to check on my kids and found them sound asleep. I tucked them in and kissed them goodnight. What an incredible contrast.

'There' is my mommy at the end of her life and 'here' are my kids starting their joyful existence. 'There' and 'here' - I had such different emotions.

A chameleon wouldn't have been able to change his colors as fast as I was experiencing this awful roller coaster of emotions. Was I in a movie?

I walked down the stairs and felt like I had to call a good friend of my mother. I told her: "If you want to see mom you'd better come this week." She was going to call first thing in the morning, she said.

Right after this talk I called the hospice nurse to ask whether my mom was still 'fine'. The nurse was going to go check on her. She called me back: "Your mother is sound asleep still" she said. "She lies in exactly the same way you left her" she reassured me.

Those were comforting words for me. I then decided to go to bed. After all, I had to go to the office the next morning. Patients would be waiting for me.

I have always been a good sleeper, no matter what. But…

Suddenly I was awake, wide awake… it was exactly 1.00 am.

Strange, because I was supposed to be tired, exhausted from the long previous day. Being around my mother from 10 am - 10 pm and experiencing such an emotional roller coaster didn't prevent me from opening my eyes like I was struck by lightning. I sat up in bed vertically like I was pushed by a great force.

I immediately thought: *"It is not OK! She is not OK! Mommy is dying!"*

I had to call the hospice nurse…

I was furious with myself. *"How on earth could you have gone home to see the kids when she is 'there' dying! How could you?*

Oh my goodness, please don't say she's died without me at her side! Please, please, please let this not be true!"

Since the nurse had called me back earlier that night, telling me my mother was still sound asleep, I suddenly realized I could push the button on my phone to reach back to the last caller; the nurse. That way I didn't have to go downstairs to look up the number. My youngest daughter was lying next to me, cuddling against her mommy because she had become sick an hour before and needed my attention. I did not want to risk the chance of waking her up…

So, I pushed that 'call' button, and pushed it again, again, again, and… again. It wasn't working. But… instead of freaking out I was very calm. I knew, I just knew the nurse was going to call *me*! I put my cell phone right next to my bed telling myself: "Stay awake, the nurse will call you!"

I had hardly finished telling myself this, when my phone rang!

It was just after 01.00 am. I answered the phone: "Hi, this is Leslie." "Hi this is nurse 'X' from the hospice. Am I speaking to Leslie van Oostenbrugge?" I heard her ask calmly. "I want to…" I didn't let her finish her sentence. My gosh! I knew whom I was talking to!

Had I been indeed a fool to go home? To have taken an action *against my intuition*?? 'I shouldn't have listened to that nurse!' I thought in agony. I promised myself that very second that I would never ignore my intuition ever again.

I frantically asked: "Is she dead? Is she dead?"

I thought: "No, *don't let it be too late!*" As emotional as I was, though, another part of my brain couldn't help but tell me: *"Well, if this has happened, it is ok. She must have chosen her own moment, without me."*

But hallelujah, mom was still alive! She had woken up! The dose of sleeping medicines didn't last the time it should have. The nurse said: "Your mom was restless and made clear that she wanted you."

I yelled to her: "I am on my way!"

She replied: "Take your time. Your mom will be OK…"

After the quickest shower ever, I jumped in my car and drove/flew to her.

While on my way, I thought of calling my brother and my dad. Should I drive by and pick my father up? My dad had Parkinson's disease, so it would have taken a huge amount of time to wake him up and get him in the car…

My brother had to go to work the next morning, so I decided to let him sleep. All kinds of thoughts were running through my mind.

I arrived just before 2 am. I hurried down the hallway, where the nurse welcomed me. We both walked up to my mom's room. Just before entering, I heard a strange noise (like three kids blowing into their lemonade through a straw, producing enormous bubbles).

I opened the door… there she was, her head tilted to the left, her normally beautiful blue eyes gazing into a space I could only imagine.

"Hi, honey" I said. She quickly turned her head to the right; that meant she had heard me.

I threw my jacket off and went to hold her hand.

She made some gestures that seemed to say;

"I want out of this bed."

I shouted out to the nurse, a different woman than I had met in the afternoon: "She wants to sit! She wants to sit!"

We pushed all her bed sheets aside to let her sit up straight. She sat up with her legs hanging over the side of the bed.

With the remaining energy in her body, she had been able to tell us what she wanted. I could read her gestures, like I had done my entire life.

I kneeled before her and I held her knees tightly so she couldn't fall of the bed and I could see her face; she could no longer lift her head.

I then asked: "Would you like for me to call Dad and Ronald (my brother)?" She could not give any answer either verbally or nonverbally. It was so hard to see her like this, and all I wanted for her was to go back to sleep.

We both had agreed earlier that year for her not to suffer. The risk with esophageal cancer was to choke. She actually wanted euthanasia but we had not really taken action of filling out all the forms to prepare for this. Now it was too late...

Here she was, realizing she was going to die within a limited number of days or months. I once said to her, *"You are sitting in the lala waiting for your ya ya"*, referring to the time she was waiting on her own for her death to arrive. The words are part of the lyrics of the song from Lee Dorsey *(Ya Ya, 1961,* <u>*https://youtu.be/K5LnpErE6f4*</u>*), an artist* my mom loved so much.

So I knew if she wanted euthanasia, which wouldn't be the case, she definitely wanted to at least go to sleep now.

I shouted to the nurse: "Give her a sleeping drug! Give her a sleeping drug! I do not want for her to wake up... let her sleep... let her sleep! She doesn't want this..."

The nurse said: "I will give her another sleeping dose, but she will not die from that." Well, as far as I was concerned, my mom was ready to die, but when and how? And to be honest... I wanted the suffering to end for my mother, too. How amazing to want this for a loved one. I knew she would be better off in heaven, that's for sure.

The nurse admitted the drug, enough to let her rest again. Indeed, she fell asleep.

The nurse left…

Now I was all alone with her… my mom.

The terrible sound of that what I came to know as a death rattle filled the room.

I sat next to her, on the right side of the bed, holding her hand. I was facing the wall and facing my mom.

I was in despair… and cursing and swearing! I realized she might be able to hear me. She might have thought: "I didn't raise you like this, girl. Don't swear." I didn't care; I had to express my fear and anxiety like this, I guess.

I was kind of rocking in my chair, and it wasn't a rocking chair! Cursing and swearing and rocking and listening to my mom's rattle while time passed by.

I finally decided: "I am not going to do this anymore on my own! I will not do this on my own. I am totally fed up with doing emotional things on my own."

So, I decided to call the nurse. Wow, what a decision. Asking for help.

I was going to push the red button beside my mom's bed to call this nurse whom I didn't know at all, to help me and bear with me through this.

I had never asked for help; being 40 at this point, I thought it might be about time.

The nurse came and I asked her whether she could hold my hand…

"Please can you hold my hand? I cannot go through this alone." Well, maybe I could, but I didn't want to. Period.

And, I didn't know for how long I was going to sit there.

Was she dying? Now? When? How many weeks would it take? Hours? Seconds? Well, neither of us knew.

When I had travelled with her to the hospice less than a day ago, it has been clear to me how weak my mom was. I held her head in my hand for the whole journey in the ambulance.

The ride took about 15 minutes; she was in sheer agony the whole time. The smallest bump in the road felt like climbing Mount Everest.

The ambulance driver asked whether she wanted to drive by her house for the last time. She had lived there for 38 years with my dad. She didn't want to. This showed how weak she was and realizing that made me cry even harder.

Finally, we arrived at the hospice; we knew the place where she was going to literally 'end up'.

She was terminally ill. Diagnosis: "Cancer."

Esophageal cancer. She was 62, and her life was over…

The diagnosis had been made in February, and she was operated on in May. We were all very hopeful because the so-called PET-scan showed no metastasis! Yahoooooo!

My mom was pretty healthy, relatively young and in good condition so the doctors decided to operate.

The surgery involved taking a piece of the esophagus out and doing some arts and crafts, like sewing a part of the esophagus to the stomach… and lo and behold, she would have more time to be with us.

But things didn't turn out as hoped. When they opened her up, the doctors saw that the cancer had spread all over her body…

Apparently, all the PET scan had been able to do was recognize a certain minimum size of tumor. When the doctors still thought that the cancer hadn't spread, I had wheeled her all the way down to the operation room and watched her go in with this brilliant news on our minds.

Now, I had to go tell her that her life would be over… and I did.

My brother was with me; he came immediately after I called him with the bad news.

Later my brother and I went to our dad to tell him the bad news. My dad was at a rehabilitation center, recovering from sensory paraplegia.

He had Parkinson's disease also and it was impossible for him to come to the hospital where his beloved wife had just received her death sentence.

My dad's medical conditions were the reason why my mom decided to go into a hospice. We knew she didn't have many months left to experience this life, and she didn't want to be a burden to my father, as he was unable to take care of her. So we selected the hospice in May, the one she would die in very soon.

I cried when we both first stood in her beautiful hospice room. My mom apologized to the people around us for my tears. "She is a bit upset', she explained.

Now, being exactly six months later, she sat in a chair all day long with her head on her chest… too tired to lift it.

Her colleagues had sent beautiful flowers. How lovely.

When I had to leave her for a minute, I warned her not to die!

She promised me not to.

She hadn't eaten for about half a year orally; she had been fed through a nasal tube. Since this very morning she hadn't had any fluids either; all her feeding and drinking tubes had been pulled out of her body.

It startled me at first… but, but, but; then she will die. Oh, I forgot… she has too. It was all so confusing.

I was very hungry. How could that be? I didn't want to leave my mom to eat a sandwich which I had bought in the hospital that morning. Then mom asked me, "Aren't you hungry?"

Kind of embarrassed, I answered; "Yes, but I don't want to eat in front of you." "It is fine with me", she said, "You have to eat." "Ok." So, I grabbed the sandwich… mom wanted a smell. "It smells so nice, Les", she said. This made me cry. My mommy who loved cheese sandwiches… all she could do and wanted to is take a little sniff. "I would pay a $1000 for a glass of water", she said.

I was hiding my tears, but she couldn't see me anyway. I wanted to stay brave, for her.

The doctor told me he saw a very, very sick woman. I was like: "Seriously?" How naïve of me... I just didn't want to see it.

I said to her: "Thank you for being my mom."

She nodded. She had expressed her feeling towards me earlier by saying:

"You are the best thing that has ever happened to me in my life."

She had never told me this before.

Remember, _tell your loved ones you love them every day! Act like it is your last day on earth and like it could be theirs, as well._

So now, about 12 hours later I was alone with her, and the nurse was holding my hand while I held hers.

Then, all of a sudden, the nurse let go of my hand and went to sit at the left side of the bed.

"I see a change", she said. She had been closely watching my mom's face, I guess. I screamed, "What! What? Is she going to die? Is she going to die?"

"I am not sure... ", she responded.

"What a stupid question", I thought. "How does _she_ know?"

It must have been obvious for the nurse that mom was about to pass over to the other realm, but I couldn't see that.

She now made clear mommy was indeed starting her new journey.

I was totally stressed, I did not at all expect '**the**' moment to be now.

I was now yelling at the nurse: "What can I do, what can I do?"

The past year I had driven my mom as well as my dad to and from hospitals, nursing homes, rehabilitation centers, pharmacies, home, with my dad to my mom, with my mom to my dad, you name it and I had done that...

But now? What on earth (yeah, earth...) could I do now? No more 'going tos', no more medication, no more 'I am here for yous'...

"Talk to her", the nurse said. "Oh, my goodness, great idea", I thought.

So I started talking to her, while holding her hand. The other hand was running through her dark brown hair. Not a grey hair in sight. On my head there was hardly any brown hair left. I've been grey since I was 33.

Mom's eyes were very glazed, nothing left of the beautiful blue sparkle. They stared at me but I wondered whether she could see me. I hoped she could hear me.

The nurse confirmed she could hear me. Come to think of it, I have read that the last sense to go before someone dies is that of hearing.

I told mom to go see her mom and her brother. Her brother died at the age of 14; my mom was 10 at that time. My grammy died when my mom was 21. She never got over that.

Her father had died many, many years ago also, but I knew she wouldn't want to see him, so I didn't mention his name, no way!! I didn't want her to suffer any longer.

While stroking her hair and talking to her, dark fluid came out of her nose. We wiped it away carefully. She was breathing in a very strange way, very deeply. Every breath was so hard I thought that she was gone. But she wasn't. She came back.

I didn't want her to come back, for her own sake. I suddenly felt I had to let go… physically. I said to the nurse; "I have to let her go… " She nodded.

So I took my left hand out of her hair. But… my right hand was still holding her hand.

I pointed at my hand and asked the nurse; "What to do with this one?" She said: "You decide."

Then I decided to 'let go'. I carefully let go of her hand, pulled my hand towards me from under the sheet…

I watched her… there… one last breath… mommy died.

I felt and saw her peace.

A few months earlier, after the operation, I said to her; "Actually, we should all be jealous that you are going to die." "Why?" she asked. "Because it is all beautiful up there. There is peace and no wars and just souls loving each other." "Thank you for thinking that", she said. "How lovely of you."

At that time, I thought only heaven was great.

Gradually, I discovered heaven is also on earth and life is great.

She has been dead for 14 years now.

About me

I am proud of my name: Leslie van Oostenbrugge. I do not consider myself to have a biography, for Spirit is eternal and everlasting. Anyway, a bio is meaningless because what matters is what I 'am' at this moment.

Physically, however, I do have a bio which you can find elsewhere in this book.

Half an hour before my birth, my brother decided to go ahead and see the light.

Born on the same date out of one and the same mother made us twins.

My mother told me many times; "You always had *that special* look from the moment you were a born."

My answer would be, "That's because I loved you."

I spent a great deal of my childhood in the eye-hospital for treatment of a viral infection in my left eye.

Hence, (I guess…) I decided at a very young age (it must have been around 8 or 9) I wanted to become an eye-doctor. I had a deep-rooted wish and longing to go to medical school.

But…

In primary school I really didn't know my numbers at all. I badly flunked the 'aptitude' test regarding numbers and calculating in my head.

As a result, the teacher decided that <u>my</u> level ever to be reached in secondary school would be 'a way-below- average'.

An aptitude is a _component_ of a competency to do or comprehend a certain kind of work at a certain level.

It is a developed knowledge, understanding, learned or acquired ability or attitude.

Well, the *numbers* (and in secondary school, the math) were not my friends, that's for sure…

My mother, however, decided to see whether a higher level of education instead of 'a way-below-average school would suit me anyway.

And so I started a 'MAVO' (nowadays called 'VMBO').

In Holland we have a grading system which ranks from

1 (very poor) to 10 (excellent).

I had the best grades at the 'MAVO'! They ranged from 7-10. I was awarded the '10' about 52 times in the first year.

So, indeed I outgrew the 'way-below-average-school' as well as the 'MAVO'… right?

Except, for math.

Usually when you have these grades you can go straight to the 'HAVO', but because my math grades tended to be 6, the teacher decided that I couldn't.

I remember telling my parents, "Well, I will go the long way but I will get there!"

I decided to choose to be a science student. This means that I opted for maths, which was my not-so-good subject, instead of

Alfa, the languages, which I was good at. Why would I do this? So I could go to Medical School one day.

"Oh my goodness!" You're probably thinking. "Despite your teachers strongly advising against it, you made this daring decision?"

Yes, indeed.

Anyway I finished secondary school (average grade 6… the math) so Medical School, here I come.

However…

I was *not* admitted, despite my more than devoted hard work and desire to become an eye doctor.

My grades were not good enough…

So, my dream was shattered. Thank you system!

My life took a new turn.

To understand this, you'll need to know that I had travelled to the USA when I was around 15 years old. I went with my brother and my parents for a month. My uncle lived there; he had invited us to come over and use his camper to tour through several states.

That was the moment I hugely fell in love with the USA.

More and more, over the years, I have come to know that for some reason I feel an intense connection to the US.

It appeared that my dad had wanted to emigrate to the US but he met my mom so he didn't. But my uncle had.

Anyway, when I finished secondary school and was not admitted to Medical School, I had a temporary job.

But then, in 1984, a letter arrived. (Date written; my birthday date; ain't no coincidence).

In that letter a friend of mine, who lived as an au-pair girl in a city close to New York, asked me whether I was interested in the same type of job. I would live with friends of her family.

In the US? Oh my! YES! No doubt.

Two months later I was living in Rye, NY.

The family had three kids to take care of. I learned how to cook, *express* love, iron, clean, do the laundry, receive love, drive, play tennis, play squash, baby-sit and come to terms with my broken self.

It was a 'work hard-play hard experience'.

I stayed for 22 months in this very, very loving family.

I still deeply care about this family and am in contact with them 30 years later!

I also passed my High-School exam in New York, earning an equivalency diploma,

What a roller-coaster of experiences.

I also got to spend a lot of time with my friend whom had sent me the letter. She lived about 15 minutes away from me. We talked to, or saw, each other every day.

I have known her since I was around 14 or 15 years old. We met playing handball at the same club. I was a reasonably good handball player myself, but my brother was way better. My father was a well-known (team) player! My mother also enjoyed this sport.

We were a sportive family.

Years later my brother called my living in the US 'an escape' from the nest.

I was 19, very cheerful, fun-loving, an always laughing girl.

He was right...

Our mother was a grieving woman who had had a difficult childhood. . I am saying 'grieving' and not 'dominant', for efforts at dominance can be the result of grief, I believe.

Unfortunately, she inflicted a lot of her unhappiness on me. I was not able to stand up to her behavior.

My brother is much braver than I am, and he sure did stand up for himself.

I grew up and finally left my parents' home with the idea I was worth nothing at all and pretty ugly.

About myself

While in the US, I had applied again to be admitted to Medical School but was again rejected. After my return home, I decided to study Physical Therapy instead.

So, to satisfy my eagerness to know everything about the human body, I travelled directly from Rye, New York to the School of Physical Therapy in Utrecht.

I did very well in the program, earning terrific grades.

I always wanted my grades to be perfect so that I could feel good about myself. Nothing less than perfection in every area of my life was good enough. The teachers, who were physical therapists themselves, told me I would do well in the profession.

Given how well everything was going, I was shocked to get a written remark on a report in my senior year, in which the instructor suggested it would be better if I didn't continue asking bold questions.

Why would they say this? I was eager to learn and wanted to know 'the why' of different physical treatments. I guess my asking for wisdom so frequently must have made me a pain in the butt. I hadn't realized that.

After four years of study, I experienced a terrible disappointment: I did not pass the exams.

I suspect the reasons for this were my amazing lack of self-confidence and perhaps my so-called 'off the chart questioning'.

I'm sure you can imagine how beside myself I was when I was told I still hadn't passed the practical physical therapy test after the fifth attempt. I was so upset I kicked down a closet door.

I dropped out of the program and started a temporary job in a hospital as an audio typist. I had the best time and a lot of fun with my colleagues.

But, I couldn't bear the thought that I had given up. It felt like a huge failure. After having shown so much perseverance for so many years, I had allowed other people to destroy my dreams.

I just knew I had the qualities necessary to become a good physical therapist. So I decided to recommence my studies half a year later at a different school.

My new physical therapy teachers also told me I would become a good therapist (yeah, right, I had heard that before). I was even allowed to do exams within three months.

I passed…

With honors!

It was almost, 'with highest honors', but I had been fearful and didn't allow myself to show my true potential. This had kept me from summa cum laude.

How happy I was to regain a strong sense of self-esteem and self- confidence by passing this exam. My success was proof that I deserved to give myself credit.

After this, I decided to continue studying but in a different field: dentistry.

During my stay in the US I had experienced many dental problems. And before that in Holland, I had undergone treatments because of an accident with a surfboard at the age of 12.

As if that wasn't enough, my having a small jaw meant that I had needed to have premolars pulled and had to wear braces.

I applied to Dental School at the age of 28 and was accepted!

In the first year of my dental studies, a teacher (and dentist) told me that I should drop out of the program and give up any idea of being a dentist because I had a viral infection. I am a carrier of the HS-1 virus (HSV-1). This virus can cause cold sores or fever blisters on or around the mouth or nose. I was infected around birth with this virus. This most likely happened through contact with my mother. Once in a while I experience this outbreak, it can happen when being too busy, too stressed, or having been exposed to sunlight too much.

In the first week of the start of the new study I had such an outbreak. The dentist commented on that. I was too flabbergasted to ask him why he thought I better quit the study.

Four years and nine months later, I finished Dental School.

Graduated with honors.

I started to study Dentistry at the age of 28. So, there were no grants or any other financial help for me. I worked hard to fund the study myself.

I worked as a Physical Therapist in the evening hours and during the holidays.

I graduated in June, and started to work as a dentist that August.

You form history; it doesn't form you

While we had our fights like other siblings, my brother and I got along very well overall. We and our parents had lots of fun and happiness.

However, there was a lot of grief in my mother's heart. Unresolved grief for the loss of her mom and brother as well as her hatred for her father. She didn't attend his funeral which says enough about the bond between them.

She had never learned to express or receive love.

She admitted her 'shortcomings' the moment I became a mother. The way I treated and expressed my love to my children differed very much from hers. She realized that and was burdened with an intense feeling of guilt.

I said "I forgive you." What I actually meant was "I understand you."

Because forgiving would mean I was bigger than she was in spirit, and I was not.

We are all the same… we are love.

My beautiful mother couldn't cope with her own grief. Her mother had died at a very young age, her brother died at the age of 14 when my mom was only 10, and her sister left the house early. My grandfather sexually abused my mother.

She emigrated at the age of 19 from Germany to Holland when she met my dad. They married when she was 20. I was born about a year later.

All of this formed *me.*

It led me to choose only love, and to be kind, polite, gentle and patient.

But it also formed my belief that I was worth nothing, for my mother projected all her grief upon me.

I, however, am the only one with the responsibility and duty to cut through the tortuous cycle of criticisms, verdicts, sadness, and the non-receiving and non-giving of love.

I have always had the 'knowing' that something is 'out-there'.

I know now that it is all in here! (the *palm* of my hand is pressed against my *heart*).

There is a 'knowing' and the 'knowledge'.

Knowing: you came in this life *feeling* there is 'more to it', that there are 'more things in heaven and earth'.

You just know.

This knowing came *with* birth.

Knowledge: acquired information from teachers or books or other sources, which is stacked and drilled in your brain.

This comes *after* birth.

My mother felt *inferior* to me, her own daughter. Hence the remark about *'that special look of mine'*.

I loved her so much and I really encouraged her in life. She expressed her joy whenever she noticed *me* noticing *her* doing well in anything.

It 'should' have been the other way around, shouldn't it? I don't know. I never felt like 'the child'; I have always felt 'the caretaker'…

We cannot allow ourselves to be ruled by life experiences of our ancestors.

It must not at all affect me that in the year 1680 my great-great-great-great grandfather sprained his ankle, my great-great-great-great grandmother couldn't make a fire because her spouse didn't get the branches home on time because of that, their children were cold, their being cold led to them being grumpy and obnoxious, and they were punished for this, leading to a roller coaster of condemnation.

Sometimes people have to experience things of profound meaning to remember that there is more to life than arguing, complaining, and being miserable.

Sometimes we 'need' to:

- Lose a loved one
- Lose the so-called love of our life
- Lose our job
- Get caught in an accident
- Feel betrayed
- Feel used

Or another negative experience in order to create a new turning point.

It is a huge leap to acknowledge that you see these kinds of experiences as the turning points in your life that you 'need' in order to make transformations. Frankly, if this is the case, it's a sign that you need to change your course.

I have a client who has had cavity after cavity after cavity for years. She suffered from gingivitis also. She had been working for a company 60-70 hours a week for many years.

I had warned her that she needed to take more time for self-care. Unfortunately, she did not. Clearly, she saw the expectations of her boss as more important than her teeth. She eventually had the need for root canal treatments (more on this treatment later). She was worn out, on the edge of a burn out, and her dental health was declining.

It sounds strange, but I must say how joyful I was (for her sake) to learn she had been fired for economic reasons.

We do not have to fix ourselves, for we are not broken. We only think we are. We come into the world fully whole and awake. We only need to remember or be reminded.

More of the same

In August 1997, I started my career as a dentist.

I had already investigated where to live and work after my studies; I eventually decided on IJsselstein, near Utrecht. My husband and I bought our first house.

In November of that year we moved in, and in December our first baby was born! Happiness all around.

So, in 1997:

I got a job, I bought a house, I got pregnant, and I graduated.

Yes, in that order.

Of course, as I saw all this coming on the horizon, I couldn't help but ask myself, "Who am I to deserve this?" (For I heard my mom saying: "You do not deserve this.")

"Will I really get the house?" (Owning a home instead of renting like my parents did.)

And; "Can it be true?" (For I heard my mom ask, "Who do you think you are?")

"No way; a house *and* a baby *and* a job?"

Something <u>must</u> go wrong!

It didn't. It all went well even though there were problems we had to work through at first.

After I finished Dental School I started to work with a dentist in the town I was going to live in. How perfect I had arranged it all. I was ready to roll, my work ethic went through the roof.

I was like a puppy, wiggling my tail to dive into something new.

However, this colleague saw it all differently...

The promise he made to eventually sell his practice to me was just a lie...

He did not even provide an assistant for me...

He had a vision in mind... *with me.*

He never shared that vision with me even though he was pretty sure his future included **_me._**

Working with this dentist was my first experience as a young graduate. How full of energy I was to work beside him in his office. How much was I to learn from him. Or so I thought.

I disagreed with him on many different points and issues, but I was afraid to stand up for myself, again...

After a while, I finally decided to check out what other opportunities were out there.

Would I ever have an office of my own? My own space with my own vision, my own rules, just for me?

Long story short; I worked in this dentist's office for a year and a half.

Our collaboration ended up in court...

Luckily, I soon found a new job! Just an eight-minute drive away from home. Whooohooo!

I, however, thought this new colleague was a bit odd. Her approach to people wasn't my kind of thing.

Despite this fact I agreed on starting a partnership; we would be equal partners with the same position and the same rights. My dental career had finally started. It felt like this was 'the first day of the rest of my life'.

Unfortunately, I eventually realized this partnership was not working for me the way that it should. There were things happening which made me extremely unhappy and disempowered. I'm sorry but I can't share the details here. (I hate gossiping.)

I figured I had tried long enough to make it work.

I now knew! Just knew:

<u>I no longer wanted to be defined by somebody else's opinion.</u>

I decided to leave. I just couldn't take it anymore. I was fed up with people telling me what to do and judging me for how I was. I would no longer tolerate the psychological pain.

I was now ready to start my own office.

My dear colleague wanted to settle things with me in court. We met there four times…

She was furious that I had made my own choice… **her** future changed… I would not be there.

So, in my life I first encountered my mother, then the dentist and then the other dentist…

'Woe is me', right?

What is **with me?** Why do (these) people do this to me?

I must be a total 'wrong-do-er'. Everybody is against me…

Emotional Alignment Is Easy

Yet I have always felt I am a loving, caring, helping, listening, always-there-for you human being. I have not allowed people to bring me down and I've made my own choices. But I've had guilty feelings about doing so.

My life up to this point had been: following my own choices, preparing my ideas in silence, having lots of fun, joy, and laughter, and playing sports. I've been *the quiet observer, the passionate listener, and the comforter.* I knew I would somehow, someday gain insight into the meaning of life. I knew I had to stop soaking up all these critics.

It appeared I needed to experience so many negative situations to find out that all you need is within yourself.

Sometimes you 'need' pain to realize you are 'off'! Off of what?

Sometimes you need pain to realize you can more effectively tap into your own power.

Pain is a symptom, remember? Mental (or emotional or psychic) pains and (meta) physical pains are symptoms!

These encourage **you!**

These can be wonderful **reminders that** you want to become who you already are.

Homeless

I always like to listen to stories about the 'why' and the 'how' people have created their lives. I love to hear about their perseverance.

Never ever give up! That's my motto and advice.

It's quite possible that you do not share all of my interests, but as human beings are curious and inquisitive (and dare I say, on occasion, a bit nosey), I dare to believe that you might be interested in how a dentist builds a practice. Am I just a tiny bit right? I hope so!

So, in July 2007 I made the decision to start my own practice. This meant I now had to take action.

I was so eager to contact a contractor that I made the first call at 8 am… I think he was still in his pajamas, LOL. I had known him for several years, as he had helped us with the interior of the office where I worked with my former colleague.

So the search started to find an office building. And, of course, I also had to find out what all the costs of the office would be, including all the new materials, equipment, staff, you name it.

I found a financial advisor who guided me through the whole project. He was the one who had gone through my financial details and told me I could afford an office of my own. It was this that allowed me to get a mortgage from the bank.

Yeahooooo!

I also needed approval from an official (regional planning) at city hall. I knew that might be a tough one….

We were informed about a house for sale in the center of Vianen. We went to check it out. It had housed a cute old flower shop; it was affordable but I couldn't really buy an all new interior and dental chair. Also because it was located downtown, it was not very handy with regard to parking. Later on, we found out it appeared to have asbestos in the ceilings. It was out of the question.

I frantically dragged my assistant Carolien to come see another (too tiny!) office space. She, however, realized that it was my anxiousness to escape the situation with my colleague that made me so desperate to find something quickly. This could lead to bad decision-making. She firmly yet kindly advised me not to view this eminently unsuitable location.

I found another place soon, though! I liked it. I wouldn't be able to afford to put in a whole new interior, but I told myself that perhaps this wouldn't matter.

The contractor and I walked through the house to check whether it would be 'dentist' proof. We make a lot of noise with our burs ☺. I got an OK from him. So, I got 2 'yesses'! The house and the contractor's approval. The next hurdle would be getting approval from city hall. Luckily, after a very relaxed meeting, we received a 'yes'! I didn't know it would be *this* easy.

Wow! The only thing left was to have a purchase agreement made up and signed…

Three 'Yesses' obtained within 9 months after my decision to go start my own practice, what an achievement. Unfortunately, however, it was all too good to be true.

On the day the real estate broker came over for me to sign the papers, I received a phone call.

"Hi, this is Leslie. Good afternoon."

"Good afternoon. Am I speaking to Mrs. Van Oostenbrugge, dentist in Vianen?" (Vianen is where my current office is. It is located just 8 minutes drive away from my home).

"Yes, this is she", I replied. "You are speaking with Mr. K., I am an official from the City Hall of Vianen."

I was a bit confused. An official from the City Hall? What does this mean? He continued:

"I have received notice that you are planning to settle with your practice in a house on the xyz street in Vianen."

"Yes, that's true", I said.

"Well, Mrs. Van Oostenbrugge, you are not allowed to do that!"

I was like; "WHAT? What do you mean? I have the approval of Mr. X, a colleague of yours."

"Yes, ma'am, but he doesn't work here anymore and he checked the wrong books. He had very old information to go on."

I was flabbergasted!

Here I was, one inch of ink away from being the owner of a new building and my dream was shattered.

"I'm afraid we cannot let you open your new practice at that location. Please be aware that if you go through with the plan, you will be removed by City Hall."

I was shocked and felt like a criminal. Me who always abides the law felt really threatened.

"But I was just about to sign to purchase the house! The real estate broker is here with me!"

"Yes, ma'am… I understand your frustration," he replied, *"but there is nothing else I can say."*

I hung up the phone and returned to the living room. The broker had overheard the conversation and was almost ready to grab all her stuff and leave.

No signature, no balloons, no champagne.

Now what? After she had left I called C. He felt sorry.

So, now I had to start all over again.

A few days later, my husband and I remembered an ad regarding an office building that he had seen in the papers. The paper had been thrown away, but I was able to find the listing online. It was still available. A call was made and within a day a new broker was sitting across my table.

I was interested in building #1: there were three parking spaces in front and two at the side. Brilliant! The only minus, I thought, was that it was located in an industrial area.

Well, I figured, we will make it beautiful on the inside… who cares about outside!

So I wrote an official letter to City Hall to ask approval to move over there. It would be a two-minute drive away from the current office. It was a very nervous few weeks before I heard back.

Bad news! I was not allowed to move over there either. According to the development plan, there was no room for a dental practice.

I was really getting worried now! How would I ever be able to leave my current practice? I'm not an anxious person by nature but all of this was really getting to me. I was afraid that my assistants would soon resign, as they hated being around my colleague, too.

I had no choice but to continue in my quest. I had been so proud of my decision to leave. How many people stay in a bad work-related relationship? How many people think, "Well, this is <u>it</u> for the rest of my life. I am stuck here." Not me!

I suddenly remembered: there was another dental office across the street from the location! Why and how did *they* get an approval, then?

It was time for me to make a call to the regional planning department. I asked why my application had been denied but the other dentist was allowed to practice 100 meters away from my desired location. They claimed that until that point, they hadn't been able to "maintain order like they should", and that the dentist had been at that spot for at least six years. All of this seemed more than a little fishy to me. I had to wonder: were the people at the city hall really honest? This seemed like a case of jobbery.

Being a non-judgmental person it was tough to bring it up but I did. I do not like to threaten but I finally said, "You're clearly treating me differently than the other dentist. I plan to call a lawyer to look into this." Oh my goodness! This is not me!

He gave no response, and I hung up the phone. Now what?

I put on my thinking cap and really mulled it over. I suddenly remembered that the highest official working on regional planning was an old acquaintance of mine! Could I really be this lucky?

I decided to write her an official letter with a very friendly note attached. In the letter I asked for approval to move my clients, dear assistants and myself over to the industrial area. In the *note* I was very amicable. Would 'her knowing me' help in my situation?

Well, it was weeks before I heard from her.

In the meantime, it happened I had a client from my colleague in my chair for treatment. He was a member of the board of City Hall. I suddenly realized he might talk to her about my search for a new office. With this in mind, I told him about my plans and asked him to please keep it a secret from my partner. I knew the remainder of my time in this office wouldn't be a lot of fun for me or my assistants if this got out.

There was a moment where I thought that neither my old friend or my colleague's patient would be able to help me. This was when I got a call from City Hall again telling me that my application could not be approved for the same reasons as before.

I asked Jose, one of my assistants, to contact the broker to call the whole deal off.

But then the phone rang again. This time it was my colleague's patient from City Hall. He asked, *"You just had a call from City Hall, right?"*

"'Right", I said. *"Well, Leslie, the outcome might turn out differently than you probably expect. That's all I can say"*, he said.

After the conversation was finished I screamed for Jose. *"Please Jose, call the broker again! Tell him I've changed my mind and want to have the option to buy the office building again!"*

Jose, feeling like a puppet on a string, ran to make the call. I had to go back to a patient who had been waiting for me in the chair.

I really was in an emotional roller coaster. I have never been on a roller coaster but I have seen those monsters and know I never want to!

Now what?

It appeared there would another meeting in which City Hall would discuss my application. Ok, there was hope again!

Four weeks later, I knew the result of the meeting would soon be in. Being somewhat irritated that no one called me, I decided I could wait no longer. What was the answer:

"It is not a 'yes', but it is also not a 'no'…"

This didn't make sense. They clarified, "We now have to publish your application in the paper, so that anyone opposed to your plan has to communicate this to City Hall."

"So if none of the neighbors has any objections then I can have my office there?"

"Yes, ma'am!"

I was trying not to get too excited but things seemed hopeful. As it was an industrial area, it seemed unlikely that anyone would object. It was full of concrete and noises much louder than that of my bur!

Well, finally after six months of writing, calling and begging I finally succeeded!! Yeahoooo. Ready to go.

The next step was to tell my colleague that I was leaving! But when and how would I do this?

The accountant

Of course, I also had to contact our mutual accountant. He was responsible for the contract made when we (former colleague and I) decided to start the practice together.

I had to find out whether there was anything in the contract that could interfere with my move. He assured me that there were no restrictions of any kind, no non-competition clause or goodwill to be paid. He said that he admired my courage to leave.

I still hadn't actually told my colleague that I wanted to leave the partnership. Why? I must admit that I was scared.

Luckily, out of the blue our accountant asked, *"Would you like me to make this announcement?"*

You can imagine how relieved I was. I accepted his offer. I must admit that I felt like a coward in doing so, but I couldn't resist the opportunity to avoid facing my colleague's inevitable displeasure.

He said he'd talk to her first thing in the morning.

I would be starting at 9 am because I had to take the kids to school first. I knew that she would already have the information by the time I got to the office.

Colleague

Just as I expected, my colleague totally flipped. Her reaction helped to confirm that I had indeed made the right decision in leaving.

I still respect my colleague despite what I went through with her. I love her as a human and remember the fun times we had over cups of coffee.

What was the problem, then? Outside of the office she was a very, very different person than inside. It was almost as if she had a split personality. We had diametrically opposed opinions on dentistry, the running of a practice, and social contact with patients that continuing on with her was untenable.

This story is absolutely not meant to make her look bad in any way. As said before, we often 'need' difficult people or (bad?) situations as an ignition to change our lives. It is a sign to finally, finally make a choice to achieve better things in life and not stay stuck in a situation that make us unhappy.

We often meet people who are our 'teachers' (spiritually spoken) in life. It is a gift to be able to perceive this and be led to make decisions that will benefit us.

A year had already gone by since making my decision to leave in August 2007. It was June 2008 now. It was holiday time. When I started my three-week leave, I found a lawyer's letter *in the mail.*

It is law!

It appeared that my colleague was incredibly angry. Talking to me seemed out of the question to her. A lawyer was apparently the answer.

This scared me.

So nervous I almost tripped over the stairs, I made my appearance at his office.

Why did all this have to happen? We could talk ourselves, couldn't we? Well, no, I guess not.

Did I have to go through all of this because of a personal choice I made for myself? What was it all about, anyway? She didn't have a case, did she?

According to my own lawyer, there indeed was no case! He had set up a meeting with himself, my colleague, her lawyer and me. Keep in mind that while all this was happening, we were still working together in the same office.

It appeared that she was demanding money. She wanted to be paid for the clients I was going to take with me.

She also wanted me out of the current building as of January 1st, 2009 since that was the date chosen for the end of our partnership.

The money part didn't worry me; our contract stated "no good-will to be paid", just like the accountant said! Her request for me to leave the building by December 31st didn't really frighten me, as she had no control over this. We both rented the current office from another dentist, and I thought that the current agreement meant that I could stay there until January 2011 if I needed to. My new office would be ready far earlier than that, though, in August 2009.

Well, it turned out that I was mistaken about this. My lawyer explained that my colleague actually did have the right to ask me to leave by the last day of the year. I couldn't understand why but he assured me that it was true and didn't seem willing to fight it. I was flabbergasted. He was **my** lawyer! Wasn't he supposed to stand up for my rights?

So, the frantic search for a temporary home started.

I wondered if the best thing to do was rent a dental port-a-cabin. Wow! Good idea Leslie. But it seemed way too expensive.

Then I had the idea of renting a dental bus! In the 1970s in Holland, there were pediatric/school dentists who rendered complete dental care in such busses.

Unfortunately, though, this was done in such a way that a high percentage of the now grown-ups have dental fear!

When *'that bus'* showed up in front of the school the kids would run home or hide in classrooms to avoid being dragged into the bus to see Mr. Dentist.

And *'the bus'* seemed to be even more expensive than the cabin. It took me three weeks to find this information. But I was desperate…

One morning, I took a long walk, worried sick about the future. I even called my assistant, hoping for comfort and reassurance.

She said it would all be ok, "sunny side up" like her eggs at Sunday morning breakfast!

Another patient of mine, a logistics manager in transportation services, worked right across the street from my new office building. I knew that his workplace had a huge parking lot for trucks.

It occurred to me that this parking lot might have room for a dental truck to house my practice. I made inquiries but unfortunately found it would not be possible.

I was utterly desperate at this point. The situation was getting way too big for me. So, I decided to let it all go. I gave up. I didn't care anymore. I was fed up with the frantic searches and stress and worrying. Being this anxious and frantic wasn't like me at all.

The only thing 'left' for me was to go to my office each day and do the job I love. After all, it is my passion no matter what. Working with lovely assistants and being part of a team with great clients; that's the passion. I decided now to focus on the good stuff.

But then, a few days later, I received an unexpected phone call.

It was K. He said he might have a temporary office space for me… WHAT? You must be kidding!

"Can you come now? I can show you the space we have for you!" I was flabbergasted. *"Of course, I will be right there!"* I said.

I grabbed the kids from school and off they went with mommy to see what might be her temporary dentistry shelter.

It appeared K. had office spaces for rent that I didn't know about.

He showed me a huge space, big enough for us to work in. The 'to be' waiting room was as big as a football canteen.

It was fantastic! Too good to be true?

The rental price was terrific. But…

But? Yes 'but'.

Was I allowed to practice in here according to City Hall? Had I go through that ordeal again?

K. said, *"Don't worry, it will be ok!"*

"Yeah, right K., you know what trouble I had to take to come this far!"

"I know", he said, *"but don't worry. It will be fine, I promise you."*

Well, I wasn't sure at all. City Hall; I am back again.

K. was going to call the officials for me; he would get back to me the next day.

And so he did.

He announced that I would be able to rent their space.

I was stunned.

It appeared that City Hall had changed their development plan. After they had given me the approval to settle in my new office building, they apparently declared that the entire area would be open to dentists and other medical professionals in the future.

It appeared that my 'fight' served a bigger goal than just mine. How fantastic.

I was all set now to go and start a new future.

On December 18th, 2008, I moved all my gear into my temporary home.

I had my own practice, my own office with my lovely assistants, Carolien, Jose and Claudia.

In October 2009, a year and a half after my decision to change my working life, my new office building was ready to receive us… and we made it beautiful on the inside. We sure did!

One for the money…

The contractors, the plasterer, the carpenters, all the hard-working men who moved in all the dental equipment, the assistants who painted the place with me, you name it: we were a team.

I did all the interior designing myself. (Do you need my number?)

We had an opening party with a few hundred people in attendance. What excitement!

From the beginning, we had a great time in my new practice. Our clients loved the office. Well, maybe not the treatments, LOL! Everybody seemed to know their role and be happy with it.

2010 arrived. I was still in seventh heaven with my gorgeous new work-space, and couldn't imagine a better way to ring in the New Year.

I thought things couldn't get any better, but it turned out that my situation was perhaps not as perfect as it seemed.

It became clear to me that money was going to be a much bigger problem than I had imagined. The costs involved in opening a new practice were huge. And then I also, of course, had the burden of:

Paying two mortgages, my house and the office building, but I also still had to pay the rent from the mutual building until January. At the same time I also had to pay rent for the building I needed to work in for a while since my colleague did not tolerate me in the mutual building anymore.

There was also a mountain of unexpected costs and costs I hadn't properly accounted for in my budget. As a result, I found I couldn't pay the IT-bill, the bill from the contractor, the bill from the carpenter. I can tell you these were thousands of dollars.

While in the temporary building, I had been forced to spend a lot of money making it workable. A few thousand dollars were used to rebuild an office I would only be in a few months.

On top of all this, I still had to pay a lot of money as result of the law suit. You'll remember I mentioned that my former colleague demanded that I compensate her for the money she would lose by my patients leaving the practice.

Although I <u>*knew*</u> that everything would be ok in the end, I was experiencing severe emotional effects because of the stress. Especially because <u>*'the bank'*</u> was complaining a lot. They were very concerned and let me know it almost every month.

I was so worried that I would come into the office crying every morning. I couldn't just enjoy what I had built, what I had realized; I was cursing the money. Why couldn't we just exchange our services in life? I will fill your tooth and you will give me a bread…

Courthouse, bills, unexpected financial losses, threats with financial consequences from my former colleague, a broken washing machine, oven, and dishwasher at home; <u>more money to waste.</u>

I was in despair. I could no longer see all the good in my life. I had a totally new office building, lovely kids, a great husband, good friends and family, two cars, a house, lovey staff, good health, 'being' a Dentist, Physical Therapist M.Sc., yet I was still not happy?

This feeling must have gone on and on and on for months until I was suddenly struck by a thought. It almost seemed like a voice:

**"Leslie, you have to make a change!
A change inside of you."**

Where did this come from? Change inside? Where did this voice or thought come from?

Obviously not from myself…

My reaction was: change *inside?* What does this have to do with **money,** for crying out loud?

Being an intuitive person, I immediately realized that my thought was intuition, while the reaction was from the reasoning mind.

The choice was mine. Which one would I make? Follow my intuition? Or do what most people would do and dismiss it?

Would I choose to *continue* to *feel* this way? To keep on seeing the things I see? To keep *feeling* like the victim of my past, whether it was yesterday or in my childhood?

I knew, I just knew! For once and for all!

I was totally fed up. Totally fed up with *feeling* ugly, *feeling* a victim of the past, *having* the money shortage.

Although I didn't know what change on the inside had to do with receiving money, I decided I was going to change.

But how?

"<u>*READ!*</u>" the thought or the voice said!

Read? Oh, ok. I am good at that. I am a book-worm.

I have had books on 'spirituality' or 'healing your life' for years on my bookshelf; I assumed the voice was referring to those. My staff knew about my love for this subject and for books in general, and they had given me a book on this subject years prior to this moment. Why had I not read this before?

I had not taken the time to read that yet. Or perhaps it just hadn't been the time yet?

Now was the time!

Think and grow! It is Law

I came home from work and immediately ran up the stairs to look for the book my assistants had given me. My eyes searched the bookshelf. There it was; *'The Power'* by Rhonda Byrne.

Of course, I had heard of *'The Secret'*. But because everybody seemed so obsessed with it, I chose not to be. I thought it must be a 'hype'.

I live my life my own way. I don't follow the herd.

Beside the book were others I still hadn't read, such as titles from Louise Hay, Wayne Dyer, as well as Deepak Chopra. The only reason they weren't covered with dust was because I had cleaned them a few weeks earlier.

I picked up *'The Power'* and started to read and read and read and read.

I took the book with me to the office and read in between treatments.

I encountered the following:

It is a common belief that money and spirituality don't mix. That 'if you're spiritual, you shouldn't want money. People who want money are greedy and materialistic'. But this way of thinking can hurt you.

Well, that hit me! Indeed, I did have this belief!

Money is the root of all evil/When lots of money is earned it must have been through criminal means/Why does somebody need that much money?/Money smells.

I would even throw pennies away while cleaning!

I considered myself to be spiritual. Spirituality for **me** meant:

Knowing there is more in heaven and earth, seeing the good in every person, refraining from judgement, helping people around you, being kind, being polite.

It had seemed to me that this was incompatible with money. It turned out that I was 'wrong'. I had flawed ideas on the subject of money.

I learned about the Law of Attraction.

Simply put: the Law of Attraction is the ability to attract whatever we are focusing on into our lives. It is believed that regardless of age, nationality or religious belief, we are all susceptible to the laws which govern the Universe, including the Law of Attraction. It is the Law of Attraction which uses the power of the mind to translate whatever is in our thoughts and materialize that into reality.

In basic terms: **all thoughts turn into things.**

If you focus on negative doom and gloom you will remain under that cloud. If you focus on positive thoughts and have goals that you aim to achieve, you will find a way to achieve them.

No man can attract money if he despises it, I learned!

The fact that I had such money problems suddenly made sense to me. I hated money and despised it. I had cursed money and had even thrown pennies away!

I was flabbergasted by this knowledge. Of course, I had heard of the 'like attracts like' but I didn't really know we could **use** this law to create our lives ourselves.

My negative ideas about money had been created in my childhood and adolescence. Perhaps this happened to you, too? Perhaps there were parents who kept telling you to 'save your money', 'buy nothing new before the old has worn out'. Having two, or worse even three pairs of shoes was almost criminal! Hoarding and saving was the motto. 'Study hard', 'Go get a good education' are phrases we all know. 'Have a good job and work your ass off' also, right?

When there is enough money people will love that money. But the same people will hate money when it is gone.

I was ready for the change. Nothing to lose, right?

I had now read tons of success stories of people deliberately using this Law.

If 'they' could do it, so could I.

Change the thought and the situation will change!

New Thought is New Life

I am an eternal student, so I love to browse the internet and study books to discover tips to help improve my life. So what I found about 'The Law of Attraction' (or: The Law of Allowing) was that you are a creator, you create with every thought.

The LOA is among many the most popular of the Universal laws. Advocates of this mind-power paradigm generally combine cognitive reframing techniques with affirmations and creative visualization to replace limiting or self-destructive (negative) thoughts with more empowering (positive) thoughts. A key component of the philosophy is that in order to effectively change one's negative thinking patterns, one must also **'feel'** (through creative visualization) that the desired changes *have already occurred.*

This combination of positive thought and positive emotion is believed to allow one to 'attract' positive experiences and opportunities by achieving resonance with the proposed energetic 'Law.'

Despite the fact that the LOA has no scientific proof that so many of us believe we need, there is evidence that emotions are associated with significant changes in the body!

Even *<u>acting</u>* our emotions cause a medical shift in our bodies.

Researcher Paul Ekman of the University of California, San Francisco has shown that people who willfully contort their facial muscles into expressions of happiness, fear, or anger will soon come to *<u>feel</u>* happiness, fear, or anger. Immunologist Nicholas Hall and his colleagues have reported immune changes associated with acting! Their findings suggest that acting is more than an act; it exerts effects on the body that may have important consequences for our health. The scientists measured changes in the immune systems of two actors before, during and after they performed in two plays. One was a comedy and the other one was a serious, depressing play. The researchers started drawing blood and measuring the heart rate before they even read the scripts. They monitored the actors through rehearsals and during all the subsequent performances. Hall and his colleagues measured the responsiveness of the immune cells called T- and B-lymphocytes. The data suggested a correlation between the type of personality being performed and immune responsiveness!

You probably already know that Shakespeare said if all the world is a stage, we are all actors and every life is an act! But, then, which role shall we play? In my opinion, the best role to play is the _**"act as if you are loving"**_ -role. I know, at first it sounds like a recommendation for false behavior but I can assure you, you will eventually go through life loving even the people whom you hated. I have been practicing this same role. It doesn't change "the other person", but it changes YOU who will eventually _experience_ that person in a different way.

As writer Marguerite Yourcenar says in her book, *Memories of Hadrian*:

"The mask, given time, comes to be the face itself."

New data

So now what to do with this profound knowledge?

When you have had certain thoughts all your life, they have been stored in your *subconscious* mind (more about super-, sub-, and conscious mind in the next chapter). It's kind of like a computer with a lot of new data. This old data is useless. It must be removed. This is accomplished by squeezing it out with new data to take its place and create a new program. So, you have to add new information to your subconscious mind.

This part is important: don't focus on removing the old stuff, as thinking about it will only attract more of the same. Get it out of your brain by adding new things.

Each book I read referred to a new one which I devoured. It tasted delicious and I wanted more of it.

I came across the book written by Florence Scovel Shinn titled *The Game of Life and How to Play It*.

This is a *must read*. Schools should absolutely include it in their curriculum.

Why do we learn about history? Does that make us happy really? We better study happiness.

I have had a bible since I was twelve and ever since then I have had the urge to read that. Every time I started, though, I gave up because I just didn't understand it.

Emotional Alignment Is Easy

When I read Florence Scovel Shinn's book, however, my urge to read the bible totally disappeared. She explained what Divinity is.

Just like with *Sermon on the Mount* written by Emmet Fox, I learned about who we really are and what the real meaning of life is.

I discarded old information about myself. (I am ugly, I do not deserve this car, People do not like me, I am fat). I accomplished this by adding the new! I constantly told a new tale to myself all day, day in and day out.

Affirm the new! Affirmations help purify our thoughts and restructure the dynamic of our brains so that we truly begin to think nothing is impossible! The word "affirmation" comes from the Latin *"affirmare"*, meaning "to make steady", to strengthen. Affirmations are proven methods of self-improvement because of their ability to rewire the brain. Much like exercise, they raise the level of feel-good hormones and push our brains to form new clusters of "positive thought-neurons".

In the sequence of thought-speech-action, affirmations play an integral role by breaking patterns of negative thoughts, negative speech, and, in turn, negative (re)actions.

Affirmations do not make things happen; they make things *welcome* to happen!!

I learned to change my thoughts about lack of money. I started with an affirmation from Florence Scovel Shinn's book:

"I cast this burden of lack to the Christ within and go free to have plenty

I cast this burden of lack to the Christ within and go free to have plenty

I cast this burden of lack to the Christ within and go free to have plenty"

I affirmed this for days, every morning when I was barely awake and every night just before I fell asleep (moments when the subconscious is most susceptible), for months until I understood and indeed believed that "lack" doesn't exist.

What is meant with "the Christ" is your *sub*conscious or the "Absolute Spiritual Truth".

Reversing your thoughts and changing within is NOT an easy task. It takes time and perseverance. Remember, it took time to put the crap in there too!

So how did I manage to take the time to reprogram my mind with a busy family, three kids, husband, dog, fitness hours at the gym and a busy dental practice?

The answer is I set the alarm clock an hour earlier than I used to and decided to stop watching television. Even a few minutes a day of TV-time now felt like a waste of time to me. I used to watch the news but I didn't like the way that we are supposed to always believe what "they" are telling us. Negativity all over. I was not going to literally buy it anymore.

Of course there are many, many affirmations you can do to help with "lack of money" or "debt".

For instance:

- Money comes to me in unexpected ways
- I look in wonder at the money I will receive
- My bills will be paid in a wondrous way
- I deserve all the money I need
- I am awake to see the sign of money coming my way
- Money will find me because I am a Divine being
- I am all good, I am Divine therefore I will receive good
- Money flows to me from many different sources

Of course, in the beginning you will be like, "yeah, right, it is all bull-do. Just by saying things like this, your bills will be paid? Have you been hit by a windmill?", you will ask me. "No, I haven't", is the answer.

Because I am living proof: *<u>my bills were paid!</u>*

Just keep reading! This is just the beginning of your transformation, if needed. There is more to come… Start slowly and gradually.

Please take the time to start your own affirmations in case you want to try it. Do you need guidance in choosing your sentences or words? Good affirmations are positive; they need to lessen the tension. So, an affirmation like: *"I am not angry"* will still register a negative impact in the subconscious mind because of the word "angry". Replace that with: *"I am loving"*, for instance.

Do not hesitate to contact me in finding the right words. I am here to help.

Again, it takes practice, practice, practice!

It is like going to the gym: you have decided to grow some muscles or lose weight.

You cannot expect to accomplish this in one week!

The next few pages are for you to write down your affirmations.

Pick an affirmation, mentioned here or written by yourself. It must resonate strongly with you. Just make sure that your only job is to affirm! The "how" and the "why" is being taken care of by the Universe!

No more excuses…READY? SET? GO!

My affirmation for today

Leslie van Oostenbrugge

My affirmation for today

My affirmation for today

Leslie van Oostenbrugge

My affirmation for today

My affirmation for today

Leslie van Oostenbrugge

My affirmation for today

My affirmation for today

Leslie van Oostenbrugge

My affirmation for today

My affirmation for today

Leslie van Oostenbrugge

My affirmation for today

Emotional Alignment Is Easy

My affirmation for today

Leslie van Oostenbrugge

My affirmation for today

My affirmation for today

Leslie van Oostenbrugge

My affirmation for today

Well, 14 days have gone by; 14 days with or without affirmations, with or without wasting your time on TV and negativity.

I'm so happy you've decided to continue reading this book. .

Wasn't it fun to find out the strength of your perseverance?

Time flies, doesn't it?

Have you noticed a change already?

Or maybe you didn't do the exercise. Did you give up?

Well, you have a free choice!

You are so free you can choose bondage.

Well, you ought a know one thing!

I am not giving up on *you*!!

Are you out of your mind?

There are three departments of the mind.

Sub conscious mind

Conscious mind

Super conscious mind

Can I draw this? Can we make a drawing to visualize the location of the mind? Where is it located?

Is the mind in the head? In the brain? Just outside of the head? In the air? Who cares?

Well, **mind** *(verb) that the mind is not the brain itself.*

Superconscious:

'All is well/ everything works out for me'
'You have to make a painting' = intuiton

Conscious:

I am going to buy a brush

Walking to a store

Subconscious:
'I like it let's do it again'.

Emotional Alignment Is Easy

The <u>subconscious</u> mind lies below the level of the conscious mind. It is a life recorder. It tapes all activities and experiences. Nothing is hidden from or forgotten by this system. It is a huge *storage* room; it has a lot of yottabytes. (YB). It is simply power without direction; it does what it is directed to do. It has stored all whatever the human being *feels* deeply. It is also called the immortal mind. It carries out orders without questioning.

The <u>conscious</u> mind is what we *operate* *with* during our waking hours and daily activities. It represents only a tiny, tiny part of our *three* consciousness's. It is the mortal mind.

The <u>superconscious</u> mind is the All-knowing power of the soul, of the universe. This "mind" perceives truth directly (with no interference or disturbance)!

It is your *intuition,* *your received dreams or thoughts…*

Part of the above I had been taught in high school.

I understood this… I thought….

But it turned out, I did not at all. For I didn't know I could change my own subconsciousness.

If I can do it, I know you can for sure!

The subconscious is, again, your storage cabinet, your garage just before the sale. There is a lot of necessary stuff in there as well as unnecessary.

Your subconscious is nothing but your past! It is history.

<u>The past is only an activated thought.</u>

<u>By changing your thoughts, you can change your past.</u>

The mind is like an iceberg:

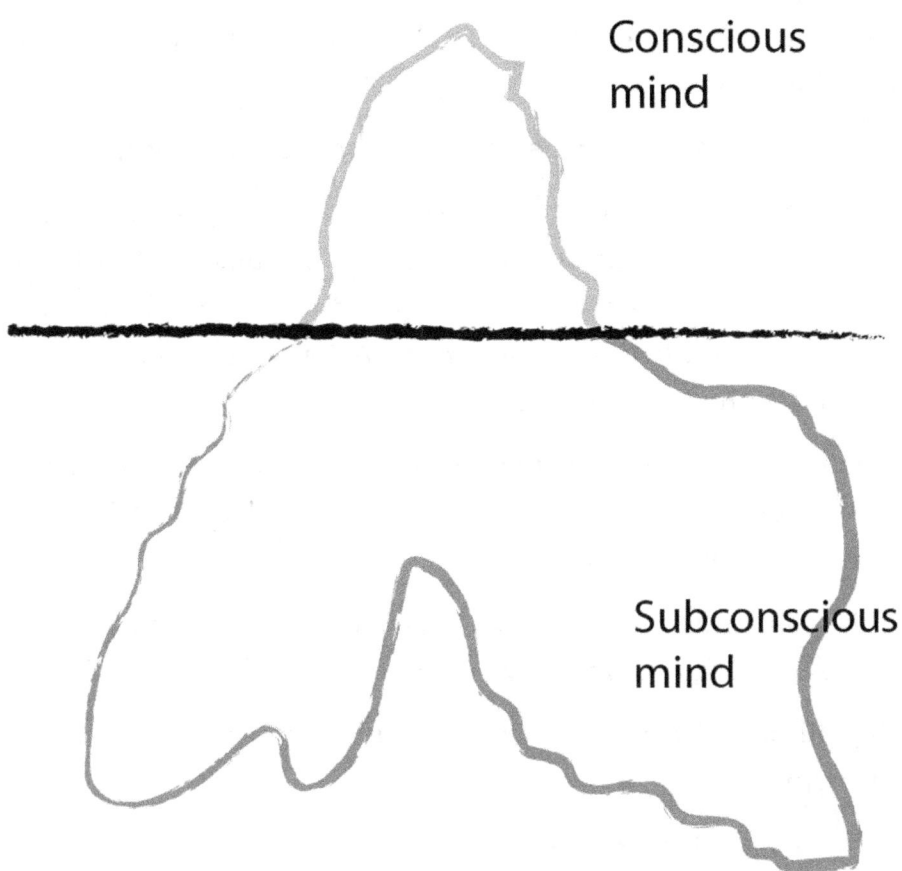

You see, life is ruled more by your subconscious than your conscious mind.

In your <u>sub</u>conscious mind, all the information from your past lives, memories from childhood, habits, pleasant and unpleasant experiences is stored.

Also stored is the knowledges of how to talk, walk, drive a car and so on. Pretty handy so you do not have to learn everything again every day.

Without the subconscious mind, you cannot recall anything.

Learned behaviors and (limiting!) beliefs are also in there!

Beliefs and behaviors have been learned through practice and repetition.

The <u>conscious</u> mind gives orders and makes decisions.

Superconscious to the conscious: "you can ride a bike, all is well". The conscious starts to pick up the bike with a lot of muscles. The subconscious says it liked it very much. You fell but got up and learned much more. After a lot of lessons, you now know how to ride that bike.

Good news: since (limiting) beliefs are stored as a result of repetition and practice, they can be replaced by NEW beliefs through renewed practice!

This all sounds like you have heard it in a previous chapter; I know but I cannot emphasize it enough.

Repetition is learning. Learning is invisible; only the *result* of that learning is visible.

Einstein and Bashar stated:

Keep practicing a <u>*new*</u> thought which has a different vibration so you will catch up with a new vibration and this new one will be stored in your subconscious.

Don't get upset if it takes you a few weeks or even months! You might have practiced the upsetting stuff for ten years.

You have to use:

Your free will to direct your attention!

Positive affirmations

Visualization

Subliminal audio/video

Meditation

Habit

I am happy to be able to show you how to use these techniques.

I am an experienced expert. I cured my back pain and solved my money issues.

I would also love to describe approaches to dental fear and dental pain.

Of course, they can be applied to any kind of situation you want to use them for.

For instance: school issues, hospital fear, phobias, working environment, stressful business, family relations and more…

A new dimension

A dimension is not a space. It is a state of being.

Every matter, thought, experience and emotion has a vibrational frequency. I already wrote earlier that thoughts and emotions create a change in your immune system. Since immune cells run through veins and blood vessels run through your teeth, you might realize now what the effect of thoughts might be on teeth… especially if you think 'I hate my teeth'.

It is difficult for people to understand that we can create shapes from thoughts. In the dimension we live in, the 3rd, things often have a physical appearance, like size or form. Let us say we are talking about a table: it has a size and a form. The table is matter, and it is built up only of atoms and electrons. Atoms and electron are energy particles, so the table is made of energy. Because of the density of the matter, we do not "see" the table as energy with its own, in this case, slow vibration. This 3rd dimension is specific because the sense of duality reigns (we only recognize; good/bad, off/on, male/female, dark/light and black/light). If the soul becomes more aware and sees that there is more in heaven and earth (you must have sensed that sometimes!), matters will be perceived differently.

A long, long time ago, it was very natural for a soul to connect with higher dimensions.

The fourth dimension is the way up to the fifth. In the fifth dimension the most beautiful and precious state is the opening of the heart. The vibration (frequency) is therefore higher than in the third. In this dimension, we learn to forgive and we learn to see the importance of matter. Once your heart has really opened and you look through the eyes of love you do not want to go back to the third dimension. You are responsible for your own soul growth. You still experience duality like good/bad, off/on, male/female, dark/light and black/white, but you know how to be able to transcend this. The problems in your life are caused by duality! You really do want to work on yourself because you really want to mind your own business.

Once you have experienced the fourth dimension you can transcend duality, and the concept that *"we are all one"* (in spirit, not in flesh) can sink in. We are all equal; we are all energy from the same Source.

Our conscious grows! According to ascension teachings, the earth and all beings living on the earth are in the process of shifting into a whole new level of reality in which a consciousness of love, compassion, peace and wisdom prevails. More light is present and solutions to problems become more and more clear.

If people want to feel better, they have to make a choice. If people want to stay stuck and sick, that is also a choice.

Sickness and dis-ease only come forth from hanging onto duality.

Are you hungry for more knowing through knowledge or do you want to stay stuck in duality world?

"Then how can we transcend to the fifth dimension", I can hear the really eager to learn-people ask.

In this dimension, manifestation through thoughts become possible; thoughts turn into things. Emotions are still present but you no longer let them fool you! You are your own master. Are you still whining about a friend who didn't show up when you needed him so badly? In this dimension, your heart is in charge!

The higher Self is (your soul) is now matched with the heart.

Love rules because the heart rules.

Things that can help you find your way to the fifth dimension include:

- Listening to light workers,
- Reading spiritual guidance books,
- Talking to healers,
- Joining spiritual groups,
- Realizing you can only help yourself.

The proof that you reached this dimension:

- You tend to find feathers everywhere. Do not look for them, they will show up. Once I had a session with a friend of mine, a paranormal healer. When I stood up from the chair I found a feather! We were both stunned! Where did that come from in the living room on a chair. It was not there when I came in.

- You tend to see numbers or combination of numbers. Numbers are energy (more about this later), they show you at which emotional point you are in life. I came to see the combination '1:11' at the clock or just the '1' or '222' or '44' all the time. When I started to see this all I started wondering what it meant and looked it up. I found out that this was 'Numerology'.

Numerology is any belief in the divine or the mystical relationship between a number and one or more coinciding events.

- You tend to find billboards giving you the answers

I found a big "YES" on a billboard when my question arose whether to write this book.

These are all tools to awaken you! Lots of people are still asleep and think this is life. No, it isn't. It is the dream. You are supposed to be the dreamer of your dream. I once said to my mother, "Once we are dead we will really know the meaning of life." I sensed something back then. Now I know, death doesn't exist (transformation of energy) and the meaning of life will be shown to you once you transcend the fourth dimension, like me.

We are the dreamer of the dream…

Conscious

To be *"awake"* in life means we are fully conscious in the present moment. Whatever we do, we do it fully consciously, focusing with all our attention on the activity we are actually performing. When you eat, eat, when you work, work, when you are ironing, iron. Taste the food, experience the work and feel the steam. No distraction! But how many people can say that they are fully conscious, or present in every moment of their lives?

We often identify with thoughts and emotions. But, hey! You *are not* your thoughts or your emotions. You just *experience* them. Realizing this is of huge importance and ignoring it is the source of many dis-eases!

Because you identify with emotions and thoughts that appear in your mind, you believe that you are a separate, illusionary person:

AN EGO

When you think your way through life, you give power to the EGO. So you keep the illusionary self alive; you try to stabilize it! But in this world, nothing can be stabilized. That is Law! The law is that of the law of change which stipulates that in the world everything is in the process of constant change. So is your EGO. Ego is just an idea!

Your sufferings are caused by the fact that you attempt to stabilize something which is made up by yourself. You totally forgot that you are pure Energy, pure Consciousness and free of identifications!

There is only one factor in life that doesn't change and that is the sense:

I am!

As a result of identifying with your mind and its function, the emphasis shifts from "I am" to "I am this...or that".

I am a female, I am Dutch, I am a dentist, I am a spouse, I am a mother, I am a divorced woman. Those are just earthly sentences. These nouns do not tell you *who* you "are".

There is only one thing not subject to change, which is the beyond *"I am", called "consciousness": the real, unchanging, stable Self.*

But *how* does the shift take place? It cannot be imposed on me or on you (by me), this shift from "identifying" to "Self". Well, first of all it doesn't happen to just a few chosen people. It happens to everybody but not everybody can or wants to "see" the shift. It is an experience that simply happens to you!

At the moment when the shift of attention takes place (shift from the "mind" to "love"), your alertness emerges. A new space appears in you; you have the ability of *"seeing"* and you contemplate what is happening to you as an external observer!

You woke up and realize you! are the dreamer of the dream. You are the creator of your life. You choose the experience you want to have!

Again, this is *not* the result of the analytical work of the mind but a series of insights inspired by the inner *"quiet"*.

Bridge over troubled water

Dr. Masaru Emoto (July 22nd, 1943-October 17th, 2014) was a Japanese author, researcher and entrepreneur.

He claimed that human *consciousness* has an effect on the molecular structure of water.

His belief was that water could react to positive thoughts and words. He also claimed that troubled or polluted water could be cleaned through prayer, positive thinking, meditation and positive visualization.

Water was a *"blueprint for our reality"*, Dr. Emoto believed.

Emotional energies and vibrations can change the physical structure of water.

Please check his amazing video! Go to my website www.theawakeningdentist.com. If you prefer you can visit this direct link:
https://m.youtube.com/watch?v=TWAuc9GIvFo

I wonder why Dr. Emoto wasn't named "Dr. Emot*i*o"

It is brilliant!

Emotions can change the energy level of water as well as the structure.

The water, with positive messages addressed to it, such as love and gratitude, formed beautiful crystals!

The water with negative messages addressed to it, such as hate and anger, became ugly and malformed.

Aren't we all <u>*watery*</u> beings? Our bodies consist of approximately 80% of water!

So, if the findings of Dr. Emoto imply that thought can do amazing things to water, *imagine* what thought can do to us?

Teeth are part of this living watery body. They are not some piano-key-like thingies (yes, sadly some people have black teeth...) sticking out of your gums. Your watery blood runs right through them.

Imagine... imagine... imagine... imagine... imagine!

LinkedIn

Each person's teeth are their own individual link, their evolutionary link to existence itself. The teeth can store memories; they are even a personal Akashic record of everything that has happened to an individual during their whole evolution. To me that is very clear, for aren't the teeth the 'left-overs' of the body when the body is Spiritless? In other words, when we have died?

The remains of human teeth play a major role in Archeology, Anthropology and human identification (forensic dentistry is an important part of identifying a deceased person)!

The oldest fossils of humans which were found were in Israel. The jaw and the teeth were 194,000 years old!

The dentist is one of the professionals most commonly called on to identify a deceased human being! DNA can be extracted from the root, fillings tell their own stories and form, size and shape are willing to tell you a lot about the deceased person.

What is an Akashic record? The Akashic records or "The Book of Life" can be equated to the Universe's super computer system. It is *this* system that acts like the central storehouse of all information for every individual who has ever lived upon earth. The Akashic records contain every deed, word, feeling, thought and intent that has ever occurred at any time in the history of the world.

"Every thought has already been thought"

So, don't think you'll come up with something new, LOL. All ideas already exist: some just haven't been expressed yet!

The record is also called *"God's book of remembrance"*. It contains the entire history of every soul since the dawn of Creation. We are connected through these records; they are the inspiration, the dream, the idea. They draw us towards us or repel us.

Some people can give you accurate readings; they tap their information out of the subconscious mind of the client and the available Akashic records.

You can tap into these records too, you know. They are yours!

Sometimes the most terrifying discovery is who you really are. I once asked my friend (cause I saw her pain) to go to a "soul retreat". She immediately said no. She was afraid that messy consequences would arise.

Everybody has his or her own level of existence. You cannot push anyone into healing themselves.

This reaction of my friend can only come from someone who doesn't know who she really is. I am just witnessing this, while I myself am in bliss.

Without this connection to Source we indeed do not know who we really are. The road map back home to Source are the Akashic records.

So again, to be sure you understand this:

The Akashic records (Book of Life) are an ancient energetic record or <u>database</u> of every thought, emotion, feeling, word and action that has ever existed, is already existing or will always exist.

I call it the:

'I-consciousness cloud'©

Your I-cloud of consciousness.

Just tune in, get your Wi-Fi installed and receive this Galactic information!

It is easy: you just have to get rid of some trash from your so called 'past'. The past is just a thought, remember?

According to "A Course in Miracles", all time is at the same time. Past, Now and Future exists at once. You definitely at least once had a thought like "I knew this would happen", right? Now isn't this "future"? We live parallel lives. It is just that as humans we think linear thoughts. We need to step out of the control of one's ego mind in order to create a better life.

Think differently and see your world change.

I did it, so you can, too. Just link in to your higher Self.

Crystal clear

I sometimes feel alone in my role as a dentist. In most dental magazines you see the brilliant technical sides of Dentistry. I felt inferior to most dentist because I am not doing this technical work that much. In my office the rate dental caries is very low. I am proud of that and proud of my clients. I realize that teeth are an expression of consciousness so every treatment has to start within this consciousness.

On my path to enlightenment I discovered the book from Osho's dentist Swami Devageet called: "The First Buddha in the Dental Chair". Osho was his patient. I read the following which Osho stated and it absolutely resonated with me.

"And our body remembers! Memories are stored in the DNA of each cell. Each human body contains memories. It remembers our evolutionary history back to the beginning of time, long before there were human beings."

Osho stated that each persons' teeth hold memories and connect to the human collective unconscious minds.

Teeth record all that is happening, even now. Why are these memories in teeth? Well, the enamel of your teeth are made out of millions of tiny crystals. Crystals can store information, just like the crystals in your computer, the chip; the enamel of your teeth absorb a lot of energy! The brain is a computer and the teeth are storage rooms for memories going way, way, way back in time.

Now, knowing this, isn't it very clear that curing the tooth means curing the body?

Literally: it is possible to find the _roots_ of many diseases in the teeth?

Taking out the right tooth, extirpating the right nerve, treating the inflammation of the gum; all of this can help getting rid of your dis-ease. Release the memories they hold, and you will be free!

I myself have had a problem with my lower first right molar. My dentist started a root canal treatment which didn't work. I knew something else was going on. I figured I had to release something, but I didn't know what. . After a lot of reflection, the answer came to me through Osho:

"Release the memories of my mother"

Osho himself too had an issue with the same molar!! He pointed out that within the same tooth the different root nerves are connected to different people and different events.

The root canal treatment didn't work for me. I did make an appointment with the oral surgeon to have the molar removed and have an implant. But then I decided to cancel this appointment and knew I had to work on something else; release and forgive my mother, although I thought I had done that sufficiently already….

<u>Working with the teeth is very healing for the whole person.</u>

Parents

When it comes to our families, especially our parents, we allow ourselves to create attachments to them. Well, for sure I did. Do or did you value your parents' opinion of you over your own? Oh yes, I did for sure! It is very possible that family karma might hold you back.

The law of Karma maintains that every action has a "cause and effect", meaning that each action produces Karmic energy that will eventually return to you.

Whether you like it or not, the connection you have to your family, and especially your mother, is much greater than just the genetic one. When you are born, you are literally attached to your mother through the umbilical cord. This cord is the connection between the mother's sacral chakra and her child's solar plexus chakra. A chakra is each of seven centers of spiritual power, or major energy centers in the human body.

A mother typically feels a strong emotional connection to her child because the sacral chakra represents the emotional center.

So, mothers can wrap a huge invisible leash around us; be aware of that now. This leash can be tightening and frightening but also loving and moving. Be aware that this chakra helps to shape the child's self-identity and personal power!

When my mother died, I experienced the unleashing of this energy. This was such a powerful experience! After the moment she died, I walked around leaning forward with my hand firmly touching the area just below my breastbone for at least 15 minutes (solar plexus).

It was unexplainable why I "had" to do this. It wasn't until later on that evening that I realized: *our physical cord was cut!* And it hurt deeply.

After my dad died, I had another terrifying emotional experience. I am certain that it was related to the trauma of losing my father.

I woke up one night and I couldn't breathe. My self-supporting system of breath had left me. I was wide awake and I felt my eyes bulging out of their sockets. *"What the bleep is this!"*, I thought. I couldn't breathe. I was about to choke.

I managed to recover by deliberately and consciously drawing my breath through my nose, ensuring I felt the air in my chest. I desperately needed fresh air, so I jumped out of my bed in the dark of the night and reached for the window. Frantically, I pulled up the blinds so I could open my window.

Staring into the pitch black of the dark night through my window, I encountered my reflection in the glass. What I saw is a face I will never forget…

It was me, or more precisely, *it was my face,* staring back at me. This face had huge black circles around its eyes. The eyes were bulging out of their sockets and looked frightening! My face was desperately crying for help! I was trying to recover by breathing deliberately and deeply, using all the muscles in my shoulders. It took a few hours for my normal, involuntary breathing to return.

Experiences are warning systems. They tell you whether you are on the "right" (positive) track or the opposite. Don't say to yourself, *"why me?"*. Rather, ask *"what does this experience teach me?"*.

This experience told me I had to work on myself. I had to remember that every pain in the body has a link to a specific emotional state.

The revelation of Osho (he found that certain teeth contained memories with his mother, father and other relatives) made me realize I still had to resolve mine with my mother. Osho and I had problems on the same molar.

Since I gained the knowledge that memories even before our physical life are stored in our bodies, I knew that I had to dig deep.

I went to see a regression therapist; I was ready to release ALL blockage in every area of my body.

Past life

Edgar Cayce, Brian Weiss, Sandra Ann Taylor and Carol Bowman are four among many writers with books on past lives. Brian Weiss' books *Many Lives, Many Masters* and *Same Soul, Many Bodies* are absolute must-reads. We all know the Deja vu experience, right? When we suddenly remember something like we have seen it before when we are at a certain place or do a certain act. Or, when we meet people and we feel like we have met them before.

Are you experiencing unexplainable pains in your shoulder? You might have fallen off the back of the horse when you were a knight in shining armor in the year 1560.

If you tend to be depressed, you may have been emotionally beaten down when you were young, but there also may be lingering feelings of hopelessness from <u>preceding</u> existences!! Low self-esteem may have some of its roots in a previous life filled with criticism.

You are impacted by past-life influences, present-life upbringing, and ongoing unresolved emotional issues.

By releasing the feelings, clearing the Karma, and in my opinion above all restructuring your belief system into healthy assumptions and intentions, you will not only restore balance to your personal energy field, but also bring a dramatic new direction to your life right now and to your Soul's future!

My desire to achieve this was the reason why I was there, lying on a therapy bed, breathing in and out, in and out, in and out…

… until I reached this mindless state…

… and saw myself in the year 1680.

I went back to the moment I saw the frightening face in my window. The therapist asked me to look deep, deep, deep into those eyes and then even go deeper and deeper and deeper. Then! There I was…

I saw myself jumping around in the woods with my little skirt jumping with me. I had to get wood for the fire stove. I must have been 6 years old. I was a happy little girl, skipping and jumping and singing. I looked very happy! I could only see myself from the back. The sun was going down and darkness was falling into the woods. I had to go in there still to gather the wood! *"Hurry Leslie, hurry"*, I said to myself. My mother was in the little house with smoke coming out of the chimney. My dad was outside, running after me into the dark, dark forest. I didn't see myself coming back.

The more deeply I sank into this mindless state, the more I *"saw"*. I saw myself as a little baby in the year I was physically born in my present life, in the 60's. I had a visitor in my room….

The therapist asked me whether I wanted to stop the session. *"No way"*, was my answer. I was going to finish this session today. *"I'll float 'til I drop"*, I said to myself. I had to know the truth!

I suddenly saw a face peeking over my right shoulder. A very familiar face! A friendly, happy, bearded face. I instantly knew who it was!

GOD! It was GOD! Oh my goodness. I knew what this meant immediately: <u>*"I AM GOD"*</u>, I said to the therapist. <u>*"I AM GOD"*</u>.

We all are God, because we are part of him. He made us like Himself.

That night changed my life for the better. I knew who I was! I never had a breathing issue like the ones I had experienced again.

We started at eight o'clock in the evening and were finished by eleven thirty at night.

Your family is your gift

Before we were born we choose our family, our father, our mother, our siblings. We choose them to get the best out of our lives, not the worst. Remember that we live in a friendly world!

Of course, the newspaper and the journalists on TV will tell you otherwise. They need you to believe that the world is full of horrible and sad news and very little good. Why do they do this? They need to sell papers and attract viewers, that's why. Every evening, millions of people curl up on the couch with a cup of coffee for another eight o'clock news indoctrination.

Whenever you feel an energetic tie is present, you can release it by physically pulling it out of you. Pull the rope out of your body and visualize the emotions leaving you. You might need this after the news broadcast.

You are 50% your dad and 50% your mom. To "accept" your mom and dad on a deeper level is very essential for a child. Because you will always be their child. If you inwardly reject your parents, you immediately install a new pattern within yourself. The pattern that you do not want to be "like them".

But guess what… eventually you will be like them! That is LAW! The most important thing to remember is this: the more you let your parents be who they are, the more you get to be your Self and you will not turn out *"like them'*.

Now here is the pitfall for many people, including me. I didn't accept my parents the way they were. I took over a lot of responsibilities from them, took care of my brother, tried to please my mother and did my utmost to make her love me, and never actually talked to my dad because he was on mute a great deal of my life. He was unable to express and show love, like my mom.

But taking over responsibilities that aren't your own weakens you as well as "the other".

You have got to honor your mom and dad and honor the space they are in. You know immediately when you are not doing that: you tend to

Look for love and recognition and want to prove yourself

You don't need to do that for *"being"* is all encompassing. There is no need to search, as love is here for you.

So cut the crap for you are wasting time, energy and teeth!

I forgave my parents through affirmations and I walked the labyrinth in Turkey. You don't have to go to Turkey for that (LOL), but while I was on holiday there and had spare time, I decided to draw the labyrinth myself in the sand on the beach with the sun nicely tanning my body.

The labyrinth is a walking meditation, a path of prayer and an archetypal blueprint where psyche meets Spirit. A labyrinth can be a source of solace and can quiet a distracted and overactive mind. It can help resolve your inner discomfort and still your mind enough for you to clarify what is going on.

Remind yourself that you are not your thoughts and you are not what you think your parents think of you.

You are not responsible for what happens to you in childhood. You are responsible for healing that childhood pain as an adult!

Like Carl Jung said: "I am not what happened to me. I am what I choose to become".

After having walked the labyrinth inside and out twice, I stopped in the middle, raised my arms up to the beautiful sunny sky and yelled out loud; *"mom, dad, thank you for being my parents. I forgive you"*. It is "the moving through" as an adult which is crucial to our well-being and maturation!

This was a healing moment I will never forget…

The sacred privilege to be a mom

My three lovely children are a joy to watch. I crack up most of the time because of their sense of humor :-)

Many people have lots of problems with adolescent kids going through puberty. Honestly… I don't!

You will only have trouble if you try to control them and want them to behave the way *you* want. Also, when you want to make them believe what you believe! This is impossible. All I can do is give all my love, show them my power and "teach" them why they experience things in life. It is all for the best. Even my own death will be for their sake. I hope Keij, Max and Eef, the three of you will read this book while I am alive. For sure you will read it when I am dead. See? The three of you needed my transition to get out of your own way.

I am trying to raise honest, expressive and happy children while maintaining my own sacred joyful God-given space. Love yourself, then love you being a mom!

Let me share the 7 bits for kids:

1. Communication! Talk about what is really happening at home. Share what your thoughts are on running a household, raising children and having a job. Talk about your plans, encounters, life and friends.

2. Express love! Show them you love them! Say to them every day: "I love you". Even when it is tough for you. You can do it; it just might take some practice! Forget the fact *your*

mom didn't say that to *you*. Take your responsibility and love!

3. Show authenticity! Tell them who we really are. Not just a bag of bones but pure energy, love and light. Everybody is unique and has special gifts.

4. Praise the kids! Do not praise them for having good grades, but rather for who they are! Focus on strengthening them. Focus on the fact that a problem is the solution in itself. Every so called "problem" is just a mind shift closer to Self. Do not criticize! Just <u>witness in bliss</u>!

5. Never compare your kids to one another! This will demolish your child's self-esteem! My mother used to say to my brother: "look how well your sister is doing!" Guess what? It destroyed my self esteem for **<u>I became the one</u>** who felt guilty because my brother felt bad! This combined with my mom telling me "who do *you* think you are" was enough for me to totally shut my feelings up towards my brother. I felt guilty for many, many years. So comparing your kids may not only affect the "accused" child but also the "eulogized" child! For God's sake, please accept your children as they are. My brother went to university in his late 30's and got a terrific business degree! I was happy to see him wear his mortarboard! My mom wasn't physically around anymore at that time. It was only then, when I started doing my affirmations and got rid of my guilt, that my brother and I really reconnected again in the most splendid and beautiful way! Again: it is all your own wish and your own work.

6. Organize a family meeting once a month! In this meeting let every family member say out loud five positive things about every other family member. It is incredible to hear this. It is wonderful to watch each member straightening their back and to see the twinkle in their eye and sparkle on their teeth. The family vibe is raised! If you hear your son telling your daughter: "Keij, I was so happy that you helped me out with my homework without asking. Thank you for that", you might cry from joy and utter bliss. But if you would rather see them sit in front of the TV with sad faces after a fight then that is ok, too. See? It's all choices. The movie will be over in an hour….

7. Take care of Self. You cannot take care of them if you don't feel ok! It is just like putting on an oxygen mask on a plane: yours first, then your kids'! Don't choke on all your chores, must-do's, have-not's and what-if's.

Healing is the portal to abundance

Forgiveness and self-love will allow you to release negative energy, making room for the positive.

There was more to work on for me: money! I had judged money all my life. I had seen it as my enemy.

I had to turn my thoughts and beliefs about money around; I had to choose to create good feelings about money.

I came across the following books: *Think and Grow Rich* by Napoleon Hill, *The Essential Law of Attraction Collection* by Esther and Jerry Hicks, *The Sermon on the Mount* by Emmet Fox, and *The Master Key System* by Charles Haanel.

They all provide the same advice for how to see money in a positive way:

- Pay your bills with love
- Write "thank you for your service" on your invoice
- Write "thank you for the money"
- Whenever you receive (even the smallest) payment, write "thank you"
- Feel love when you pay for your goods in the store
- Say "thank you for my groceries" to the man behind the counter
- Realize you help people keep their jobs because of your payment
- Pet your credit card like it is your puppy
- Feeeeeeel rich

- Give money away with love
- Feel happiness while buying a too expensive toy
- Do the happiness workout, good will follow
- Keep a 100$ bill in your wallet and spend it mentally ten times a day
- Clean out your wallet!! It is not your garbage bin
- Clean your house; make room for the money
- Say thank you for the money you will receive (affirmations)
- Feel happy when you give, feel happy when you buy!
- Order your bills; stack them neatly in your wallet
- Shout out to heaven when you find even a penny, "thank you universe"
- Money is energy; just like thoughts, like attracts like.

I can proudly tell you I have done all of the above. Yes, it takes perseverance! When you try to learn tennis, you might not like the game at first if you cannot hit the ball. But you will learn to hit the first ball and the next and the next. Then the game begins.

Let the games begin.

I cleaned my wallet of all the 3, 2 and 1-year old receipts, and threw away coupon cards of stores I hadn't gone to for the last year or so. I still do pay at the cashier with love and say or think *"thank you for the beautiful stuff"*.

I sometimes put a stack of bills worth 150 dollars in my wallet to *feel* rich. Sometimes I take them out and pet them or play with them like mafia bosses play with their stacks. When I find pennies, I thank the universe. I sometimes pay for the customer behind me even though I don't know him. I buy drinks for people I know whenever we happen to be in the same restaurant, all for the fun! I recently paid for an elderly woman's groceries; she was in heaven. I surprise people with flowers and chocolate.

Life experience teaches, words don't.

Soon… my results showed!

Now remember, the process takes at least three months!

Believe it and you will see it.

But first… how do you love money if you don't love yourself?

I love me

From a very early age, people (usually your parents) teach you what to believe. Often because of their own upbringing, stress, experiences or lack of love, they try to impress things upon you. Unfortunately, most of the time they succeed.

It is a flawed premise that because my parents are my parents and were here way before I was born, they must know better than I do what is right or wrong for me.

Of course, we all understand that parents must provide us with food, shelter and a safe physical environment. But why do we think they have the right to determine our life's purpose?

We were all born with our *own* guidance and intuitive system!

I just had the lovely experience of being on holiday for a week. Although I hardly ever listen to conversations between other people anymore (95% is complaining), I happened to witness two conversations between mother and child.

Well, perhaps I shouldn't say "happened to". Sometimes you overhear things for a purpose; maybe they are needed for your own growth.

In the first conversation, I overheard a mother forbidding her child to take home two (small) beautiful stones she found on the beach. She was only permitted to take one. The discussion as to why she couldn't take both went on for around 15 minutes. It ended up with a "you just cannot".

May be the child's energy resonated very much with these two stones. She was now cut off short of experiencing this on a higher level. She didn't ask to take 100 stones….

Another conversation: on a balcony, a little child about 3 years old was very lovingly and carefully putting cream on her mommy's back. All of a sudden, the mother shouted, *"don't you know what is enough? Do you never know what is enough?"*. No, she doesn't know what "enough" cream is. She doesn't know what "enough" love is either. Love is endless… it came to the mother through the cream. Needless to say, the child stopped…

A zillion examples are available, of course.

Well, I grew up and realized I didn't love myself at all, hated my body, was insecure, didn't really think I was smart… you name it. I eventually graduated cum laude in Dentistry as well as Physical Therapy and still thought I was not smart enough. As if that wasn't bad enough, I thought I was ugly, too.

Compliment your kids, tell them you love them, and hug them every single day. Include your partner in this process. If you cannot do this, it is not because of *your kids!* It is because of *you.*

When I had kids, my mom admitted she wasn't able to really hug, squeeze or say *'I love you so much'*. She saw her past in my future…. I forgave her and asked her to try again the act of loving with her grandkids. I asked her to try it for <u>herself</u> to learn and realize how beautiful it can be. Try for <u>me</u> in the second place so I could feel the love towards me through my kids.

She couldn't…

I was judged, and I learned to judge myself.

I let myself deviate from my own guidance system.

A+! That's the grade I would have received for judging and hating myself, yes indeed. Actually, I would have passed cum laude.

When I received the thought (yes, we receive them) about changing within, I immediately knew I had to start loving myself. I was fed up with hating myself. It seeps through into your whole life.

I had heard about the existence of "Mirror Work" (we should call it "Miracle Work" because it *really, really* works). I started to do **this work.**

Every single day I would stand in front of the mirror saying beautiful things to myself.

Obviously, you have to start with the things you *believe* in and really find very beautiful! (If you *believe* you have a fat stomach, you cannot suddenly like that, right?). There must be something beautiful about you!

So I said to myself:

- I have beautiful eyes
- I have terrific hair
- I have beautiful strong hands
- I have strong biceps
- I have beautiful triceps
- I have a great height
- I have a good clothing size

- I have beautiful size feet
- …

Of course, it takes time and yes again, practice, practice, practice. Gradually you will see the increase in self-love and will be able to see more and more beautiful things in yourself and your body.

It's important to create a schedule for self-work exercises that works for you. You'll find that many books provide set schedules and tell you to abide by them, but it's best to take the lessons that really resonate with you and invest an amount of time which is comfortable for you. So for example, I didn't follow instructions to stand in front of the mirror three times a day. Instead, I spent one moment a day in front of the mirror.

When going to the gym for the first time you will probably not go busting your ass for three consecutive hours until you throw up, will you?

Because there wouldn't be a next time, that's for sure. Your exercises have to fit into your daily schedule.

I generally did my mirror exercise right after my morning shower. Wrapped in a towel, I would gradually unveil my body and choose to love it in its entirety. The full unwrapping took a few weeks….

This process led me to the feeling I have today when I look in a mirror. I laugh with joy and say to myself, I know I know **I am** beautiful.

<u>Mirror, mirror on the wall you don't have to tell me anything at all,</u> hahaha!

Chapter closed.

Closed at the age of 48.

If you do not love yourself and find yourself *not worthy, worth* cannot come to you! You are blocking it.

If you do not have any confidence in yourself you will always struggle with limitations and fear, and you won't recognize great opportunities right in front of you!

Well, I was healed and ready to receive. I had the strongest desire to begin changing and allowing the healing.

The next page might be of help to you in quick starting your use of affirmations.

Again, affirmations are statements that you repeat over and over and over again. During these affirmations, you **must** *feel* good.

Whenever you cannot reach the *"feel good"* feeling, just try to remember a great situation, a great love in your life, a funny experience. The trick is to keep the butterflies (which is the demonstration of feeling good) alive and get them flying again!!

The universe knows what you <u>feel</u>. Feelings are energy. The universe will respond to that, for IT IS LAW!

Affirmations for you

- I enjoy feeling good
- I am totally good stuff
- Thank you for this body that takes me everywhere
- I can be healthy at any size
- I love my legs that carry me all over the place
- I like my eyes because I can see beauty
- I like the color of my eyes
- I love my curls, and the way they dance
- I love my straight hair and the fact it is easy to groom
- My body can do awesome things
- Only I have to like me
- My body loves me
- My ears are able to hear my children
- I give thanks to my belly, as it protects my organs
- My head is keeping my brain safe
- Breathing through my nose lets me smell my food
- My hands work to keep me young
- My eyes are seeing all the wonders
- My butt lets me sit when I want to
- My butt doesn't hurt when I am sitting
- I am happy I chose this body
- I love my back as it always supports me
- I love my hips because they carry me to my friends
- I love my mind
- I love the wrinkles because they show me I have had fun
- I like my funny smile

Emotional Alignment Is Easy

- I love my teeth because they are smiling back at me
- I love my gums because they are pink, like the color of love
- My teeth are great because they help digest my food

Chemistry of "feeling good"

Because feeling good is an essential part of life, I want to talk more about it. I want to emphasize it, actually.

"Feeling good" can be measured.

When you have joy, it creates a good, most often terrific feeling….

Usually you have the terrific feeling first and you recognize this as being "joy" within a thousandth of a second. It is recognized by the brain.

But how?

There's a molecule called **"NO"** (nitric oxide). It is the boss of the neurotransmitters, including endorphins, dopamine, and serotonins, for instance. It regulates the release of all these chemicals.

Nitric oxide is produced by cells in the brain, blood and its vessels. It is also produced in the lungs and your *gut. (Gut feeling.)*

Their production is triggered by *laughter* and other pleasure experiences. *Bodily exercise* also releases this molecule. Have you heard of (or experienced yourself) the "why" of why runners get a "high"? It is produced by NO.

Meditation also triggers the production of "NO".

"NO" relaxes blood vessel-*walls*. These walls widen and then more blood can flow through the vessels. Your heart can really skip a beat from it.

Your vessel walls will become softer, more relaxed. The more relaxed **you** are (meditation? exercise?), the more relaxed your walls, and the more your blood flow will increase.

Imagine; more blood flow -> more oxygen in your organs and muscles -> more muscle relaxation, and so on.

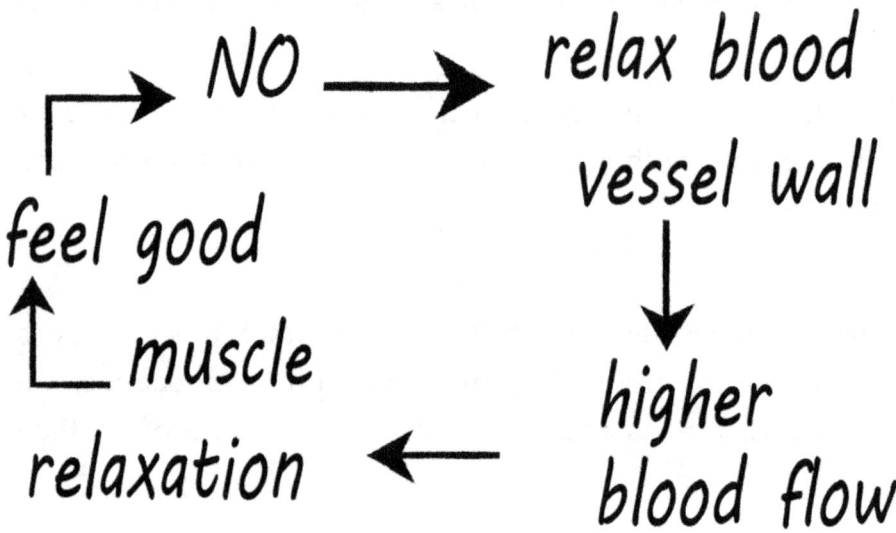

Note: it is a 'NO-brainer'. This process happens unconsciously.

The muscles, including those in your jaws, relax. Muscle relaxation might reduce headaches; it could even might reduce _referred_ pain to the teeth.

So what if you "choose" to feel good on purpose? I mean choose with the mind and then influence the brain and _let_ your body act accordingly. (Study by prof. Ellen Langer, next chapter).

You can _choose_ to feel good, feel joy.

But… it takes practice, and more practice, and more practice.

Our *inborn* nature is one of joy and love! But nowadays people tend to be ashamed of having fun and being joyful. When my friend and I are having the greatest fun on vacation, people asked whether we have been drinking. We said "Yes, water! We don't drink alcohol". People tend to step back when having fun and huge laughter. "What if… someone sees me", they think.

We have forgotten to really enjoy things. Now it is time to step-up and remember.

What's (*the*) matter?

All matter is made of molecules which are a series of atoms. The body is made of atoms also. As a matter of fact, the atoms of our bodies are traceable to stars. We are chemically connected to all atoms in the universe. We are biologically connected to every other living thing in the world. This smart talk doesn't come from <u>*my*</u> brains. Enough research has been done and can be found online.

What I learned in school about matter, atoms and molecules is that they are energy packages.

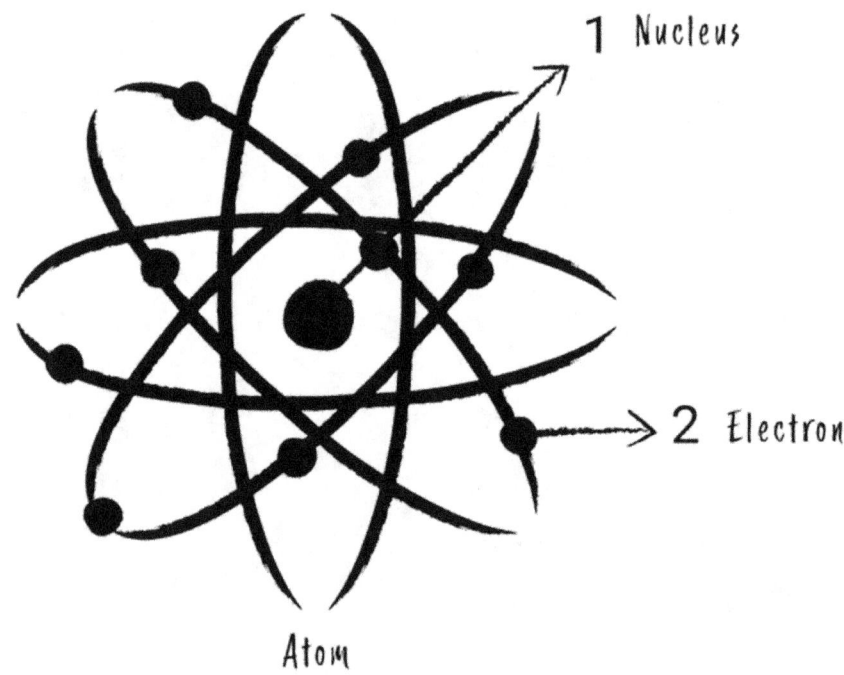

Atom

So an atom is the smallest constituent unit of ordinary matter. The atom's nucleus contains protons and neutrons, and electrons circle around it.

Quantum physics says: the atom is made of energy.

Proton: *a subatomic particle with a positive electric charge.*

Neutron: *a subatomic particle without a charge ('no net charge').*

Electrons: *a subatomic particle with a negative electric charge.*

Description of a molecule: at least two or more atoms brought together by chemical bonds.

For instance, water: H_2O-molecule, which is a chemical bonding between two hydrogen (H) atoms and one oxygen (O) atom. .

Water Molecule

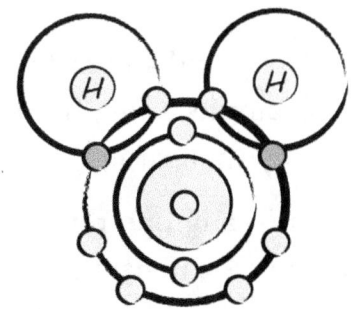

Remember, the human body is 70% water.

The human body can be considered matter. We consist of different types of atoms; combinations of these are molecules and combinations of the latter are matter.

Who is the matter? You! You are matter.

Emotional Alignment Is Easy

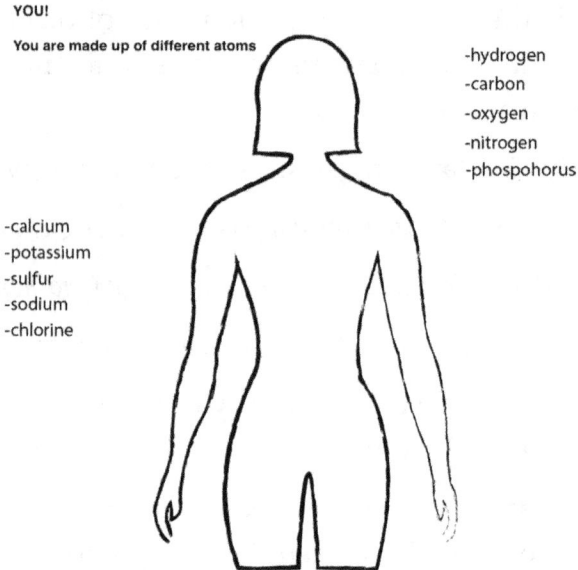

Yet according to quantum physics, a quantum atom is made of energy, molecules are made of energy, water is made of energy -> people are energy!

Energy is *not* matter.

Energy is all around you and interacts with you constantly. You can see it; for example, sunlight. You can touch it; for example, vibration. You can hear it; for example, music.

Energy isn't made up of any one thing…it is a very abstract concept. It is a force **field**, is invisible, and has a big influence in the physical world.

We are energy beings. We are vibrational beings (actually it is only the trick of the light that we see ourselves as human beings).

We are capable of influencing energy particles to go where we want. Energy particles can behave differently just as a result of being observed.

The double slit experiment by Thomas Young (1773-1829), a British physician and scientist, showed proof of this. Please check this link and be amazed.

https://m.youtube.com/watch?v=zKdoE1vX7k4n

This is an orderly universe. Nothing happens by accident. The images you plant in your marvelous mind instantly set up an attractive force which governs the result of our life.

You are a living, breathing magnet.

Spirit meets science, hi!

Spirit just knew science would catch up.

The English word *"spirit"* comes from the Latin word *"spiritus"*, which means "breath".

It is often used to refer to the consciousness or personality. The notions of a person's spirit and *"soul"* often overlap because they both contrast with the body and are believed to survive bodily death in some religions.

Spirit is experienced through:

Love, children, connection to something great, your ease, your "just knowing", saying the right things at the right time, the "how did I get that idea" kind of experience, receiving a thought, and feeling things like cold/warm air suddenly passing.

It is not that the body has a soul, but the soul has a body.

Our body is a physical vessel for our spirit while here on earth. It is energy even though it looks solid.

Quantum energy and spirit (energy) are on the same plane in the Universe.

We are in an energy field that gives us shape.

We are all part of that field. We are not separated from each other or from nature!

So your field, thoughts and energy shape your life.

Einstein said: the field/mind is the sole governing agency of the particle (or matter).

The new thought movement was a mind-healing movement that originated in the 19th century in the United States. Its fundamental teaching is that spirit is more real and more powerful than matter and that the mind has the power to heal the body.

But the New Thought movement was preceded many years by Wallace D. Wattles.

Quotes by Wallace D. Wattles from *The Science of Getting Rich*:

"There is a science of getting rich. It is an exact science, like algebra or arithmetic. There are certain laws which govern the process of acquiring riches. Once a person learns and obeys these laws, he will get rich with mathematical certainty."

"Every thought that goes forth from the brain sends vibrations into the surrounding atmosphere and moves the realm of things to action."

"All is Mind. The things that appear are expressions of Mind."

"If we lack anything it is because we have not used our mind in making the right contact with the super mind."

"Science is at last proving what Religion has taught from the beginning-that God gave dominion, and that we have only to understand and use dominion to become the Masters of our Fate, the Captain of our Souls."

There are many "New Thought Practitioners" that say the same thing. In fact: the Bible also does so.

The Bible involves the laws of the universe and it, in its turn, describe the nature of how God works. Jesus said, "Pray believing that ye have that ye may receive." "Pray believing and feeling and sensing that you already have it, and then you're available to receive it."

The Bible represents "nothing but" the science of the mind….

Mind boggle.

The mind is capable of healing the body.

A very famous study about the power of the mind was done by Harvard professor Ellen Langer, Ph.D. (*Book: Mindfulness,* Addison-Wesley, 1989).

She and her colleagues took <u>two</u> groups (in 1981) of men in their seventies and eighties, brought them to an old Monastery in New Hampshire and dropped the *first* group into an environment which resembled the early 1950's. The men watched black and white TV shows from that period (they went 30 years back in time!), and read newspapers and magazines from that time. They saw pictures of themselves when they were 30 years younger, and listened to music famous at that time.

The second group, who arrived a week later, were told to stay in the present and live in that era, the 80's.

Before and after the experiment:

Both groups took many cognitive and physical tests including, for example, weight, height, gait, hearing, blood pressure, eyesight, memory, intelligence, and so on.

The outcome of the experiments surprised her and her team.

After <u>one</u> week there were dramatic positive changes.

<u>Both</u> groups were stronger and more flexible! Height, weight, gait, posture, hearing, vision and even performance on the intelligence test had improved. Their joints were more flexible,

their shoulders grew wider, their fingers more agile and longer and less gnarled by arthritis.

While it's true that both groups experienced positive effects, the men who had acted as if they were actually thrown back in time to 1950 showed significant **more** improvement! In other words, those who had impersonated younger men seemed to now have bodies that actually *were* younger!

These physiological results provided evidence for a simple but invaluable fact. She stated:

"The aging process is surely less fixed than most people think"

And:

"Wherever you put the mind, the body will follow"

"It is not our physical state that limits us. It is *our own* mindset about our own limits, our perceptions, that draw the lines in the sand", she declared after the experiment.

Our fixed ideas, internalized in childhood, can affect the way we age.

Our bodies are designed to thrive and jump for joy!

Alas, in our education system we get pushed in the chair and warned: 'You'd better sit still or else… Well, from the ages of 5-12 in school it might be tough to keep your joyful, jumping little body within these restrictions.

Sounds like my son Max's body. The teachers in *every class* reminded him he talked too much, he jumped up and down too much and did too many gymnastic exercises in the classroom. It wasn't unusual for him to enter the classroom cartwheeling. ("Why do they build such small classrooms mom?").

His eighth grade teacher had the best comment:

"I didn't care whether you were sitting or standing in class, because you always paid attention and that was what counted for me."

Every one of his teachers also wrote: "we will miss your joyful presence." I can tell you, this hasn't changed in high school. He is always laughing and funny! One teacher admitted she simply cannot get mad at him. **"Join the club!"**, I thought. He is 18 now….

Luckily, he hasn't changed!

We are not designed to sit still in chairs, stare at screens (except when writing a book…), and create problems with RSI's, hernias, and headaches because of the stress.

Your experience is your proof!

So having the *knowledge* as a result of reading tons of uplifting self-help books, watching movies related to this subject and listening to uplifting stories, as well as the *knowing,* and all of that is within me and I am all that is, I started to see **proof.** Proof of the Universe backing me up.

Many people want to see proof before they believe something. I am convinced that you can change your approach to "believing is seeing". I am living proof of that, as are hundreds of thousands of other people on this planet.

While it's critically important to do the affirmations for self-love and money, it's equally so to have an "open mind" so that you can see and hear proof of the Universe backing you up!

You studied for an exam, wrote the exam and now you want to see the results, right?

What is "an open mind"?

It is focusing on the situations and people you encounter and *translating* these encounters on a <u>spiritual</u> level. Allow yourself to receive the information; allow yourself to receive the answers. Ask yourself: "why" did I meet this person today or "why" did this situation occur? Not *"why did this happen to me?".*

Every Friday morning, for the last 10 years, I have gone to my spinning class. Spinning is an indoor cycling sport. You race and sweat but you don't move. The bikes are fixed on the floor. After class, I used to drink coffee with a few cycling friends.

The weather was great, so we sat outside. I had to leave the table for a few minutes, so when I sat with my coffee it was cold. I decided to go inside and order a new cup of coffee.

The woman behind the counter said; "Hey Leslie, coffee, black? This one is on me".

In a flash, my mind said *"it was **me** who let the coffee go cold/who am I to deserve this coffee for free/you cannot get coffee for free, you **have** to pay for coffee"*.

So the guilt, the lack of self-love and the blame pervaded my mind and the brain was just about to absorb it until the truth struck me:

*Wait a minute!!! This is IT! THIS is A SIGN! The woman giving me the coffee for free was the proof or result of the affirmations concerning the self-love and money coming **to** you.*

When was the last time (or was there ever a time) I received a cup of coffee for free in a restaurant or bar from the owner herself? Other than a "thank you for being my guest" gesture, I mean.

I realized this was the moment to *allow* and *receive* the feeling of worthiness that came with receiving that cup of coffee from her. This was also the moment to *allow* to get something for free, no money. So the money was coming **to** me, right?

So, I did not let the "old" mind trick me again into hating myself and telling myself you are not worthy enough to get a present.

In a split second I adjusted the ego and spirit took over. As a result, my answer was: *"Thank you very much, Fiona. That is so kinf you"*, instead of saying the old "nothankyoubecauseitismyfault".

So I walked outside with my first demonstration:

A cup coffee for free.

Do I sense some skeptical thoughts hovering around your head? That is because your mind is tricking YOU right now.

Trick or treat?

This first awareness might have been just a baby step, but I felt like celebrating.

I continued acquiring more knowledge, and affirming and practicing what I learned.

Then the next proof showed up: I received money back from the energy company. About 400 euros. I didn't see that coming. *"Money will come to me in many different ways"*. The Universe doesn't just hear what you say; it hears what you mean.

The Universe doesn't trick you, it treats you!

But.

You can trick the Universe!

"Match the frequency of the reality y o u want and you cannot help but get that reality" *–Bashar*.

You'll remember I mentioned the teachings of Florence Scovel Shinn (September 24, 1871 – October 17, 1940), an American artist and book illustrator from Camden, New Jersey who became a New Thought spiritual teacher and metaphysical writer in her middle years. In New Thought circles, she is best known for her first book, *The Game of Life and How to Play It* (1925).

Shinn expressed her philosophy as:

"The invisible forces are ever working for man who is always 'pulling the strings' himself, though he does not know it. Owing to the vibratory power of words, whatever man voices, he begins to attract"

Emotional Alignment Is Easy

So I learned that if a man is in debt or experiences lack, it shows that a *belief* of debt is present in his *subconscious* mind.

So I better turn that around, right?

I had a huge number of bills to be paid. I didn't know how to pay for them.

I knew I had to ask the Universe for help.

I started to repeat the following sentences every single day, day after day after day…I eventually knew them by heart so I could repeat them during sport activities, walking the dogs and even during patient treatments.

1) "I cast this burden of lack on the Christ within and I go free to have plenty!"

2) "Infinite Spirit open the way for me to let me receive me what is mine by Divine right. Let me receive love, health, wealth and self-expression"

3) "I deny debt. There is no debt in Divine Mind, therefore, I own no man anything."

I wrote the next statement down on paper for months in a row: *'at the end of the year ALL my bills will be paid'*.

Do not ask the Universe: *"How"* or *"Why"*, just trust the process. I repeated this sentence also over and over just before going to sleep.

The best time to do your affirmations is just before you go to sleep and *immediately* when you wake up the next morning. The mind is still 'still' at those times.

So instead of thinking or trying to remind yourself of negative things, such as: "Oh yeah something went wrong yesterday, what was it again? How could I forget! Yes, now I remember" again, lovingly and gently force yourself to focus on something else. Otherwise you might start again where you last finished: in low vibe city!

It is just like hitting the brakes of your bike going downhill; it is better to stop on top of the hill instead of trying to hit the brakes while going 40 miles an hour downwards.

Stop your thoughts from controlling you. You must be the boss of your own thoughts. This was my goal. *HOPE* is not good enough of a goal. I reached for a higher vibration.

FAITH.

Hope looks forward but faith knows it has already received and acts accordingly.

So I started to act like I had paid all the bills.

I showed assurance of having enough money.

I *w r o t e*:

"Thank you for delivering the goods to me. I am happy to be able to pay you."

"Thank you for letting me continue my business."

"Thank you for fixing my car so I can go to the office."

"Thank you for your support so I can treat more clients."

"Thank you for cleaning my office."

I showed faith; I even went for a luxury dinner, bought some new clothes, and so on and so on.

Like Einstein said:

"Imagination is more important than knowledge. Knowledge is limited, while imagination circles the world."

I tried to keep an open mind and open vision to receive the answers and solutions from the Universe.

Off course

Of course, it was very hard for me to break through my learned and "overtheyearsconditioned" behavior.

It became an everyday practice for me to focus on the good.

One day, my husband and I were cycling a beautiful route, the weather was sunny and birds were singing and the sky was clear blue. In Holland, this kind of weather makes us fly out of our houses like birds that have been kept imprisoned in their cage for months.

It was a fabulous day! As you know, I am really very sport-minded and I was in heaven on my bike.

I was appreciating the green grass, the cloudless sky, my bike and my good-in-shape body. The coffee and apple pie in the sun tasted very well after having passed our first 50 miles.

Then my cell phone rang....

At first, I thought I was not going to answer the call but then I realized it might be one of my children.

It was the bank! My bank! The bank who had given me the loan to start a new office. The bank that had shown faith in me at the start (or knew it was going to receive lots and lots of interest money from me in all the coming years perhaps?), but also the same bank that had become worried when I asked for a small loan to cover totally unexpected expenses.

I knew I would be totally out of debt if they could lend me some more money. I had faith in myself and my dental practice to be able to pay it all back. It would let me be a bit more relaxed and even have a vacation to re-energize myself.

But the bank figured they had lent me enough money.

The mortgage was based on historical numbers and not on the amount of money I was making now. At least… that was *my* vision. Despite the fact *"they"* said I had a thriving practice they didn't act like it: *"they"* were putting me on a black list! *"They"* were planning to put me under *"special asset management"*.

This was despite the fact I had never failed to pay either the mortgage on my house or on my office-building or failed to pay any other kind of money I owed the bank. *"They"* were scared I would go bankrupt.

I decided I was not going to pick up the phone! I was so proud of myself. I refused to pick up the phone and listen to their accusations. This was a huge step for me. I chose to feel good at that moment. I wasn't going to feel like the victim. I knew, just knew I was financially going to be ok. When? Why? How? Well, that was also still a mystery to me.

This is what it was all about! I choose to feel good! Keep the vibe high. I was able to totally focus on the course I was cycling and not go off the course I had decided to follow.

I continued focusing on the landscape and on our terrific day off. I was in heaven.

But… we are also on earth… a choice we made as a soul before birth. We wanted to experience this earth and all its miracles and beauty.

So… I called the bank back a few hours later. But now it was <u>me</u> who decided to have the conversation. It felt better but on the other hand I was still very nervous.

Remember, I had been doing my affirmations only for a little while at this point. It had only been a month or two, maybe three, since I started changing my thoughts. . So I was not very stable at all concerning the money belief.

I sat on my bed, far away from the kids' noise, and talked to "*them*". "*They*" again were very worried about my financial position and didn't want to mention the word "bankrupt", so **I** did. "*Well, Mr. X. Do you think I will go bankrupt?*"

"*If you continue the way you are doing now…well, uuuhm, I don't know…Leslie*". "*Mr. X. I assure you it will all be ok!*", and… again there was the threat of moving my "case" to "special asset management".

I said: "*You go ahead and do your thing*".

Then we hung up the phone, leaving me a nervous wreck, but…less so than I would have been without my affirmations and growing new belief.

After all, at this point I had reason to be happy the bank hadn't lent me the money. I would never have discovered all the good that life has in store for me. At this moment, though, I didn't realize that.

Many of us fall into the trap of thinking someone else is responsible for our issues in this world. This was how I felt about the bank. But then something inside me said: "*the bank is not responsible; you yourself are*".

In the midst of "trouble", please know something better is in store for you.

I realized I was getting stronger inside. I was not alone: the Universe, GOD, inner being, you name it, was with me, always.

You are never, ever, ever alone.

Source energy

Many people do not understand that they existed *before* their physical birth. Or they might think that when they were born they stopped being "non-physical". They think it's the body that has a soul, but it's the other way around: the soul has a body!

The body is energy; we can only come from energy, called Source energy.

Before the moment of birth, we are vibrationally connected with the Energy Source or what we might otherwise call "God", or "all that is", "all- encompassing love", "all-encompassing light", "higher being" or "higher self"

Whatever you name it, it doesn't matter. Hopefully you understand! For that is the most important part.

In the moment of birth, a part of the consciousness that is *you* focuses itself into *your* physical body. The "rest" of your consciousness will stay "non-physical"!

Like Emmet Fox (1886-1951), writer of *The Sermon on the Mount* (and one of the foremost spiritual teachers of the twentieth century) wrote:

'Man being a m a n- ifestation or expression of God....'

Also:

"God individualizes Himself in an infinite number of distinct focal points of consciousness, each one quite different (hence all the different people on earth!), *and therefore each one is a distinct way of knowing the universe, each a distinct experience."*

The word "individual" means "undivided". Emmet Fox states: *"The consciousness of each one is distinct from God and from all others, and yet none are separated"*.

Well, how can this be?

How (on earth, LOL) can *two* things be *one* and yet not one and the same?

You might be getting confused here!

Well, the answer is that: in matter, which is finite, they cannot; but in Spirit, which is in-finite, they can!

To me this is the explanation of the fact why we sense that "we must have met before" or "it seems like we have been friends for ages".

As you know, energy cannot be destroyed; it can only change form. So at birth we as an energy life form enter the (finite) body on earth. When we die, as an energy form, we enter the infinite realm also called "heaven".

This present limited three-dimensional life on earth means that we cannot see this, but intuitively we do know that it exists.

So, we are all a part of God Spirit, of source energy.

In my life long questioning I also found the answers in the teachings of *"Abraham"* by Esther and Jerry Hicks and *"The Seth Material"* by Jane Roberts.

"Abraham" is a group of uplifting Non-Physical teachers. They present their Broader Perspective *through* Esther Hicks. Her husband Jerry Hicks made his transition back into the Non-Physical in 2011. In other words: he died in 2011.

Why would this "material" and teachings be true for me? Because it resonates so much with me!

Now I know what life is about. Now I know the purpose of life. Now I know why I sense people's energy. Now I know why I said to my mom that we should be jealous that she was going to heaven. Now I know that heaven is beautiful, and that heaven is on earth also. Now I know why I had all these life experiences up until now….

Why didn't the Bible or "the church" contribute to my truth? Because it did not resonate with me. For instance, why should there be a hell? Why should anyone end up in a place like that?

There are some things in the Bible, though, that I appreciate. For example,

Abraham says: *"In the moment of your birth, a part of the consciousness that is you focused itself into your physical body and your first relationship began, the relationship between the physical you and the NON-physical you."*

Now we are talking! I get it now!

It is all about *"the remembrance"*. I had "forgotten" who I was and what I came here for, on earth. I was now starting to remember.

I had been visiting my clairvoyant friend for years to "search" for the meaning of life. During those visits, my vibration was the highest ever but I couldn't always continue that feeling because I lost the connection.

This discovery made me cry…it reminded me of the questions I had all through my childhood. I was like a wheel not attached to the bike. I knew something "must" be out there to make me whole and to help me function properly and vividly, full of speed and energy, ready to roll!

I am connected to my non-physical part "up there". That part which wants the best for me sent me here to experience all the best: JOY, LOVE, HEALTH, WEALTH, SELF-EXPRESSION, you name it we can have it. Do it or be it!

But how do I know my non-physical part or "God" or "Source Energy" wants the best for me? Just by reading this No, not just by reading this, but by *__feeling__* this.

Give Love and receive Love, that is the only real thing in life.

So this is "it" right? We came from source energy, since we "are" energy. Whenever we feel "off", it means we do not remember our own guidance system (our non-physical part/God/Soul/ Heaven), which shows us the way by giving us *signs* and *intuition* or *inner guidance*.

Emmet Fox wrote: *"whenever the Christ (that is the True Idea concerning anything) is raised up in thought by anyone, healing follows-physical healing, or moral healing, or even intellectual healing, as the case may be."*

And indeed, it did. I cured the old back-pain I had experienced for 15 years just by remembering this, doing my affirmations and ruling out my ego.

I also learned a lot from people who recovered from a near death experience (NDE).

One such NDE is that of Tommy Rosa, as described in this book, *Health Revelations from Heaven and Earth* (co-written by Dr. Stephen Sinatra):

"Your heart should lead you through life. It is through your heart that you can truly connect with your Creator and your Divine self. Living through the heart keeps you fearless and egoless and connected to all things Divine. When the mind leads and the heart shuts down, a person is in danger of losing his or her way. True faith can elude the mind but never the heart. Living through the heart allows an individual to keep a high enough vibration to maintain optimal, vibrant good health."

Tommy Rosa is a Bronx-born plumber who died after being the victim of a hit and run incident. (A restaurant owner being a witness even saw Tommy's spirit rise out of his body!) Well, he came back after an amazing encounter with his loved ones and Jesus!

Like Anita Moorjani wrote in her book, *Dying to Be Me*:

"Just look at my life path! Why, oh why have I always been so harsh with myself? Why was I always beating myself up? Why was I always forsaking myself? Why did I never stand up for myself and show the world the beauty of my own soul?

Why was I always suppressing my own intelligence and creativity to please others? I betrayed myself every time I said 'yes' when I meant 'no'! Why have I violated myself by always needing to seek approval from others just to be myself? Why haven't I followed my own beautiful heart and spoken my own truth?"

Dear all, we do not have to die (and come back) to accept this truth, do we?

Sleeping beauty

This awoke me even more! It shook me WIDE awake! In fact, it slapped me awake!

This was what I had been doing all my life: rejecting myself, punishing myself, calling myself ugly, judging myself for not being perfect... Punishing myself for not getting an A! For not studying hard enough (cum laude... remember?). For not getting an A+ on that filling, when that was the best I could do with an uncooperative client. For not being able to be the daughter my parents wanted me to be, for not being the deferential colleague, for not being what "they" want me to be. For not being able to pay all the bills.... I was tough! I was the tough woman, right? For me that meant: "no weakness"!

But what is weakness? Is it perhaps just the lack of ability to conform to the demands and/or wishes of others? Conform yourself to the demands and/or wishes of *others?*

I have always lived from the heart and refrained from judging *others*. I got an A+ judging myself, though!

Well, sleeping beauty is awake now!

Never, ever again will I let myself be guided off of my own guidance system, inner being or GOD. God isn't a man with a beard; it is a state of being.

I am prouder of myself for finally having reached this state of being than I was when I finished Dental School and Physical Therapy School put together! I take more pride in getting an A+ from my higher self than any other source, such as clients, friends, or family.

Calibration

I do not want to describe an emotion as being intrinsically "negative". For why should *crying* or *being mad* always be negative? Actually, these can be terrific experiences, because they tell you that you are off of your inner being or guidance system.

You can call something "hot" because you know what "cold" is. You can call something "big" because you know what "small" is. You can call something "negative" because you know what "positive" is.

We have decided in our language to call feelings "positive" when feelings feel good. We have decided to call them "negative" when they do not feel good. Although a good cry can "feel good", I assume you know what I mean.

So there must be a calibration system! For to call an emotion "negative" their must be a "positive". This system is your emotional guidance system. You were *"delivered"* with it when you were born.

You were delivered with an A +. You were born into your physical body, leaving your greater part behind, in the non-physical realm. This has only good stuff in store for you.

Recently my dearest friend's granddaughter transitioned. This was, of course, a tragic experience for her as well as her daughter and son-in-law and the other family members.

My friend's daughter was 21 weeks pregnant when she "lost" her baby. They had their precious little girl cremated. The father said; *"There is no such tiny little baby-girl who gave and received so much love as our daughter did."*

She was not trained off of her guidance system. We grown-ups are! How come? As described earlier, parents, teachers, bosses, governments, **doctors, dentists,** caretakers, you name it, "think" *for* us.

<u>Why do they do this</u>? *They* have often entirely lost touch with their own guidance systems. They've forgotten where they come from and their purpose in life. They have forgotten the message of Jesus. They wouldn't act this way otherwise.

We wouldn't have wars, shouting parents, killing teenagers, jealous friends, or angry neighbors if everyone was 'aligned' with their higher being self. The all-compassionate part of themselves. The "ALL IS LOVE".

love, joy, passion, happiness, optimism, trust, peace, faith, admiration fear,

---

sadness, aggressiveness, remorse, anxiety, anger, disgust, hate.

Any emotion experienced below the line feels bad; anything above the line feels good.

When you experience 'negative' emotion, please **at that moment** realize: *"Hey I have strayed from my true self.* Ask yourself, *'what can I do to go back to where I came from."*

Of course, *experience* your emotions but know source is there for you and wants to guide you back.

Recognition *of* your emotions tells you *where* on the scale you are…

Emotional Alignment Is Easy

You can train yourself back above the line. How? First and best of all, by believing you can!

> *"You don't look out there for God,*
> *something in the Sky*
> *you look in you"*

-Alan Watts-

Emotional alignment

Sometimes we have experiences that do not seem 'good' but are part of or serve a greater good. So amidst all the apparent problems in your life, keep your faith!

Alignment is the process of applying the knowledge that you are one with your higher self or God.

It is the training into this high state of being. It is the stripping away of the garbage you have gathered during life. By garbage, I mean the opinions and judgements of others and your own negative judgements of yourself.

Do your training, and step-by-step you will get back there! No excuses! Train your feelings to get up there.

Remember, it isn't easy to get from the emotion of fear to joy. A psychologist said to one of my patients: "focus yourself on the next ten minutes. In ten minutes, the fear will be over". I asked her whether that advice was effective. The answer was no! This is demonstration of caregivers must never assume, but rather ASK what the client thinks he or she needs!

This client came from a place of total fear. She would not come into my office. She would stay in my waiting room for like half an hour, then it would take another half an hour for her to go sit in the chair. We trained together (took a few visits) so that she could come to my chair within two minutes! You'll remember her therapist had said that she should focus for ten minutes. This was impossible for her, and we could both see that. I asked whether she thought she could manage to focus for five *seconds*. She thought she could, and indeed she did. While I was drilling, I'd count to 5 and then stop. It went great.

I helped to train the patient into a more positive outlook. I did this by letting her say out loud, for instance: *"I can leave any moment I want to"*, *"I know I do not like the dentist but I will try to stay for five minutes"*, *"I know I can trust Leslie"*, and *"this filling will keep me from hurting any longer"*, and (of course) *"I trust myself in this process"*. (Remember? Don't give your power away).

So, as you can see, I now apply teachings I used for myself to help other people.

Only *you* can decide what is good for you. But also remember, **you** are guided!

Practice no force

Here's an example of my own game with the Universe.

Since energy cannot be destroyed...

I have a dog named Ollie, she is five years old now. She is such a loving furry buddy!

Right after the transitioning of my dad, she came to live with me and my family as a puppy. She has beautiful dark brown eyes. There are a lot of times when I look in her eyes and I see...my dad.... I have said a few times (very, very softly...), *"Hi dad"*.

I never told anyone about this because I knew they'd probably think it was far-fetched. I didn't even tell my family.

I believe the non-physical can have a distinct focal point of consciousness in animals, like my dad has in Ollie.

Just like with my mother... it didn't feel like "<u>dead, over and out</u>".

Every once in a while, I play the game with my parents: I "call" them. One day when on a long walk, I stopped at a beautiful place in the middle of a park, looked up in the sky and said: *"Hey mom, hey dad, I know you are out there. You know me... sometimes I am a bit stubborn (stub born) so even though I know you are there, I am asking you for a sign. I am here in my physical body, and sometimes I still need the 'proof', mom. So please show yourselves to me..."* Then I continued my walk.

Just a few minutes later, it happened...

When I go for a walk, or just before I go to sleep, or while driving in my car, and right after I wake up, I listen to or read uplifting material. Just like this afternoon I was listening to a high vibrational speech on my iPhone. In the middle of the speech, the sound stopped. Mute… nothing… no sound, which was odd because that never happens unless there is no signal but that was not the case. My earphones were still plugged in. What could be 'wrong'?

I pulled the phone out of my rear pocket, checked the screen and was flabbergasted. Captioning of speaker's text was showing on the screen. Maybe it was a service for hearing impaired people. Anyway, when I checked the screen the word 'momentum' was there. It said **"mom"** across the screen…

I took a screenshot of it…

Then… two miles or so ahead I saw a woman sitting on a bench. I felt compelled to talk to her. I felt the urge to ask whether the name "Dirk" (my father's name) would ring a bell to her. Although I felt very awkward, I walked up the hill (thinking she probably think I was nuts… see… I wasn't stable enough yet in my thoughts) and asked her indeed whether the name "Dirk" rang a bell. Well, she knew a "Dirk" but… I even forgot the answer. It didn't resonate with me!

But the answer didn't really matter. I realized suddenly that I was *forcing* an answer… forcing an answer from Dad.

The Universe doesn't know force... it only waits for your allowance. You need to get into a different frequency to see the signs.

I said goodbye to the lady and walked away, asking myself, *"Leslie, you were compelled to talk to her. You are so good in following your intuition, so why did this not resonate with you?"* The answer came: *"Well, Les, the answer indeed didn't resonate with you, but the lesson you learned is bigger than that and that did!"*

The Universe is not force able

I did not realize that at this minute, though. I realized it later when at home and sitting down to read a book.

There it was, on the first page. It said the name... "DICK".

My dad's name was "Dirk", but he had always called himself "Dick".

Emotional Alignment Is Easy

op de camera
n Tijden
are locatie
u kunnen zijn
hebben
chew **Dick**

I cried in happiness and gratitude for the sign the Universe and my father had given me.

Be still

Before the time I started to read Florence Scovel Sinn's *"The Game of Life and How to Play It"* (around August 2010), I had a very odd experience.

One day upon arriving at the office, I felt very, very overwhelmed. My heart was pounding in my chest and I had trouble breathing. What was going on? I didn't know. All of a sudden, I was scared to open my mailbox.

Although I was scared, I still did. I was sweating all over but I did open my mailbox. Why? To find out who needed me and what for, I guess…

At this time, I also had troubles opening my physical mail. I was also experiencing difficulties in answering questions, especially at the office. My heart would beat like a heavy metal drummer.

Around that same time, my youngest daughter, Eef (then 6 years old), didn't seem very happy. I have always felt she was "different". Highly sensitive is what she is. It was hard for me to "read" her. My other two kids are very easy to "read". I always instantly know what they want, how they feel and what I can do to contribute to their happiness. With Eef, though, I had "troubles".

In the classroom she would throw her pens and pencils and scream, throwing tantrums.

The head of the school would ask me, *"Who does she have it from"*. As if it is a genetic thing.

Of course, I wondered whether it had something to do with the death of her grandma, my mother. I thought that perhaps her young mind hadn't been able to process it.

Although I know it is ok for me to show grief, I never did so in front of the kids because I didn't want them to see me sad. So I kind of stupidly assumed they didn't really experience my grief. Me, who knows there is more in heaven and earth and can sense people a mile away, was thinking this?

I decided to bring her to a psychologist, an old acquaintance who I knew was very good at her job. After a few visits she wanted to talk with me. She said: *"Eef is suffering"*.

I felt pain permeating my heart. *"Suffering"*, I asked? It was not at all what I'd expected. *"Suffering? My goodness, My baby"*.

She asked me, *"When will you stop the interrogation"*.

Interrogation? I wondered? I only ask my kids how school was, how the teacher was, how the bike ride was, how… how … how… and how….

I suddenly realized this was causing stress for my children. I soon recognized that I was asking all these questions to *sense their wellbeing in a place where I was not*. Get it?

It struck me that my own hypersensitivity had gone so far (it was my protection system from childhood on; I 'read' my mom and acted accordingly!) that it affected my kids!

Although I am a mother who lets her kids lead their own lives (I generally only advise when there might be danger), I indeed plead guilty of doing the thing the psychologist had accused me of: interrogating.

From childhood on, I had used my senses to 'feel' people.

I was going much too far with this, though. It used to be a protection system but I had trained myself too well and used it everywhere. I wanted to 'know' answers to meaningless questions such as: who was the person sitting in the car in front of mine, who was the guy across the street, and who was the woman behind the cash register. I wanted to "know" the license plate numbers on cars. I once recognized the number from a friend's license plate before I even knew it was her in an approaching car. I was literally sick from more than 40 years of energy waste. I'd never realized this, until now.

Up until this moment, my heart would beat out of my chest when doing something as minor as opening my mail… I have had too much… too many stimuli.

My life had been an emotionally tip-toeing game. And yet things had still been great in many respects!

Despite my upbringing, I was a clown, I had fun and usually I was the life of the party. When I was quiet, everybody would wonder what was going on. Well, *nothing!* Of course. Everything I had set my mind to I succeeded in.

I knew for sure now that I had always lived to 'please' others, to say "yes" instead of "no". I wanted the other person to feel good and didn't care about my own feelings. *"When they are fine, I am fine"*, was my motto. At my home, my parents' house, at friends' and for sure, at my office.

Everybody happy (but me)?

It had taken its toll.

I had to change this! I had to quiet down my senses.

The therapist had sent us to a psychiatrist! My goodness, our daughter and us! But Eef did not want to speak; I quietly applauded. Why? Because if the questions I asked her at home caused problems, how would she respond to an "interrogation" from the psychiatrist?

She had a few sessions… without a word! Isn't that amazing? This highly sensitive child is without a doubt an Indigo child.

We stopped the treatment. It didn't work. This was ok with me because I knew I would be making important changes that would help my daughter.

Eef was born five and a half weeks too early, only weighing six pounds. She was rushed to intensive care, and at day five I feared for her life. Almost two weeks after she was born I got to take her home… healthy and happy!

It was from this moment on that I was a frightened mom. Checking on her a zillion times. My other kids were chubby ones at birth but Eef was fragile.

My care for her and my *"I am going to love my kids to pieces because I missed out"* made me gradually kind of overprotective. This resulted in still dressing her every morning until the age of six. This was in contrast with my other two which I always encouraged to be independent earlier on. It also resulted in a tantrum when I didn't dress her.

Again, I needed to change!

I organized a family meeting. I talked about the visit to the shrink and my wake-up call. I asked the kids whether they thought I asked them too many questions too frequently (in other words, all day, every day). Their answer was "yes". Wow.

I had thought I was being a good mom was, in fact, harassing them. Harassing them and only able to feel a glimpse of **their** well- being.

So I said that from this very moment on I would stop asking all those questions and leave them alone.

I was also planning to stop trying to acquire any kind of information which I did not need to "survive". I stopped asking questions other than those important for my job. I stopped checking out cars, people, and situations unrelated to me.

I decided not to watch television, hear and watch the news, read newspapers (all negative crap) and listen to conversations and gossip.

My assistant Jose was getting scared: *"I hope we will get the old funny and sincere Leslie back"*, she said. I sat down with my assistants to reveal my intentions.

In between every patient I was going to read a sentence from an uplifting book. The books went with me to the office every single day. Many times, I would lie down on the floor in the room next to my office and do my affirmations. I would repeat the affirmations during drilling and filling. Nobody knew, but being still was my new mission.

At home I abruptly started not to get Eef dressed anymore. What I would say to her was; *"Mommy loves you so much, baby!*

It would be so nice to have breakfast together before you go off to school". Then I would take a shower, and go to breakfast. She wouldn't show up. I would get dressed and then go to the office, leaving her crying upstairs.

(NOTE: daddy is home;-))

The same night I would come home and say to her: *"Honey, I love you so much. Too bad I didn't see you downstairs this morning"*. The next day it would be the same. I went to my office, crying. It wasn't easy. It was the big letting go.

I also did not call my husband to avoid any stimuli for myself. It went on for a week or so. Then the *shift* came.

First of all, the kids started talking. They were sharing things from school and their time with friends. This was a sign for me that they were kind of "cured".

Eef started gradually doing better, too. She would still get out of bed, take a shower, get dressed, and eat breakfast too late, but I complimented and encouraged her. I continued telling her I loved her so much and was sad we didn't have breakfast together.

Then, sooner than expected... Eef and I had breakfast together with brother and sister and daddy.

The *shift* was there!

Her as well as mine. My mirror and me.

My shift resulted in a remark from my dad: *"You are not my lovely Leslie anymore..."*

"Well, dad, I still am but I have come to define __my__ borders."

Much later I read in "The Game of Life and How to Play It": *"Mothers often, unconsciously, attract illness and disaster to their children, by continually holding them in thoughts of fear, and watching for symptoms."*

Nothing left to say here… besides that, I felt I was on the right track.

Ask

I was feeling much better. I felt less tired.

One reason for this was the time and energy I was saving by being still, while the other was the fact that I now knew my life's purpose and was rejoicing in it. Finally knowing that I am an extension of source made me less tired, too. No more "holding onto", "striving", "fighting" or "pushing". Now it was more like: "let it be", "allow", "all is well", "ease into it" and "God is with me on this".

I remain extremely happy about the "road" I took. . Whatever I concentrate on, I succeed in. **So can you, too!**

Now, my next mission: "the money".

The bank didn't loan me the money.

You know that this led me to reading my books, affirming the high vibrational sentences and listening to very uplifting material.

In August of 2012, a few months after my nervous call with the bank, I was surfing the Internet to find more uplifting material.

I came across a seminar which seemed very interesting. I checked to find out what this course was all about. I was thrilled to find out it contained practical application of all the theories I had studied for a number of years now.

The curiosity in me arose; I straightened my back and my heart started pounding somewhat faster.

The contents of this seminar looked exactly like theoretical lessons coming alive in a practical exercise. Like dentistry: studying and applying the knowledge.

So I wanted to find out where I had to go to attend the seminar. Yes! The USA. You know I love this country so much so no obstacle here…

How much do they charge? Nothing!

When is it taking place? In November; check! Fine with me.

November is always a special month for me. My mom was born in November; she also died in November.

Where is it being held? Burlingame, California. Ok… Burlingam … *whhhhaattt…? Burlingame? California? They must be kidding!*

Burlingame is the city the/my (I like to call them "mine") American au pair family lives today. *"This cannot be true!"* Coincidence? Coincidence doesn't exist.

Co-incident! That is what it is!

How come that in my month of birth (August), I find a seminar to go to in the month of birth and dying (November) of my mother which will be given in Burlingame?

I had goosebumps all over my body… they are signs of truths. I knew, just knew I had to go there!

Amazing!

So my heart said; "you go for it, girl!" My wallet said, however, "you cannot go, because no work-no money".

I had a tough one to chew on here. This choice was going to be very challenging.

The question was: did I out-train my brain well enough about the money issue. By the way, I didn't call it "issue" or "lack" anymore because words come from thoughts and they have vibration. "Issue" and "lack" have low vibrations so I preferred not to use them.

Had I trained myself well enough to be able to follow my heart instead of following my wallet?

Was I strong enough to hold onto my faith, *"there is no debt?"* Or was I going to choose a lower vibration and not accept Einstein's wisdom in saying:

"Imagination is more important than knowledge. Knowledge is limited; imagination circles the world"

Or Florence Scovel Shinn when she says:

"All obligations are now wiped out under grace in a miraculous way." (see her book: Your Word is your Wand 1928)

Or the Bible when it says:

"Ask, and it shall be given you, seek, and ye shall find, knock, and it shall be opened unto you" (Mat.7:7)

Or Catherine Ponder when she says:

"God in me is my prospering power. God in me is always worthy"

I still felt wobbly in my choice of whether to attend the seminar. In fact, the score was 70% GO and 30% STAY.

I had to contact Berna "my" clairvoyant friend. I needed a helping hand… still.

Another absurd thing had happened simultaneously: I had NO patient appointments scheduled on the current date, September 4th! This was very unusual for a Tuesday! There had initially been some bookings, but patients had called and cancelled for a variety of reasons. Another sign was the fact that the date 09-04-2012): Angel number "3" has a lot to do with this date. *"You are doing something right"*, it says.

I asked clairvoyant Berna whether I should go to Burlingame. She immediately answered, *"YES"*.

Berna said: *"Well, look at the date: this is the day you have to prepare for the trip you are going to make in November."*

Well, wasn't she right… again…

I made the decision to go to Burlingame, attend the seminar and see my old friends.

Berna was happy for me. She said: *"you will see the color green"* and *"you will be on stage"*. She would probably be right.

*Sig*nature

In the weeks before the seminar was to start, I had amazing encounters. I experienced signs.

What is a sign, exactly? Well, when I looked it up online, this was the definition I found:

"Spiritual meaning of (subject)…"

Encounters of the Universe or signs or messages or Angel callings. You name it…I call all of these things signs. They were pointing me in the direction of Burlingame. Just one example is the fact that many of my patients came into the office wearing shirts with the American flag.

Another flabbergasting sign happened as I was driving to work one day. You know that I had trained myself off of letting unnecessary stimuli overwhelm me. Yet at a traffic light, something caught my eye.

When anything "catches" your eye, please be aware of the message the subject gives you. This might be in the form of a word on a truck maybe. An animal perhaps in the middle of a street. A stack of wood at a strange place and so on and so on.

Keep an open mind and start questioning: *"Why do I see this right now?"*

Again, at the traffic light something caught my eye.

It was the license plate of the car in front of me. *(I trained myself off of checking license plates, remember?)*

But this one I had to see.

84-P**-6

** Not revealing the initials here on purpose.

84-P**-6? This is so amazing! But why was I still amazed at occurrences like this? Didn't I now know the Universe conspires to let you receive all the good? Did I still need proof?

The "84" referred to the year I went to New York as an au pair girl to live with the American family.

The "P**" is the initial of the first name of the mother of the kids and my employer! The "6" referred to the amount of people living in the house.

All of this couldn't get any better. It just couldn't! I had to go to the conference!

Another strange (co)incident happened around the time before the trip.

One Friday morning (usually I am out but today I wasn't), the doorbell rang. It was the postal carrier. He came to deliver the three DVDs I ordered.

"DVDs I ordered?" I thought. *"Mister, I did not order any DVDs." "The label shows this address"*, he said. *"Well, they were not ordered by me"*, I said. *"So, you have to take it back I guess". "Well, yes ma'am, ok".* So he tried to beep, beep, beep the return of the DVD's into his little computer with his scanner but somehow it didn't work. He was not able to "un-deliver" his delivery. He didn't know why the system didn't work. He told me I *had* to take the DVDs otherwise his boss would be angry with him. There was no invoice to be found on the package.

It was a weird situation. The mailman requested me to please accept the package, and said that no invoice would follow. He couldn't trace the right name or the right address.

I decided to accept it; I didn't know why actually, because it wasn't mine.

When I opened the package, I found that one of the DVDs was called *"Autumn in New York"*.

Wasn't that where I was going to be on a layover for my flight? I ran up the stairs to check my E-ticket: my flight to Burlingame, California would indeed have a layover in New York!

Oh my… did I need more?

I never unwrapped them the DVDs. They are still in a drawer…

Flying high[2]

Finally, off I went on Wednesday November 13th, 2012.

Burlingame here I come!

My family in Burlingame knew that I was coming for a visit while there for the conference.

This opportunity to see them was really huge for me. Kind of inviting myself (I stayed in a hotel, however) was a big step. Coming from a place of low self-love to this high-flying place was still new for me. I really stepped out of my comfort zone.

"Relax Les, relax…breath in…breath out…". I was a good actor, so it's likely that no one else could perceive this inner struggle.

"You can only become a new kind of being through a new kind of thinking" -theawakeningdentist.com

P. was going to pick me up from the airport. I was so happy to see her again. I couldn't wait!

19 hours later…touch-down. Safe landing. Ready to go on my adventure. Now, off to get my two suitcases. One was filled with famous Dutch Stroopwaffles for my family as well as chocolate, "Delfts blue" ceramic cups and more for the kids. I was feeling anxious.

I was as happy as a little kid when I arrived at the luggage belt and stared into the crowd looking for P. She must be somewhere out there. She must…she must…right…?

She wasn't…she wasn't there. How could this be?

She was supposed to pick me up, wasn't she? Or had I completely misunderstood?

My wobbly vibration showed up.

Ego spoke to me:

"See, you are not worth it! Who do you think you are to invite yourself and think they will spend their valuable time with <u>you</u>? They need all the time they have to live their own lives."

I had to stay calm and breath through this. I knew that Source says: *"You are worthy, you are loved, by me. I am here. The fact that you are alive means you are worth everything."*

Life is all about this choice:

Ego or Source

We are an extension of Source (energy). Source is focused in you and through you. We are an extension of love. We are love. Every moment of the day, look through the eyes of love; in other words through the eyes of Source.

Make *that* choice.

Your ego likes negative talk. It enjoys putting you down.

"Breath in... breath out... feel your feet on the ground, Leslie (I was telling myself). *It is not about you... choose Source... choose Source..."*

So I focused on the good stuff and didn't let the negative self-talk get to me. This talk was based on make believe. Left-overs from the past. Left-overs; no meals anymore...

So, instead of feeling sad I focused on the journey I had taken so well by myself. On the safe trip I had experienced. On the transportation which was going to bring me to my hotel. About the nice people helping me find the way around the airport.

Within an hour I arrived in my beautiful hotel room. I grabbed a quick bite to eat and decided to get some rest.

Just before I fell asleep, I got a text message.

It was "P": she was so sorry she hadn't picked me up at the airport. This message appeared to have been sent earlier on, so I guess it must have been delayed. She had been confused about my time of arrival.

I am glad I choose Source. See, everything always works out for me (and for you).

We decided to meet the next morning.

Source hears no evil sees no evil.

Ego is the worst invention in human history.

"God individualized Himself in an infinite number of distinct focal points of consciousness, each one quite different; and therefore each one is a distinct way of knowing the Universe, each a distinct experience."

-Emmet Fox in *The Sermon on the Mount*

So He created infinite kinds of consciousness through people, with each person having their own special plan for them to have a joyous life on earth. We were created with a free will. Too bad humans so often choose to use their free will in negative ways.

As you know, I have used my free will in many negative ways in the past. Now, however, I am in tune with the Universe. I am counting on its flowing *through* me by way of ideas, hunches, goosebumps, intuition and signs.

We have our ears, eyes, nose, taste buds, and fingers to receive information from the Universe, and we use our body as a vehicle to take action accordingly.

Like the example of seeing the sign of the automobile's license plate which "told" me to go to Burlingame.

Let us check out why the ego is not our friend:

Ego	Source
Absence of love	Only love
Force input by others	Force within
Make believe	Real
Temporary	Eternal
Can feel bad	Only feels good
Doubt	Secure
Fear	Joy
Changeable	Unchangeable
Fake you	Our true self
Self-criticism	Self-love
Man-made	God made
Brain	Gut-feeling
Image you have of yourself	God's image
Mask	Un-mask
Worth depends on external things	Birth makes worth
Action	Allow
Sin	Sinless
Mistakes	Growth
Time	Timelessness
Seek and ye shall NOT find	Seek and ye shall find

Your ego misleads you every day. It tells you to follow others in their beliefs, it tells you there is sin, it tells you to take action on getting stuff so you will finally be happy. It makes you think you will be happy by having this stuff. It will tell you to jump into a relationship so you will feel better.

It says you will be complete if you marry as soon as possible; best before you reach your 30's. The fact is; if somebody can complete you it means somebody can *un*-complete you, which is nonsense. You are complete as you are, and have been from the moment you were born.

The ego is changeable, yet it doesn't like change.

Sounds a bit strange, doesn't it?

It loves familiarity and is threatened by change; change in your attitudes and opinions, changes in your perception. It is scared you might choose something which *will* serve you. All excuses will be made up to define the *known* as preferable to the unknown.

This is why you continue eating unhealthy food, stay in abusive relationships, keep that job or stay in your 'comfort zone' every day.

It all seems safe (for now). Ego has created a world (the world doesn't actually exist) in which you think that to predict is to be safe! I have always said as long as I can remember: *"When men predict, God laughs up His sleeve."*

I have changed that idea, however. I have come to know that *God, or inner being or higher self or soul,* doesn't acknowledge "bad" or "sin". "They" are totally unaware of it!

We have to return to our Source. Be like little kids and do what makes us feel joyful.

The ego delays happiness whenever the opportunity to experience it presents itself. It leads us to believe there is always some type of change needed before we are able to relax and be joyful. First we, (especially women?) have to clean off the table, get the dishes done and dust before we can sit and enjoy a cup of coffee in our beautiful backyard.

Do not misunderstand, though. We still need the ego. It is not evil, and you should not discard it. Why? Because while it makes a lousy master, it can be a terrific servant!

Do not allow the ego to make big decisions in your life. Your higher mind/self is there to serve you in this area. So allow the higher mind/self to do its work, and then take action. While it's true that the ego is true for action to take place, you need to be the ego's master!

"The moment you become aware of the ego in you, it is strictly speaking no longer the ego, but just an old, conditioned mind pattern. Ego implies unawareness. Awareness and ego cannot coexist."

-Eckhart Tolle

Timing is on your side

Ego tells us to look into the future instead of the now. But every decision we make is in the now. Not in the future. The future doesn't exist, because every moment is now. The so-called future is but a collection of many, many, many now's. The ego wants to escape the present, hence its flight. This is why we desperately have the urge to plan and take action to ensure our secureness in the "future".

> The heart of man plans his way
> but the Lord establishes his steps.
>
> ~ Proverbs 16:9

Be secure in the now by realizing that you are safe in this moment. The next moment is not yet here.

Ego tells us that *time* exists. This isn't true either.

Einstein concluded in his later years that the past, present and the future all exist simultaneously.

Einstein proved that time is relative, not absolute, like Newton said. Einstein's own Relativity Theory let him to reject time.

Another highly recognized American physicist, Richard Phillips Feynman (May 11, 1918 – February 15, 1988), described *time* as being simply a direction in space.

We all know that a belief is just a thought you keep thinking…

We invented time to be able to stick to our earthly agenda. But the heart doesn't want to be rushed.

It will respond one day by telling you! … It will slow down…

Time tends to separate us from ourselves. Being in a hurry doesn't contribute to you living your most joyful state.

> Set your minds on things that are above,
> not on things that are on earth.
>
> ~ Colossians 3:2

"**Timing**" is the word we should acknowledge.

Timing is the regulation of occurrence, pace, or coordination to achieve a desired effect, as in music, sports, work and so on. Set your mind on Divine Timing!

The Universe is famous for its Divine timing.

"And it shall come to pass, that before they call, I will answer and while they are yet speaking, I will hear." (Excerpt from the Bible).

This means that our prayers are heard; your wish will be granted. The timing will be at its best but you must be patient.

During our time on earth, we are obliged to act within the constraints of time in many instances. For example, there are certain times in which we must work, take part in sports, walk the dog, iron, do the laundry, and wash the dishes. But let us <u>*use*</u> this time to also express love with whatever we do.

<u>**Make sure to use time to:**</u> get up early so you don't have to rush to work. Take time to listen to the birds outside. Take time for a long shower and be in the present moment while scrubbing and *feeling* your skin. Take time to listen. Take time to express.

Emotions are manifestations

Negative emotions are the manifestations of having chosen ego instead of Source.

When you use your free will to choose Source, or love or God, your emotions can only be those of love and joy and happiness.

Shift back as soon as possible so your cells can heal. Know that your life is bigger than your experiences!!

Holiness created me whole

Kindness created me kind

Helpfulness created me helpful

Perfection created me perfect

Love, which created me, is what I am.

~ ACIM A Course in Miracles

Instead of letting your ego rule, seek and find and affirm the evidence of your "innocence".

You are "innocent" of guilt and shame and worthlessness because you created this flawed premise yourself!

Many people have become addicted to seeking and finding proof of their guilt, weakness, shame, worthlessness and so on.

This used to be me. I would wake up in the past and immediately return to the bad thoughts of yesterday. In a split second I would run across my negative thought center and remember the negativity of the day before even more intensely. The, *"what was wrong yesterday again? Oh, yes..."*.

Have you ever experienced this?

It turns out that people in many cases *seek* to experience self-pity, pain, humiliation, victimhood, and putting themselves down. Why?

There is a biological explanation!

<u>Negative emotions and pain activate the reward center of the brain, which causes an *un*conscious addiction to those negative emotions and pain!!</u>

The same area of the brain that seeks out pleasure also seeks pain.

Feelings of self-pity, anger, hate, and so on seem to activate beta-endorphin and dopamine pathways.

Chronic jaw pain (essential for dentists to recognize and acknowledge) and painful thoughts activate these pathways just like addictive drugs do.

Cocaine, meth, crack and heroine, and cigarettes cause a joyous vicious circle in the pleasure centers of the brain because they activate the beta-endorphins.

Negative emotions have negative effect on the cells they release cortisol and mediate dopamine release. But why are beta-endorphins released? After all, these are the "feeling good/runner's high" chemicals.

Well, the beta-endorphins are also powerful painkillers (analgesics). You are in a high state of being; you won't feel pain until you have finished that ten-mile run with huge blisters or have done the 100-mile bike ride with a more than sore butt.

When you are home you suddenly hurt everywhere.

We engineer our own suffering!

For heaven's sake, get out of the dungeon!

Stop the game of blame, guilt and self-pity; instead, accept your own responsibility, correct your "mistakes" and turn grief into soul accomplishments.

You need to start your own NA (negativity anonymous) to get rid of your addiction. Ask yourself, for instance:

- Is it hard for me to be around happy people?
- Do I feel comfortable around people with drama?
- Do you find yourself becoming suddenly angry, especially when all goes well?

For me there were three yeses. I was able to turn them into three nos.

The Miracle

Thursday… I was so happy to meet 'P'. She picked me up from the hotel. I was sure to bring them the typical Dutch treat: "Stroopwafels". Cookies with molasses. About 120 of them because the whole family was in desperate need of this treat.

Off we drove to her house, just outside the center of Burlingame. I couldn't believe that I was really here.

Pinch me….

We sat at the kitchen table and had coffee and fresh fruit; delicious. Her house felt like mine. I was home….

I had seen "P" a couple of times since 1986. Once they had asked me to come back and babysit while they went on a cruise. Like a fairy tale, indeed, being invited to New York (they moved to California approximately 20-25 years ago) to babysit!

I had visited them in 2008 with my husband and my three kids, which was absolutely fabulous. Can you imagine? **My** kids playing with the kids of her eldest son? (He was 11 when I left in 1986).

Four years later I was back, on my own.

Back to the present visit. "P" was eager to know about my life and how I was doing with my dental office. She knew I had started my own office, as I'd told her that in 2008.

I took a sip of my coffee and fired off…

As you know, words are energy. Mind your words. Use only high vibrational ones. As you know, you need to tell the story like you *want* it *to be*, not *like it is* and for sure not at all *how it was*.

Keep the vibe high!

That's indeed what I did.

I choose not to tell her what I had "been through", the law suit, the lack of money, the hostility of my former colleague, the pains, the self-pity and my role as a victim. After all I had been out-training myself of those thoughts since 2010.

Anyway, I no longer thought it was appropriate to think of my experiences as something I had "been through". They were a gift. I wouldn't have grown the way I have if I hadn't experienced them. My colleague's hostility was only a sign to me that she was not at all aligned.

At some points in the conversation, I did feel a little bit wobbly. I made it through, though.

"My practice is thriving. I am doing so well. I have lovely assistants; we are a great team", I told her. *"I had such a great team who built my office; it looks terrific."*

On questions regarding my former colleague, I had to answer that I really didn't know how she was doing. I only said that I had to face her in court.

"The kids are terrific, Keij is 13, Max is 10 and Eef is now 8 years old. They are my sunshines. Sjaak is doing well also."

When the conversation turned to finances, I told her I was doing ok. Why "ok" instead of "wonderful"? It was too much of an emotional leap to go from terrible to terrific, but "ok" was manageable. I said, *"I am doing ok; I would love to go on vacation again with the kids one day* (wobble)...*"*.

Then it happened...

She raised her hand and said: *"STOP, STOP!"*

I stopped talking.

"I want to help you", she said.

"What do you mean?", I said. *"Well, I want to help you financially...!"* she said.

I was absolutely shocked. Stunned. Flabbergasted.

I dropped my head in my hands. In a split second, I realized her saying this to me was

The work of the Universe!

Through her I was going to receive money to pay off my debt! Hadn't I written down *"at the end of the year, all my bills will be paid'*? Did I not ask myself *"how?"*.

P. said, *"Well, I may not be the Universe but I will help you."*

The Universe works through people like it was now working through P.

This was a reward from the Universe/God/inner being/Jesus for finally allowing myself to love myself, to stop criticizing myself, to accept help from others, and most of all: ***find myself worthy.***

My choice to realize that because I am alive I am worthy had resulted in this manifestation of money.

...that you would walk worthy of God who calls you into His own Kingdom and glory.

-1 Thessalonians 2:12.

How can you walk worthy if you are not worthy?

You can't! But He wants you to walk worthy, so what is going on? What are we doing to ourselves? What have I done to myself? You and I are worthy, but you must also make the choice to see yourself that way.

As a man thinketh, so he is.

-Proverbs 23:7

You all know that I have shifted my thinking.

It became clear to me that because I had followed all the signs, intuition, gut feelings and the advice of Berna, I was now receiving money I couldn't have earned my office in months

Thank you, Universe. Thank you, Universe.

Thank you, P., Thank you P.

She asked me how much debt I had; I couldn't tell her at first. I was too embarrassed, afraid she would think I was terrible at handling money.

Later on, of course, I had to tell her. She was proud of me for being such a strong woman and getting through such difficult circumstances.

Dent-art-ist

Like I mentioned before: you are not your profession.

Sometimes a profession can distract your focus off your "being" though.

In dentistry, it can be quite a challenge to stay focused on one's self-love, self-esteem, worthiness, and equality. There is a lot of stress in this field. Apparently, dentists have an alarmingly high incidence of cardiovascular disease, hypertension, colitis, lower back pain, eye strain and mental depression. A Dutch dentist even chopped one of his fingers to get money from the insurance company (the case was investigated by the police and insurance police; he was found guilty of attempting fraud). Why did he do this? He felt he couldn't handle the stress anymore.

WHY? Why is our profession so prone to these problems?

The fact that being a dentist can involve a high level of stress is being shown by data gathered by Steven Stack, professor State University in the USA.

He made a list of the 13 most suicidal jobs. Check it out:

1. **Dentist**
2. Musician
3. Actor
4. Dancer
5. Author
6. Photographer
7. Artist, sculptor and painter
8. Carpenter

9. Doctor
10. Performer
11. Mathematician and scientist
12. Skilled manual laborer and machinist
13. Semi- and unskilled manual laborer

Dentists are 5.45 times more likely to commit suicide than the average of other professionals and workers. Doctors' rate is 1.94. The other professionals in this list are between 3.60-1.46 times more likely to commit this act than the average.

Why is the dentist at number one? (I don't need a trophy, thank you. I was acquainted with a colleague who killed himself).

Because of the:

- Stress of perfection
- Economic pressure
- Time pressure
- Treatment frustration
- Patient anxiety
- Dentist's personality
- No exercise

Stress of perfection:

We want everything we do as dentists to be perfect. Unfortunately, though, this cannot always be.

Example: saliva gathering around a difficult place to reach in the mouth when the patient will only open it like half an inch is difficult. The same patient complaining he is drowning makes it even tougher.

Making a perfect restoration doesn't mean it will stay perfect on its own. The owner has to keep it clean. Not keeping it clean and showing up two years later might mean we have to do it all over, which means more stress because the restoration probably reaches below the gums now…

Economic pressure:

In the Netherlands, our dental rates (and thus our fees) are fixed by the government. They decide how high our incomes can go.

We get paid by the procedure. Last year our pay was cut by 5%! The costs, however, keep rising and rising.

Keep your chin up, dear dentist.

Another problem is that of trying to close a practice for a two or three-week vacation. No office hours mean no income. There's also no time to be sick. It costs money. The insurance rates are huge.

Time pressure:

Don't get behind schedule. Patients are generally very intolerant of delays. No catching up your time usually means no lunch.

Once a client said to me: *"You often run late, but when I am in your chair you always take the time for me no matter what."* That is true…just ignore my growling stomach!

Compromise treatment frustration:

Sometimes/often we have to do a treatment that isn't the best solution for the patient. He or she doesn't have the money to have the best option available. Or he or she for whatever reason simply chooses an option that is not the best possible one. Often, people choose the lowest insurance possible but expect me to give them the best available treatment.

This is stressful for us, believe me.

Patient anxiety:

There is evidence that dentists experience patterns of physiological stress responses (increased heart rate, high blood pressure, sweating, and so on) while performing procedures, and that these are related to the response of the patient. So true!

Sometimes the client jumps because he/she is so stressed and we jump with them. We really have to recover a few seconds from this before proceeding.

Some noises, and even words, evoke the patients fear and anxiety. I am very careful in the language I use, day in and day out.

Sometimes sweat runs from between my shoulder blades right into my pants. When the client leaves, I have to go get a towel.

Despite my efforts to alleviate your anxiety, many of you keep on stressing. You tend to continue blaming the school dentist from 40 years ago, a big guy with huge hands, no gloves, big glasses, no operation mask and assistants even worse than the he is, in a camper you still might feel tempted to set on fire.

I am a friendly and cheerful woman with small gloved hands, wearing a colorful mouth mask in a gorgeous office, working with assistants well-worth hugging.

Dentist's personality:

This is a biggie!

Compulsive attention to detail…extreme conscientiousness …careful control of emotions (!)…unrealistic expectations of herself.

Oops! I plead guilty.

I must control my emotions when I am doing procedures, so my patients will not perceive them and possibly become anxious. It's like being an airline attendant: you can't show your anxiety about high turbulence to the passengers!

While necessary, hiding my emotions in this way is very stressful. Sometimes I ask patients to close their eyes because I'm afraid they might see some anxiety in my expression. Trust me I will inform you about what I am doing. I always describe every step of my procedure.

No exercise:

This one I am not "guilty" of! I work out four times a week. I stretch connective tissues and work on endurance and power with the muscles. On the weekends when the weather is pleasant, I add in hiking and bicycling.

We dentists are very confined to a space; the room we work in is small, and the area we work in (your mouth) is significantly smaller! Meticulous work in small, restricted places, in a static posture, often leads to back problems and circulatory disorders.

How do I deal with all these causes of stress for dentists? The most important things I do are:

remembering who I really am
aligning with source
rediscovering my love for myself
rediscovering my self-worth.

In the next chapter, **Office Spirit,** I will describe a challenging office encounter and detail the emotional/vibrational reaction.

You'll see how I deliberately chose Source over Ego.

Office Spirit #1

I usually start my appointments at 9am on Thursdays.

I was therefore surprised to see a car parked in front of the office at 8:20. Pretty early for a client to show up but I imagined they must have had their reasons. We have coffee and up-to-date magazines so be my guest, I thought.

When I entered the waiting room, I found there was no one there.

"He went for a walk", Jose said. *"Ok...who is?"* I asked. *"The first client of today"*, Jose replied. It turned out that he had thought his appointment was at 8:30 rather than 9. *But I was convinced I'd said nine o'clock on the phone when he called to book the appointment.*

Well, usually we are right concerning the appointment times, but once in a while we do make a mistake. We are human, too.

At 08.40 am, he came back from his walk.

Now in the past I would have thought, *"Let me get him into my office because **I** made that mistake. Most likely, he will be mad at me so I'd better start the appointment now"*. Hear my ego talking?

I choose love. I choose love instead of fear since fear is a lower-fragmented energy.

I choose the only useful purpose of my body: to be a communication device through which I extend love. Love is the only reality. All the rest is made up!

Emotional Alignment Is Easy

I finished some administration, and then at 9 I invited Mr. J. into my office.

He stood up from his chair with such a force that the seat was almost thrown against the wall. While ranting and raving, he grasped his jacket from the table and without shaking my hand rushed into my office. He sat down in my dental chair.

I was in a higher vibrational state than he was, obviously, so I wanted him with me "up here" and certainly not the other way around.

So, I skipped the usual first question, "How are you?". Instead, I immediately starting focusing on the fact that J. also comes from the loving Source and had just picked up a lot of noise during his years, some of which he was projecting on me.

I complimented him on the way he looked, he was wearing really nice clothes and has seemed to lost a lot of weight. (to help him raise his vibe…). He totally ignored it.

I decided that *his* actions could *not* determine my experience.

I went on doing my work, focusing on his teeth and doing my affirmations: *"All is well", "If it isn't mine, I don't want it", "God is the only power and that power is within me"*, over and over again. My vibe was getting higher.

The game started for me.

I asked him about his daughters.

He kind of lit up but answered politely, not enthusiastically.

I went on with the check-up.

I went on with my affirmations.

He had two cavities and calculus. I asked politely whether I should fix that for him now.

"Yes, please", was his answer.

"My pleasure", I said. *"I am happy to do this for you. I will remove the calculus for you also so you don't have to come back."*

So, we went on and completed the procedures.

My focusing and my treatment lasted 45 minutes. I kept on being polite and very friendly.

He suddenly said: *"Thank you very much for helping me today. I'm happy you were able to do both fillings."*

"Thank you for always helping me so nicely."

My game had succeeded; I had been able to raise him up and make him leave the office happy instead of grumpy.

As you know, I have always had a lot of difficulty in being around grumpy people. It may be that you don't have this problem. Everybody starts exercising from a different level. I thought I would share my experience with you though, just in case.

Survival guide for the dentist

It is very easy to get overwhelmed at the office. Questions, tasks, accusations, clients, personnel, money, government rules, expectations, time, choices, demands: all ingredients to bake an overheated dentist.

Survival guide for the dentist:

- **Show gratitude**
- **Write down what you want to happen**
- **Write down what you want to feel**
- **Breathe and feel your lungs inflate**
- **Meditation during medication**

1) Show gratitude every day, whether you are the owner of the office or not.

   One day a long time ago, you chose to study dentistry. I hope you remember why. Be thankful for that. Say it out loud!! (If you don't want anybody to hear you, yell it when everybody has left the office or hasn't come in yet).

   Say (for instance):

   "Thank you so much for giving me the opportunity to express my love for teeth"

   "Thank you so much for this office space"

   "Thank you so much for the all-day-long ringing phone; it means clients are interested"

   "Thank you for my assistants; we are a team"

   "Thank you for my paperwork; it means I have a job"

Leslie van Oostenbrugge

"Thank you for this beautiful dental chair"

"Thank you for my beautiful instruments"

Prescription for the dentist:

tandartspraktijk 'het tandenhuis'
Plactiweg 2
4133 N L Vianen
t. 0347 343131
f. 0347 344154
e. info@hettandenhuis.nl

Naam ALL DENTISTS

Adres

Woonplaats EVERYWHERE

Rp/ " WHAT DO I WANT "

" WHAT DO I WANT "

S/ 6dd thought change
apply in-head

De praktijk die z'n tanden in uw gebit zet!

2) Write down (for instance):

    "I want to make a beautiful restoration"

    "I want to look through the eyes of love"

    "I want to relieve this client from his pain"

    "I want to see my assistants as my co-owners"

    "I want to experience my client as my compliment"

    "I want this encounter to be a miracle"

3) Write down (for instance):

    "I want to feel excited in my work"

    "I want to feel divinely guided"

    "I want to feel confident in talking to clients"

    "I want to feel connected to the client"

    "I want to feel connected to Source"

    "I want to express myself"

4) Breathe!

    I found that I was holding my breath during many dental procedures! When giving anesthetics, when pulling a tooth, when imagining a procedure might hurt…

    It seemed like I wanted to take over your pain.

    Breathing stops way too often. Please start being aware of your breathing pattern!

    If you're like many of us, you'll probably discover that you don't breathe properly.

Not breathing properly means less oxygen in your blood than needed, and less oxygen for the muscles, which will cramp.

We dentists usually sit statically or are bent over most of the day. Imagine the effect of this being made worse by failing to get enough oxygen.

5) Meditation during medication

To keep your mind off of worrisome, unwanted and discouraging thoughts, you need to block all negative thoughts and focus on the ones that bring you joy.

MWM® (meditate while medicate) is the name of my meditation exercise.

With the "medicate" in dentistry I mean everything that we administer and apply, including when we give anesthetics, apply medication to stop bleeding, apply the filling, give the loving tap on your shoulder to ask whether you are ok, and provide cleaning instructions.

MWM® (Meditate While Medicate)

Whenever I feel my back hurting, I think I am the luckiest woman on earth! One to chew on, right?

Because of this:

When I have back pain, I am being reminded of my separation from Source. This might happen when:

- I feel upset about a filling not being perfect
- I feel guilty about running late
- I feel harassed by clients insisting on a procedure I don't feel is appropriate
- I feel bad skipping lunch for the 876th time
- I feel sorry for sending the invoice
- I feel overwhelmed with a full waiting room

"Hey you, <u>Source</u> is calling.", "Well, High, I mean HI! It is Leslie here."

"Well, Leslie, I just called to remind you of the following facts:

- *The filling is fine; the patient can chew with it and the tooth doesn't hurt like it did.*

- *You run late because you l i s t e n e d and took care of the previous client.*

- *Clients want things to be fixed which cannot be fixed by YOU; t h e i r mind.*

- *Don't feel bad; make a choice!*

- *You took care of the problem, you paid Dental School a lot of money yourself. You spent more than a lot of time fixing the patient's problem. You are worth the money you charge. With the money you receive, you can invest to help out more patients."*

"Ok, thank you for calling!! I tend to forget you sometimes. Whenever I feel my back again I will think of you like I do so many times. But...I am human. My ego tends to distract itself from you. I know I a m the boss of my mind and my thoughts. Thank you for catching up with me! Bye.", "Bye now, Leslie!"

I am happy with these calls!

I have learned to take a few seconds/minutes time out, and take care of myself in between appointments.

I lay down on the floor somewhere and meditate (preferably not in the waiting room). I often read uplifting posts or parts of pages of uplifting books. This I told you before.

The other thing I have started is meditation while doing dental procedures.

I tune into myself, inner being, higher power, Source, you name it.

While doing a drill and fill, my thoughts include:

"Am I sitting on my butt? Do I feel my butt on this chair completely?"

"Do my feet feel the floor? The soft shoes I am wearing indeed make this shuffling noise to prove they are completely ON the floor and not just the toes. I can indeed hear that. Is my back relaxed? Ok, I am fine...I feel fine now..."

"Wow... amazing how the surface of the hand piece feels, nicely rounded and slightly curved... thank you sharp burr for letting me feel the ease of drilling through this old filling... the filling comes out easily with my great tools... I feel great this client is not in pain... I am fortunate to be able to carry out this procedure, I am fortunate to feel the trust of my client to have me work in their sacred space, their mouths. My gloves feel perfectly fitted around my fingers...I feel the ease of the patient... Great how I love to experience my job as an art... The presence of my assistant feels great...it feels absolutely fantastic to have a great team... I feel fortunate to have these ladies around... I feel honored that t h e y feel good to work w i t h me, I feel blessed to be able to do this work...I feel fortunate to be able to feel the patient's pulse in their lips so I know whether they are really at ease...when they are not at ease I am able to comfort them which feels terrific...I feel my heart skips a beat when my procedure is done successfully... I feel satisfied when a filling is not just a filling but again a restoration ... I feel the ease..." And so on, and so on.

We should be taught in dental school about meditation, about stress reduction for the dentist.

Usually the excuse people have for not doing meditation is: "no time". But it's actually very easy to find time to meditate, as I have demonstrated. How much ease you will gain. It will make you feel terrific. New doors will open for you.

The more ease you have, the more ease your patient has. Remember: everything is energy. The patient can feel you, too!

High energy

From day one, being in Burlingame was the manifestation of the vibration I had been experiencing for a long time. Remember that according to the Universe, everything will happen at the right time, at the right moment. Well, it did.

The second day of my stay, I got ready to go to the seminar. I was excited. About two hundred people would be there.

I was early. Then Berna's premonition of my seeing green was realized in the form a huge green screen! She had also said I would be on stage….

The seminar was practical training in the theory I had intensely studied for many months. We did a lot of exercises like: hugging each other and giving compliments. This was easy for me but I noticed that many people had difficulty. This made me cry at night.

It is very tough for many people to accept compliments. Often people receive (note that I didn't write *accept*) compliments and then immediately return a compliment themselves. But is this a compliment or a distraction?

For instance, somebody says: *"I love your hair! It looks fantastic"*. Often the reply is: *"Your hair looks great, too"*

Usually within a split second this compliment is made after you have received yours. Actually, you didn't really receive it. It bounced back on you.

Too bad. But hey I know the reason: you didn't find yourself worthy to get a compliment or you hate your hair.

See it from a different point of view; the other person really meant the compliment they gave you. The other person wanted to make you feel good. Well, how absolutely fantastic is that?

How to receive a compliment:

Whenever somebody pays you a compliment, just say:

THANK YOU!

"Nothing else? That's all?", I can hear you think.

Yep! That's it. It might feel strange at first because you want to reply within a split second, a reaction time a table tennis player would envy. But *train* yourself. Train yourself to only say, *"Thank you"*. This will also make the giver happy. So, you are both in on the happiness, the giver as well as the receiver. It is an example of co-creation.

Most people do not want to be touched by a stranger at all, never, ever. I once met somebody who really crouched when I touched her shoulder. It was supposed to be just a friendly gesture, but it scared her. I felt sorry. Not for touching her but the experience it had caused for her. She probably had a lot to deal with from the past.

So, a lot of men and women reluctantly executed the speaker's command to hug someone. Again, this was no problem for me. Wow, I guess I had reason to be proud already!

I got a huge compliment from a fellow seminar guest on the second day. He said: *"When you enter a room, the whole room lights up! You radiate so much energy!"*.

"Thank you so much", I said.

Don't bow for the arrow.

All participants at the seminar received an arrow. (After having signed a paper to not sue the speaker in case of an accident).

The arrow represented our *fear*. This could be, for example: "fear of failing", "bosses", "lack of money", "dogs", "not being able to pursue my dream", "no perseverance", "family", "fear of being in public", and so on.

In the exercise we were assigned, one person was to hold the arrow with its point facing the "victim", and the "victim" was required to "walk straight through the arrow to break it". It represented their fear being broken. The "victim" wore safety goggles and the person holding the arrow wore a glove.

At 3…2…1!!!

I took my step forward and indeed the arrow broke, of course! I mean, why not? I had set my mind to it, so I was going to do it.

No hole was punched in my belly by the arrow, and there was no effect on my sternum at all; There wasn't even a scratch. All that was left was only to hand my goggles to someone else.

To my big surprise, however, there were a lot of people not able to take the step "through" the arrow. They were unable to trust themselves and the other person.

To be able to cut through a belief, you have to start to cut through a thought train. It starts with a first step…in your mind…in your now.

Emotional Alignment Is Easy

They couldn't take that step, then, at that moment. They felt too much resistance to pull through. It may have been way too soon. Hopefully, they were able to do that later in life.

To me, again, it was a piece of cake. Let's have carrot cake; the best on earth, my favorite.

"Everybody back to their seats please", the speaker said. It was about time to have dinner, we knew. But first he needed to evaluate the exercise. He asked us all:

"Who succeeded in breaking the arrow?"

I reluctantly raised my hand to admit I did.

"Who thought it was a piece of cake?"

I now suddenly doubted whether I should raise my hand. The assignment was incredibly easy. I was not going to raise my hand, I decided. No showing off on this one. It was way too easy, come on!! I did not deserve *any* credit.

A lot of people raised their hands. Fewer than had followed at the first question, though.

Then we were surprised by an outburst from the speaker:

"So, you think it was easy, huh? You thought, what a piece of cake! A real waste of time, right? But NO, NO, NO it was NOT!" (he slapped his hand so hard against the flip over that I thought he must have broken his fingers). *"That wasn't an easy exercise at all! You get all the credit for it. You walked right into that sharp point of an arrow and think it was nothing? You were all required to identify a long-standing fear that you needed to address. You wrote it down and took the leap of faith that everything would be ok in the end.*

But now you ignore your own strength? What are you doing? You are underestimating your own capabilities and strength! Everything you reach in life is worth a big compliment to yourself, a huge pat on your own back!! Please remember this, every day, every month, every year!"

I was happy I hadn't raised my hand. He wouldn't accuse me, right?

But it all hit me like a hammer.

I hadn't raised my hand in the first place because I thought raising my hand was like I wanted to show off. Also, I didn't want to express my opinion.

I had been *scared* to do so.

Expressing my opinion had led to so many negative comments in the past *("Who do you think you are?)* that I'd decided not to speak.

This reality hit me so hard I started to cry. Sobbing is the word, actually. I had to leave the conference room because I was so emotional.

What had I done to myself all my life?

I'd thought I wasn't good enough; I had accused myself of being ugly. Graduating cum laude from my dentistry and physical therapy studies was "just" something that happened. I had always attributed that only to my eagerness to learn. Forget the hundreds and hundreds of hours spent studying. I hadn't even patted myself on the back after the brave move of establishing my own practice. To me it was normal. It was "just" a step to take and "just" a move to make.

I did not experience or acknowledge my own greatness. I had been strong enough to follow my dreams despite people advising me to do otherwise. I remember one assistant telling me I'd better think it all through again before separating from my colleague.

That comment made me wobble in my decision at first but I chose to focus on the good feelings and proceeded. Despite all the things that had happened in the past, I flourished in everything I undertook.

Focus is the keyword. Focus on feeling good.

We all have free will, remember? We have free will to choose our thoughts.

This day at the conference, at this moment, I realized I indeed am a born-under-the-star-Leo genius! Confident, Ambitious, Generous, Loyal and Encouraging. This seminar weekend was finally the time when I would allow myself to be in alignment with myself. To realize I am good and lovely just because I AM.

The $100 bill

Finally, I had learned to love money…

Money is energy! Contrary to the popular belief that money is the root of all evil, The Bank of the Universe never fails…

We were given the assignment of bringing in a $100 bill in our wallets. We were asked to lift up the bill and look very carefully for every detail on it.

Then we were asked to put the bills in our laps and listen. Three men came in the room. They were holding candles while walking silently and gracefully toward the front of the room. They carried three buckets of water with them.

The men positioned themselves; one on the left, one on the right and one in between.

There was a silence I had only ever experienced at funerals.

Then the speaker spoke: *"I want you all to stand up, keep your hundred-dollar bill ready, and walk to the front. You will then burn your money. Please walk this way."*

He pointed out a route that resembled the way you walk in a Roman Catholic church to receive the Eucharist.

All the lights went out; the flames of the candles were showing us where our goal was.

As you can imagine, I was in total shock at the request for us to burn our money. I was very confused. I asked my neighbor: *"Is he serious? Burn the money?"*. *"I guess so"*, he replied.

Emotional Alignment Is Easy

After all these months of being thankful for the money, understanding that money is energy and deliberately living by the Law of Attraction, and realizing that my negative ideas related to money were all just a manifestation of my own mental state, I was totally at war with myself. This means I totally separated my ego from Source.

I cried and cried, tears ran down my face. I didn't know what to do.

We were like sheep. I absolutely didn't want to go... I didn't want to follow. I was convinced Source was on my side. My life had changed for the better already in the previous two years, so my inner being must be right...right?

But I kept on walking, we had to leap over bags that lay in the aisles.

I couldn't stop crying. *"Why do I have to do this?"*, I asked myself. *"Source doesn't want me to, inner being doesn't want me to because it absolutely doesn't feel right."*

My neighbor convinced me to continue, so I did.

I didn't have a handkerchief; I was a bit embarrassed about my tears, but I was allowed to cry, darn it!

Then, all of a sudden, when the first person in line was just about to burn his money, all the lights were turned on, the flames were extinguished and the water buckets were being carried outside again.

The speaker shouted at us, red-faced:

"WHAT DO YOU THINK YOU ALL ARE DOING?"

It all struck me!

I had allowed ego to make me fall for a trick. This exercise had shown us how easy it is for ego to take over power from your inner being, by listening to others.

I had let other people make decisions about MY money because I figured they would know what they were doing. I had given away all my power regarding my money.

This exercise showed me to not give any power away.

During this exercise, I had wanted to go my own way but didn't listen to my inner being. I listened to the "Master" instead. But I am my own Master. You are your own Master. Get it?

"No man can attract money if he despises it. Money is God in Manifestation as freedom from want and limitation, but it must be kept in circulation and put to the right uses. Hoarding and saving react with grim vengeance." ~ Florence Scovel Shinn (*The Complete Works*).

A new client of mine felt that his former dentist had made too much money. *"The dental care he provided was below average!"* he stated. *"But the money he makes is huge!"* he complained.

I never react those statements such as these. My dental care was very different. He wasn't used to the amount of attention I gave him. The cleaning instructions I provided he had never even heard of. If he had known how to clean properly, he would have done so, he assured me. This was proven by the state his gum health on his next visit: they are pink! This patient was 85 years old and had dentures, and I was the first dentist who had checked under the dentures to ensure the health of his gums.

He connected his idea of the other dentist making a lot of money with that of low-quality care. He said, *"Money is the root of all evil"*.

I didn't agree on that.

<u>"Money in itself is good and beneficial but used for destructive purposes, hoarded and saved, or considered more important than love, it brings disease and disaster and the loss of money itself."~ Florence Scovel Shinn.</u>

I didn't charge him for the cleaning (it had been cleaned by a professional but not thoroughly enough according to my standards). I didn't charge him for the following consultation because I felt sorry for him. I felt sorry for the price he had to pay for low-quality dentistry. So a few visits were free. After that, he had to pay, yes even if his question took three minutes. Once, I had to check his records and write a letter to the oral surgeon. He was upset he had to pay!

Mind my own business

In the past, I hadn't interfered with the discussions between my banker and insurance agent, about *my* money. The agent was concerned because *his* commission was in danger. The banker because *his* commission was in danger. And I? I was scared to talk about money.

But…that was history.

As soon as I arrived back in Holland, I really grabbed my power. It is never, ever too late. Every day is a new day to start. I was eager and enthusiastic to cut the old habitual thinking.

I had never felt like doing these things before. I'd considered myself a dental care giver and not an entrepreneur, owning a business. But that's actually part of my role, too.

First of all, I undertook the task of obtaining quotes from a variety of agents, and compared their services and fees. I also did this with accountants.

Then I really started to investigate what I spent my money on. How much of my spending was out of fear and how much from love?

The underlying cause of all trouble is fear!

Looking back, I indeed made many of my financial choices out of fear.

Fear of:

- Insulting an agent or accountant by choosing not to become his or her client

- Running risks regarding staff/sickness
- Bank requirements
- Out-of-control invoices
- Taxes
- The future
- *Insurances.*

I had a disability insurance policy. I had to pay thousands of euros a year for this. Yet I was, and am never sick!

Insurance agents know how to get you to buy their products. Remember they receive a high commission. That is fine but I made a choice out of fear. They sell because of fear...

I have learned to trust my inner being, to trust the Universe. It has the best in store for you. Let go! So, I cancelled the insurance. It was possible! But I had to be determined.

My insurance agent, who had always been polite and gentle, suddenly became very grumpy. He was upset with me for cancelling the policy. I knew that his commission was 2500 euro a year...

I wrote him a kind letter in which I thanked him very much for the services rendered.

It was because of my understanding of the Law of Attraction that I decided I am not going to pay for my sickness when I am in this super healthy body. I am the one responsible for my body, not the company.

I, of course, still have all of the insurance required by law. Not because I want to but rather because I don't want trouble from rule enforcers. In such cases, I buy my relief.

Staff.

My assistants are never sick, mainly because of the love and respect we all give each other in my office. So don't worry. It is love that rules.

Taxes/Future.

I had to pay additional taxes, in the amount of 25.000 euros! I didn't yet have that money.

I found a solution: a pension plan I had paid into. I decided to surrender it, and received the 25.000 euro I needed.

I now had the money to pay the taxes. I live in the now…

Coincidence? As I've already explained, there is no such thing.

The everyday affirmation, *"Infinite Spirit open the way for me to receive what is mine by Divine right; let me receive health, wealth and self-expression",* came to fruition.

Line yourself up with well-being; do not line up with the idea of tragedy befalling you! But if you feel okay about paying for insurance, that's fine, too! The key is to listen to your inner being.

Timing is all you need. Stay patient.

Court

Maslow, (April 1, 1908-June 8, 1970) was an American psychologist who was best known for creating Maslow's hierarchy of needs. This is a theory of psychological health based on the fulfilment of innate human needs in order of priority, culminating in self- actualization. As care providers, dentists, doctors, psychologists, nurses, and so on, we are pretty much all familiar with Maslow.

I added the lower sentence in this pyramid. In this evolving world, new knowledge and new knowing arise; while we honor our ancestors, we add new elements to theories. The purpose of this is to try to raise everyone's awareness.

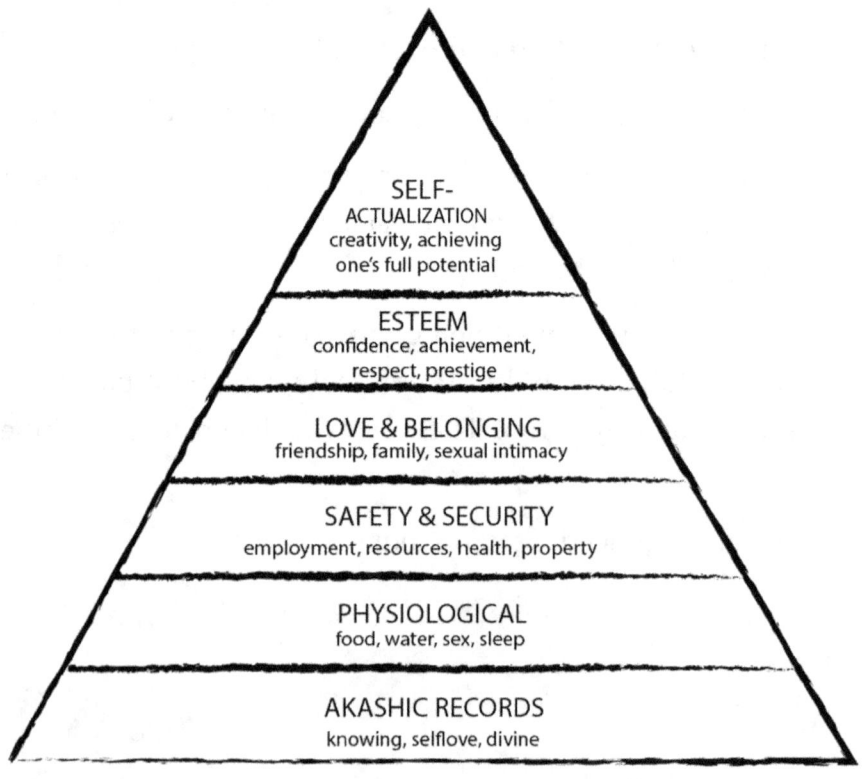

Without the "**knowing**" that there is more than we see, we will remain limited in our "thinking".

Realizing we are **Divine** and that therefore Divinity is our birthright is the ultimate "achieving one's potential".

The hierarchy of the pyramid might suggest that human needs will only be fulfilled one level at a time. On the other hand, it suggests that self-actualization is always obtained. Of course, that is not true.

Maslow called his work positive psychology. It focuses on higher human nature; the positive side of things and how they go right.

How do you know you are a self-actualizer? Self-actualizers impress us as being both authentic and wise, calm and energetic, people and problem-oriented.

Maslow's pyramid attracted my attention because of its positive approach. Its positivity harmonizes with my own approach to dentistry: I have always focused primarily on that which is healthy rather than emphasizing the negative. This is different than the conventional approach taught in dental school, where we are led to focus on what is wrong rather than right. We were not taught to give compliments to patients. We were not taught about naming the good.

People are inspired when you approach them in a positive way.

I still wonder why I chose to collaborate with colleagues. I suppose I was eager to learn the dental profession, to have "role models" in the office to show me how things work.

Emotional Alignment Is Easy

"Please teach me! I am eager to learn" and the *"I have a low self-esteem thing going on"* was the essence of my internal war.

Once I overcame my low self-esteem it seemed I got wings… I wanted to fly…away…

I could handle things myself, achieving my individual potential!

Achieving this, mixed with the imperative of getting away from a woman nowhere near self-actualization, made *me* decide to start my own practice. It made *her* decide to sue me. Now, we were going to court.

I had to choose between two options for how I would approach the court sessions.

1. Choose victimhood
2. Choose the magical approach

Well, I chose 2.

Your behavior and experience are the result of your beliefs. A belief is just a thought we keep thinking, right? So, change the thought, if you need to.

So, there is allowing…*"allowing what?"* Connection with Source. Or, there is Resistance… *"Resistance to what"* Connection to Source.

This resistance causes negative emotions, and not feeling well generally. Between the allowing and resisting is a whole range of feelings available. They are all ok! Just make peace with where you are on the emotional scale. The important thing is that you try to pick the best available feeling there is in every moment.

Abraham Maslow, said in 1966: *"I suppose it is tempting, if the only tool you have is a hammer, to treat everything as if it were a nail"*. It seemed that my colleague had fallen into this trap.

Of course, I wasn't very happy to go to the courthouse, a place full of negative vibes!

However, I knew that I am in charge of my own thoughts. Nobody can get into my head and tell me how to think. Since I am in charge of the way I think, I am also in charge of the way I feel.

I went to pick up my lawyer. Something extraordinary happened when driving through the very narrow one-way street. A cargo bike approached us.

The women driving it was going the wrong way; the street was way too narrow to have her pass the car.

While my lawyer expressed frustration about the biker's behavior, I had goosebumps all over my body. A cargo bike! This was a sign! A sign from the Universe. A cargo bike brings goods. The container was empty, it struck me. Suddenly in my mind I saw the empty container of the bike filled up with money, money for me!

What other reason could there be for this cargo bike appearing at this moment, right now in this narrow street?

What you perceive, you believe…

My lawyer was angry, while I felt at ease. We both experienced the same encounter but interpreted it differently. That made all the difference.

While enjoying the experience, we arrived at the courthouse. After a three-hour debate, the session was closed.

It turned out that in contradiction to what our business contract stated, the arbiter wanted me to reimburse my former colleague for all the clients who came with me to my new practice. Despite my argument that clients themselves choose which dentist they go to; the verdict was final. PAY!

After bargaining about the amount, my colleague finally agreed on my offer.

The arbiter must have been a dentist who had paid a lot of money to buy himself into a practice. He for sure was not letting me get away with this.

Despite all of this, though, I felt the presence of Source and I saw the cargo bike; I kept my faith....

I saw my colleague in the parking lot. At first I wanted to shake her hand and say good-bye but I figured she wouldn't be pleased with that, so I got into my car. I considered sending her a card to thank her for the time we had worked together, but I didn't do this. I figured she would rip it up and throw it away, like she had done with so many other messages.

I didn't hate her then and still don't now. We just didn't get along in the office, that's all. That's all. This doesn't mean I wasn't upset about the situation we were in; of course I was.

The main thing I was upset about was the fact that someone obviously hated me so much for making my own choice. I didn't like being hated. I didn't like her negative thoughts about me.

I send her Love and Light.

We drove back home and I cried. I cried for the incredible strength I had shown during the session. I cried for having experienced Source with me during the session. I cried for thinking, "Why did she win?" But on a spiritual level, everything is a win-win situation. There is no losing, only gaining.

The time between the initial subpoena and the final court session was four years. I wanted to get it over and done with it as soon as possible; "*Do not see the problem but come to a solution*". But my colleague decided it should take this long.

In those four years, my life changed so much. Tears of happiness will still often blur my eyes.

I had to go deep to experience what I experienced.

Today, I couldn't care less what anyone else thinks. I will love them anyway.

Reptility

Those of us who have not awakened and become emotionally aligned are part of the population of conditioned minds. Minds that resort to their brains right away. Minds that have an opinion right away, a comment or, even worse, a judgement. Thinking operates instantaneously within many people's heads. This is called the reptile's brain.

Definition of *Reptility*:

A. The nature or condition of being reptilian

B. (*Figurative*) Reptilian character or conduct;

   Devious or sly behavior; baseness

Definition of *Sly*:

A. Having or showing a cunning and deceitful nature

   "*A sly, manipulative woman*"

On one hand, we cannot help to use our intellect. The brain is there for us to use this intellect. But the intellect (which can be part of the ego) has taught itself to be separated from Source. The intellect is often the cause of actions performed out of fear, of lack, of anxiety, of feeling overwhelmed. It is sometimes called the rational approach to things. It makes us think we are unworthy. It makes us think we need to acquire evidence before making a decision.

Intuition, however, is the ability to <u>acquire knowledge</u> without proof, evidence or conscious reasoning, or without understanding how the knowledge was acquired. It is a "gut" feeling, a preconscious thing. In retrospect you don't know how you knew you knew what you didn't know before. (LOL)

The intuitive approach is the magical approach. An example of this was the approach I took in court. It is the approach of knowing that life will fulfill itself. It is a knowing, not a knowledge. To me knowledge is the wisdom you acquire after gathering facts and proof.

The magical approach takes it for granted that life will unfold in your own best interest. Your cells are impregnated with this knowing! Each cell yearns for your good! Your cells renew every day. Every other seven years, you have created a whole new cellular body. Your body is treating you well. Now it is up to you to treat your body well.

Sorrow, regret and remorse kill your cells. Show respect, use great words, forgive and show love.

Your cells love it!

For many people, the intellect often overrules the instinct. However, instinct or intuition should come first and the intellect carry out whatever evolves from the intuition.

Take your time to let your instinct/intuition tell you what to do.

I rewired my brain. By being still and not reacting right away, I trained myself into seeing and hearing signs and listening to my gut first before acting out.

This has greatly helped me in dentistry. Intellectually, I might know I could and wanted to pull that tooth. But a gut feeling said: *"don't!"* So, I didn't. It turned out to be the right decision. The oral surgeon had been busy with pulling the tooth for over an hour!!

Intuition is magical.

222

Our intuition is installed before birth, and we have the opportunity to use it our whole lives. That's what we are intended to do. "But *how?*" I can hear you ask. First of all, by being still. Do not react, agitate, comment or judge. Be quiet (be)for(e) verbalizing or otherwise showing your emotions!

Lock yourself up in some room, stay longer in the bathroom, walk in the woods, stay longer in your car when you arrive home. Contemplate! Give your mind time to be content-free! Begin with little steps. Start with 30 seconds, watch a tree, watch the rain drops on your car window, watch your kids for a minute before rushing off and cleaning the house. Follow up the next day with another 30 seconds; for example, you could stay in your car, and watching and appreciating the wheel. It is because of that wheel you are able to drive your car. The next day spend 3 x 30seconds in silence. And so on and so on. Contemplation keeps the true end (which is only love) in sight; it gives meaning to every practical act of life.

I know the meaning of life now and am awake. I know that by contemplating and focusing on the good, you will experience the good. You will eventually discover that:

- You ARE in a field of infinite possibilities
- You ARE invisible energy
- You ARE the creator of matter
- You ARE turning thoughts into things
- You ARE connected to everything and everyone
- You ARE expanding the things you focus on
- You ARE the Universe

Maybe you need proof. Proof that the Universe indeed has your back. If so, your intellect and ego are still too much intertwined.

Well, you can get the proof you need. Try the game! Really! Try. For fun. Show yourself.

Give yourself a month's time. What is a month? Before you know it, it's Christmas again, right? Time flies.

You've already read about some of my encounters with the Universe. One of the many significant signs that have been given to me was the license plate of the car ahead of me in one of the stories I told earlier. Remember? I couldn't have been much clearer that the Universe wanted me to go to Burlingame.

The art of recognizing signs that allow you to recognize that they are sent by the Universe, and are from intuition. Because we live in a *space/time reality*, we must wait for things to show up. When you are not physical anymore, everything you need will be easily evident and within your immediate reach. On earth, though, it is different. Just be patient! It will come.

In her book *E-squared (E^2)*, Pam Grout describes an elucidating exercise that you can try. She says to simply "imagine the number 222 appearing". I tried this. I visualized the number regularly and consistently. For the first few days, I did so almost every hour.

Eventually, I let the thought go and eventually forgot about it. This is the best way to do it! Ask and it IS. The Universe gathered all its components to show me the "222". It was within a month that my focusing on "222" finally showed its manifestations.

As you must now realize, this exercise doesn't only work for manifesting numbers! Visualization also works for abundance, happiness, money, you name it!

And yes, for heaven's sake, the thing that you visualize will come. When you want something, the Universe conspires and expands with you to fulfil your wishes. The process is one of focus/allow/focus/allow/let go/allow it to happen.

My personal trainer used to be the rehabilitation trainer of a famous football club in the Netherlands. He works at a physical therapy gym owned by another football enthusiast, who is currently therapist for a famous football club. Many shirts of football players are hanging in the gym. They were given as thank-you gifts. As you know, football player shirts have numbers….

My heart skipped a beat when I saw two "2s" staring at me. Not three "2s" all in a row, but I still thought it must be a sign from the Universe. My magic wand had worked again! Right?!

But I couldn't avoid admitting to myself that the "2s" did not stand beside one another. This couldn't be a sign. I had to admit it, although I really didn't want to.

My ego led me to believe that this was a manifestation from the Universe. My intellect wanted to believe that this was it, and my ego didn't have the patience to wait for the Universe.

However, I checked myself. Source must overrule ego.

Focus on what you **do** want. When it appears to be only half of that, **WAIT!** Don't try to rush things by fooling yourself.

Don't force it.

Your heart won't lie to you! That is the job of the mind. So, I reluctantly agreed with myself to wait. Which was tough. But I decided to play on. The game was still on…and on…and on…and on.

As I said before, I forgot about it. Remembering it is not your work! It is the Universe's work. You just have to ask. Your thoughts turn into things. Ask and it is given.

It was about two weeks later that I happened to glance at the wall of fame at the gym. My eyes were drawn to the shirts again. There…there it was! Thank you! Thank you!

"2 2 2" in a straight line, just like I asked!

So, try this out for yourself. Take time to visualize a hairpin, a trolley, a blue butterfly, a pink car, anything really, give it time, and see what happens. And watch. I bet you it will show up somewhere.

The moment you spot your ego is the moment you become aware. The moment you invite the Universe into your brain is the moment you will find peace.

Do not settle for less in life. Remember: Jesus wants the best for you. He wants to see you happy.

The meaning of 222

You might be interested to learn that the number 222 has a meaning. Did you know that numbers have meanings?

Numerology can uncover your destiny and life purpose.

But, remember: you are the captain of your own ship. The numbers *only* reflect back to you your emotional step on the ladder!

Have you ever become aware of the "11:11" hour at night, or the 12:12, 22:22, 3:33? Or the date being 12-21-2012, or the price tag showing $6,66?

Teeth and molars have numbers...<u>*two*</u> digits. That means double force! What does it mean if you lose a "11" or a "36"? What is your house number? I lived in a house with the number 52, and then moved to a new one with the number 32, which was eventually changed by the local government to number 42. This is an example of synchronicity.

Have you ever questioned why this kind of synchronicity happens? Today for instance I started writing at 11:11 o'clock!

My, dad, brother and I played (European) handball.

All three of us had number 9 on our backs. Perhaps more accurately, the number 9 had our back! All three of us became captains of our teams. Enough said.

"Numbers are the highest degree of knowledge. It is a knowledge itself." -Plato

Pythagoras (570 BC-495 BC) was a Greek philosopher mathematician, and founder of the movement called Pythagoreanism.) He believed numbers had souls as well as magical powers. It was said that he was the first man to call himself a philosopher, or lover of wisdom.

The Pythagoreans even divided numbers into two groups: odd and even, male and female, dark and light and so on.

Below is an overview of some of the characteristics of each number. Please be aware that this is very basic and just a tiny fragment of the spiritual meaning of numbers.

This is a compilation found on internet:

<u>Number 1:</u> New beginning, strong will, power, purity, confidence, loner, individuality

<u>Number 2:</u> Kindness, duality, balance, communication, partnership, conflict, trust, faith

<u>Number 3:</u> Magic, expression, intuition, divine, good fortune, wisdom, understanding

<u>Number 4:</u> Solidity, calmness, creation, stability, order, strong foundation.

<u>Number 5:</u> Balance, social, funny, uplifting, need of change

<u>Number 6:</u> Completeness, beauty, high ideals, trusting, caring, healing

<u>Number 7:</u> Perfection, security, safety, seeker, thinkers, intellect

Number 8: Harmony, balance, infinity, abundance, power, justice, ability to make decisions

Number 9: Magic, sacred, heaven, good leadership, fulfilment, wisdom

Number 10: Completion of a cycle, receiving an unexpected fortune, sacred

In 222, of course, the number 2 appears three times. This has a very powerful vibration. Number 22 is a "Master Builder" number. 222 means manifesting miracles! It involves keeping your balance and discovering your infinite opportunities. It tells you to keep faith and keep up the good work you are doing. Stay strong and believe in yourself.

Pam Grout *must* have chosen this number on purpose.

Armed to the teeth

Ordered to pay the goodwill money to my colleague before the end of the following month left my body a bit shaky.

I knew I was going to be taken care of so my inner being kept the faith; all was well.

I have always kept all my promises and I still do. However, this was one time when I couldn't fulfil an obligation. I'd signed the agreement in front of the arbitrary trio.

A few days later, obviously, I had to call my bank.

"THE bank", is how they refer to themselves in their ads in the Netherlands. I even have a personal banker! Whooohooo! Anyway, "my" banker (let's call him "Mr. Bank") is a very nice guy.

I had to ask the question of whether the bank would lend me the money to pay off the debt. His answer: "Well I think it is going to be tough. You just opened your new office, you are up to your ears in debt and now you come asking for more money".

Wham... a slap in my face moment.

"Although your practice is doing amazingly well, I am afraid this request will probably have to be denied", he said.

I started this phone call being in alignment and keeping the faith. His answer didn't really come as a surprise but was enough to knock me off my foot.

Yes, you read that right: *"foot"*. That means 1 and not two...

He was going to do his best and ask his superiors, he said. We hung up. After that, we had a lunch break in the office. Carolien and I decided to go for a walk. The weather was nice. I had to distract myself from my conversation with Mr. Bank.

I wanted to shout it all out and scream. I was tempted to smash one of my nice chairs. Tears welled up behind my eyes. When the heck would the financial struggle stop.

I couldn't help but wonder, maybe we should shut the place down and quit. Why work so hard? But I soon calmed down and became myself again. I don't like the idea of *"working for money"*. I prefer having an amazing job I love that will bring me money. Commit to the thing you love; don't get distracted by anything else.

But then I remembered: I had been at this emotional place before. I'd decided not to call debt "debt" anymore, remember? And I'd resolved to no longer use the word "struggle".

I don't want this feeling anymore!

But hey...I am a human being so sometimes I let my ego cut myself off from my true self.

I decided to go for a walk with Carolien, my assistant. We walked in the sun, enjoying a nice stroll. We found a feather. Feathers bring messages from above. Then...another one...and another one! Three feathers in a row.

I picked them up. The color of all three were white and grey. Remember, colors have meanings. White means to *keep the faith. You are supported by angels.* Grey is *a call to return to peace. Create within!*

Well, the feathers really gave me a lift. I was still alive. My children were safe. My husband was fine. My friends and family were ok, too. I love them all. They love me. The only true thing is love, right? The rest is illusion. I still have the highest good on earth.

I started to feel better already…. I put the feathers in my *"bills to pay"* organizer….

I didn't hear from Mr. Bank again until several weeks later, probably eight. Needless to say, I had already been meant to pay my debt. I'd managed to stay pretty calm even though I hadn't kept my promise. Amazing and surprising. I guess my alignment exercises were working….

When Mr. Bank called, he had a surprise for me:

"They", meaning "THE bank", were going to lend me the money! Under many strict conditions, they were willing to support me.

That same day (a Friday), he was going to drop the quotation papers at my house. They were supposed to be signed immediately and returned on Monday. So, the offer expired on Monday. I had Saturday and Sunday to think the agreement over.

I had been the most obedient woman on the planet when it came to following orders from "authorities".

The bank, the local government, police, former bosses, and teachers. I never argued with them. Was I going to continue with a *"be-quiet-and-do-as-you-are-told-kinda-thing"*? Like in Burlingame when having to burn the 100 dollar bill? No way, not anymore!

I had a strange feeling about the bank's proposal. First, they hadn't wanted to help me at first, but now they insisted that I sign the forms within three days. I didn't get it.

Guess what? I did not sign.

I was going to take a time out on this. I refused to act out of fear. I had acted out of fear many times in my life and I wasn't about to do so again now.

I was not going to fall for the: *"I better do this, otherwise they will get mad at me"*. I was totally fed up with it.

I want nothing but love! To give love and receive love. Wherever, whenever. In personal life and in business. I was fed up with being threatened with insecurity. Life has something big in store for me. Life is meant to be good.

I suddenly decided not to accept the offer which expired on Monday. It felt good…

Monday was here, the offer was in my bag. Off to the office.

Tuesday was here, the offer was in my bag. Off to the office.

Wednesday was here, the offer was in my bag. Off to the office.

Thursday was here, the offer was in my bag. Off to the office.

Friday: day off!

A new Monday, Tuesday and Wednesday appeared.

Then...the call came to my office. My assistant picked up the phone. She came to tell me Mr. Bank called.

Jose and Carolien know all the inside outs of the practice, which means that finances are no secrets to them. They also knew how I was going to handle this situation.

They had both seen my incredible growth.

Mr. Bank was very surprised I hadn't signed yet. I answered him by email. With a white lie, actually. I said I needed time to think, to get in alignment.

The good old Leslie didn't do what she was told anymore. At least, not right away. And certainly, if it didn't seem right to me.

So, I eventually emailed Mr. Bank.

"Dear Mr. Bank,

Thank you so much for your offer. I am happy and very grateful that you and your superior want to be of so much help.

I would like to have a nice talk with you both. I want to express my gratitude for your helpfulness, in person.

I want your superior to meet the woman who is behind Het Tandenhuis (name of my company).

I'd like to share some feelings I have about you and THE bank

With kind regards,

Leslie van Oostenbrugge, dentist"

Two weeks later, I had an appointment at their office. Carolien, my whiz woman on finances, came along.

Did I see "my" Mr. Bank trembling while drinking his coffee? Really? I didn't understand. I wasn't completely shake-free either but better than I could have ever imagined addressing one of the most fearful topics in life: *money*. Talking to "THE bank" isn't what you call very joyful.

Can you relate to this?

Sitting next to "my" Mr. Bank was, let's call him, Mr. Bank number II. A very "respectable" young man, with a blue suit and tie, and a lovely pair of shoes, well-polished, brown, and beautifully crafted.

Oops I revealed my shoe fetish (blush, blush).

After having shown my appreciation for the fact they were taking time out of their day to hear my story, I filled the next half hour with my words. I explained how I got into this financial situation.

Just moved, unexpected finances in the building, court sessions, and so on and so on.

I made clear that I was the strong woman behind the office walls. That I was their brave client, paying bills on time and never neglecting a demand from them. That I was the one who had started this great thriving practice with all the energy, love and passion I have in me.

That I was the woman who was not for even a split second letting them get to me.

That I was the woman who had attracted more than 500 new clients in the last three years.

That I was the woman on their black list, paying their penalty fees on time.

That I was the woman fighting to survive it all.

No PowerPoint, no paper…it came straight from the heart.

They nodded and watched…

They felt my energy.

Nothing left to say. What they said actually didn't resonate with me.

I felt like Gloria Gaynor: "I will survive".

When the meeting was finished, Mr. Bank gently shoved the financial offer towards me. "Would I please sign now?", he asked.

"Now? Now I will. Yes, now was the time. Now it felt great."

Please you all, t a l k, t a l k, t a l k.

Communicate without getting angry!

Remember the law of attraction; what you seed you will harvest.

You are allowed to show your emotions but keep respect for the other party. They are doing what they have been told to do. They have a boss. If they don't follow instructions, they will lose their job.

Business people often want to earn their money aggressively. I wish the banks would work in a different way; I'm certain that they would be much more successful. They would be able to grow *and* help others. Now *that* would be co-creation at its best.

Emotions have colors

The human eye can distinguish ten million different colors. But what is a color and why can we distinguish them?

A color is a visual perceptual property. It means the eye can catch a vibration or wavelength. The brain translates it into a color. The eye needs equipment for catching the different wave lengths. Each wavelength corresponds with a color.

The retina of the human eye has different kind of cells which have a variety of sensitivities to those wavelengths. *Cones* are color receptor cells and required for bright light. *Rods,* are required for dim light. Rods do not give color vision. Rods are rods cylindrical structured, cones are cone shaped.

The human eye has about 6 million cones and 120 million rods. The body is beautiful, amazing and magnificent!

A special property of the cone is color vision. There are three types of cone that differ in the photo pigment they contain. Each of the photo pigments has a different sensitivity to light, which means every pigment absorbs another wavelength of a color. These pigments are referred to as "blue", "green" and "red" or better said

"Short (S)", "Medium (M)", and "Long (L)".

You know color is energy because it comes in waves, just like sound, touch, and smell.

When these waves hit your senses, they get translated into your brain.

The main source of light on earth is from the sun.

It delivers beams of white light or visible light. Visible light is dispersed by a triangular prism to be able to transmit the different wavelengths and therefore colors.

So, light is colorless but all colors belong to light. We are also the light. Our mind is our prism. We will only experience colors when we are **in** the mind. When we "think", so to speak.

We will experience white light only when we are our authentic beings, our "selves", our higher selves. The place where we don't think but we "are".

Newton originally (1672) divided the spectrum into FIVE main colors; red, yellow, green, blue and violet. He admitted his eyes were not very effective in distinguishing colors (!) (in the mind?), and later added orange and indigo. He chose to divide the visible spectrum into seven colors out of a belief derived from the Ancient Greek sophists who thought there was a connection between the colors, the musical notes, the known objects in the Solar system and the days of the week. Well, what about the seven centers of a human be-ing: the chakras?

There are no two people who see the same rainbow, get it? It is not magic. It is simply a result of cause and effect.

As the within so the without…

Although the colors of the spectrum look (all because of the translation in the mind) like the color pattern of the rainbow, there are differences.

The colors of the rainbow are less saturated; the number of color bands may be different because of the size of the raindrops.

A color is a form of nonverbal communication. It is dynamic energy. It can change every day with an individual; it depends on *what energy* that individual expresses at some point.

Colors represent your state of MIND (not your state of being).

If you are in a positive state of mind (happy, joyful, loving yourself), the color you will attract shows with a "+". When you are in a negative state of mind (thinking too much, being grumpy, no fun in life) the color you attract shows with a "-".

Colors have vibrations; colors are energy.

Color	+	-
Red	*love, action, passion*	*anger, danger*
Orange	*courage, creativity, confidence*	*caution, sluggish*
Yellow	*energy, joy, perky, intellect*	*irresponsible, unstable*
Green	*freshness, new, money, earth, healing*	*envy, jealous, guilt*
Blue	*trust, intelligence, security, peace*	*coldness, fear, masculinity*
Indigo	*devotion, wisdom, fairness, justice*	*fanaticism, addiction, prejudice, intolerance*
Violet	*spirituality, faith, magic, awareness, wealth*	*death, mourning, conceit, instability*

You are the rainbow: the colors are in you

The covenant of the rainbow (from the new American Standard Bible):

"When the rainbow is in the cloud, then I will look upon it to remember the everlasting covenant between God and every living creature of all flesh that is on the earth."

And God said to Noah "this is the sign of the covenant which I have established between Me and all flesh that is on earth".

The rainbow is at its brightest when the clouds are at their darkest; do not fear the rain (problems) in life. God will be there. Be thankful and have faith, even at dark times.

The colors of the rainbow are in you. As mentioned earlier, no two people see the rainbow in the same way. It is your state of being that determines how the outer world looks.

Many people notice the orange and red of my office right away, but there are many who will do so only after a few visits. They are surprised by the brightness. "Did you re- decorate?" they ask me. "No, you are probably less scared today", I will reply.

Your soul has this appointment with God; through your soul you connect with God. Flesh and Spirit, heaven and earth is in us. Colors are within us; colors are within our eyes. The eyes are the windows of our souls. The nebulas of the Universe are visible in our eyes. Look someone deep in the eye and you can discover beautiful colors.

Colors are also in your teeth;

We think that teeth are white, but that is generally only really true for the deciduous teeth also called milk teeth or primary teeth). That is because they absorb all the sunlight; no waves bounce back so no colors are visible.

It makes sense that milk or primary teeth are white; it represents the purity of childhood. The "color" white is the color of new beginnings, of perfection, purity, innocence and completion.

Of course, the child had a new beginning with his/her physical body-called birth.

If a child falls or has a cavity or other abnormality, a tooth is likely to discolor.

In fact, is doesn't discolor, it does color.

Colors from teeth and gums can go from red to purple.

Grown-ups have more yellow-colored teeth. That is because the underlying tissue (called dentin, layer beneath the enamel) which is yellowish, is much thicker than in children's teeth.

A new life begins when you begin transforming from a child into an adult. On a spiritual level, you decided to "grow up"; you were born a second time.

Every tooth corresponds with: a color, a memory, an organ, a tissue part, and psychological aspects. Every tooth has its own place on your meridian.

Emotional Alignment Is Easy

Teeth and their colors (of the rainbow):

1. Red
2. Orange
3. Yellow
4. Green
5. Blue
6. Indigo
7. Violet
8. White, the sum of all colors

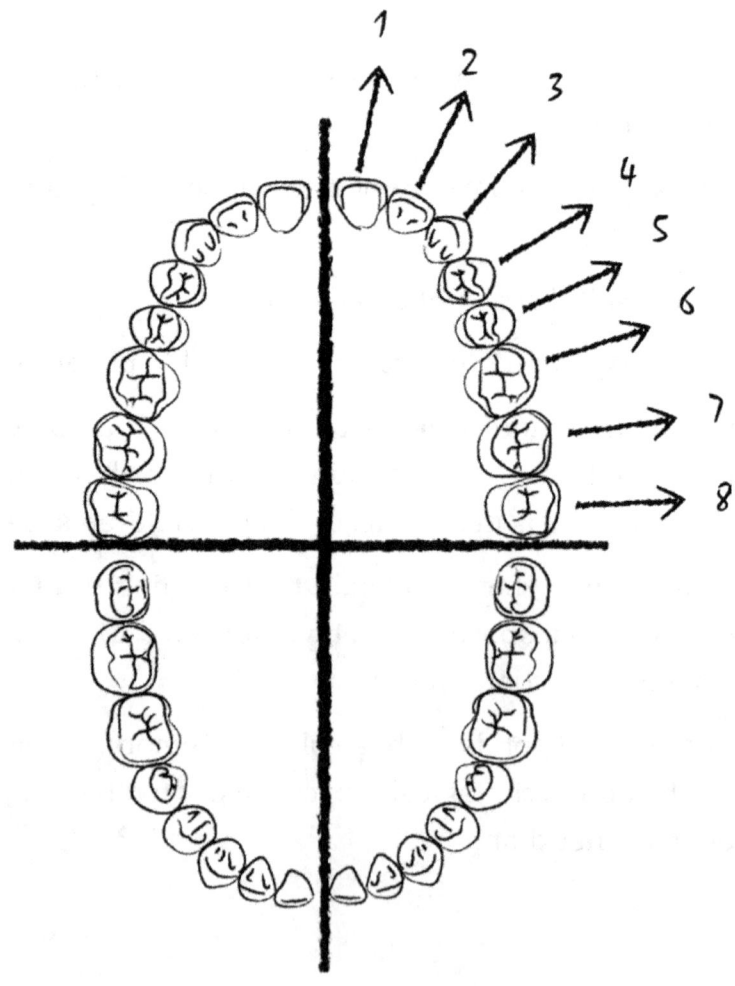

Memories are often the root of (dental) diseases!

Psychological issues often lead to (dental) diseases.

Diseases of the tissue can be expressed through the teeth.

You are about to read more about the spiritual meaning of teeth. Want a sneak preview?

I lost my front tooth! How was this possible? I am a dentist for crying out loud!

The spiritual meaning of teeth

The etheric body gives vitality and health to the physical body. It also gives life to the body and organizes it. The cooperation between trillion cells in your body is a smooth operation.

You have many bodies. Highly sensitive people have been able to perceive one or more of the bodies. They are non-physical bodies. Science is beginning to verify the existence of these other bodies.

The etheric is the subtle level of the physical body. This body contains all your energy called *"Chi"*, *"Ki"*, *"electromagnetic field"*, *"human energy field"*, *"aura"*, *"spirit body"*, *"light body"* or *"body of light"*. I like the term *"God body"*.

Your physical body is nicely surrounded by your etheric body. The God-body has the same form as your physical body. It is made of different energy channels called *"meridians"*. There are 7 major energy centers called *"chakras"*.

There are 21 minor energy centers and many more even smaller centers.

On tooth growing:

In your mother's womb; all the teeth are already constructed. So, as a fetus, you are equipped with all the tooth buds germs. I mean all of them, including those for your permanent teeth. Nature is cool.

Around the age of six <u>months</u> your first little toothies appear; in the lower jaw, the front. By around the age of three <u>years</u>, you have all your primary teeth. It's when you're about six or seven that you start to lose your baby teeth. You usually use the ones you grew in first: the tiny ones in the lower jaw in the middle. New biggies come at the scene.

Your child loses its baby teeth because the etheric body has been freed and comes to its own activity.

The etheric body has been attached to the physical body but can now express itself on its own.

A new life starts, not only in teeth-world but also for body development and growth and mental development and learning.

Do not forget: until the grown-up teeth appear, the child lives in imagination for the greatest part.

Change of teeth means a change of consciousness.

Around the age of 12-13, mostly all the grown-up teeth are visible. This is also the stage in which you grow into puberty.

Wisdom teeth can erupt in your early twenties as well as early 90's! The tooth buds for the wisdom teeth may or may not at all be present in your jaws. Wisdom teeth, also called M3's are very fickle concerning eruption in your mouth. They can erupt straight, they can erupt crooked, they cannot at all erupt while the bud is present. You name it.

Spiritual meaning of teeth problems

Mouth and teeth idioms:

Are you biting off more than you can chew?
Armed to the teeth
Bite one's tongue
A bitter pill to swallow
By the skin of one's teeth
By word of mouth
Eye for an eye and a tooth for a tooth
Fight tooth and nail
Keep a stiff upper lip
Keep one's mouth shut
Long in the tooth
Loudmouth
Like pulling teeth
Pay lip service to
Put some teeth into
Show one's teeth
A slip of the tongue
Zip one's lip
Sink one's teeth into
Down in the mouth
Born with a silver spoon in the mouth
Foam at the mouth
Have a sweet tooth
Shove down someone's throat
Cram something down someone's throat
Hold one's tongue
A sharp tongue

A slip of the tongue
Live from hand to mouth
Make one's mouth water

All idioms express feelings.

The only way your God-body can tell you that you are off-course is to let your physical body ache. This is the way it gets your attention. Let's take a look at some physical problems and what they indicate:

Tooth decay:

You are not taking good care of yourself.
Inadequate cleaning.
Not enough healthy food.
You deny yourself.
You give your power away.

Solar plexus chakra issue!

Bad breath:

You don't pay attention to your body.
Your body is angry with you.
You cannot receive, only give.

Heart chakra issue!

Teeth grinding:

You are upset with yourself.
You feel you are not "heard".

Throat chakra issue!

We have 7 chakras (energy centers) in the human body:

Emotional Alignment Is Easy

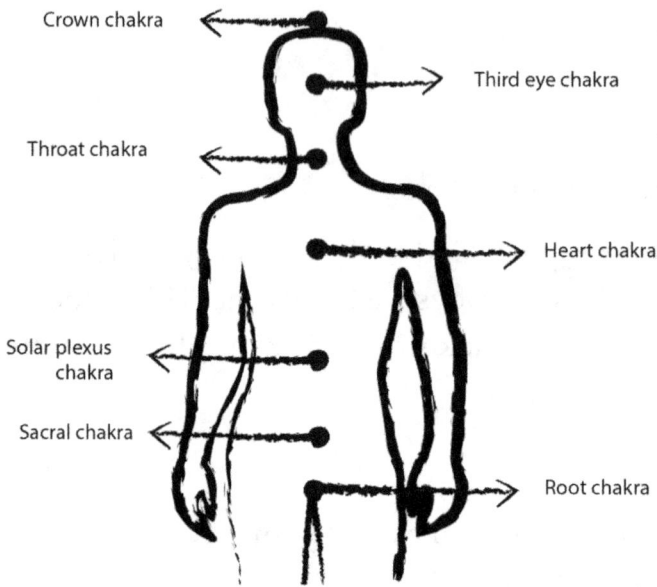

Crown chakra	: Wholeness, the God Source
Third eye chakra	: Clarity, Connection to higher self
Throat chakra	: Expression, Sound, Speak, Write
Heart chakra	: Love, Trust, Hope, Forgiveness
Solar plexus chakra	: Power, Will, Energy, Self esteem
Sacral chakra	: Emotions, Sexuality, Creativity
Root chakra	: Security, Survival, Material World

Every tooth has a connection to every chakra.

(Surpass your 12th chakra and you will reach your Akashic records.)

So, let the physical damage be repaired by the dentist but the underlying cause be cured by the lovely guidance of a:

- Yoga teacher
- Meditation teacher

- Regression therapist
- Wellness coach
- Clairvoyant helper
- Angel healer
- Spiritual counsellor
- Psychotherapist
- Reiki healer
- Chakra healer
- Aura healer
- Acupuncturist
- Light therapist
- Hydro therapist
- Color therapist
- Holistic dentist
- And more

Be thankful for the following arts-and craftsmen who repair your vehicle (body):

- Surgeons
- Physical Therapists
- Manual Therapist
- Chiropractic Doctor
- Massage Therapist
- Dentists
- Craniosacral Therapist
- Dry Needling Experts
- Podiatric Therapist
- And More

Meridians

What are the differences between auras, meridians, and chakras?

An aura is on the *out*side of our body. People who are focused and trained in this subject can see these.

A chakra is kind of a funnel of energy; chakras filter the energy into our bodies. In addition to the main ones, there are more than about 150 small chakras in our bodies. Every joint has a chakra point. If one or more chakras are blocked the system can be way out of balance. This can cause sickness and pain.

The meridians are energy tracks. This energy is called "Prana", "Chetana", or "Qi" (chi). They are undetectable with the naked eye, but scientifically proven to exist (for the ones who still need proof).

Scientists at Seoul National University confirmed the existence of meridians, which they refer to as the "primo-vascular system". They say that this system is a crucial part of our cardiovascular system.

In a study published in the *Journal of Electron Spectroscopy and Related Phenomena*, researchers used contrast CT imaging with radiation on both non- acupuncture points and acupuncture points. The CT scans revealed clear distinctions between the non- acupuncture point and acupuncture point anatomical structures.

These *"**tracks**"* transport energy through your whole body. Blockage of this energy means a stop of flow which means illness will be the result. Meridians complement each other, one Yin (energy flowing up), one Yang (energy flowing down).

Each meridian is related to an element: Earth, Metal, Fire, Wood or Water.

For instance: **the stomach meridian** is a yang meridian and is paired with the spleen yin meridian; it is an Earth element. It has its <u>physical</u> branches to the muscles, lips, mouth and saliva. It has its emotional imbalances; the stomach influences mental state.

Our energy flow affects how we feel, how we think and the overall condition of our health.

So chakras bring energy **into** your body, meridians send energy to all the organs, tissues and…teeth.

The mouth is a gateway to all sorts of microbes. To have optimal defense, you need an optimal immune system This system consists of cells that "eat" the microbes.

Your immune system depends on optimal energy. Energy is also needed for eating and proper digestion. So energy transport is important. Less energy means less defense, and a tooth can decay more easily.

There are 12 major meridians in the body:

Lung meridian
Large intestine meridian
Spleen meridian
Stomach meridian
Heart meridian
Small intestine meridian
Bladder meridian
Kidney meridian
Pericardium (Circulation/Sex) meridian
Triple Warmer meridian

Liver meridian
Gallbladder meridian

These meridians are in control of not only their corresponding organ, but also additional organs around them as well as their surrounding systems:

Endocrine, nervous, circulatory, immune, skeletal, muscular, digestive and lymphatic.

Meridians can have an excess of energy or a shortage of energy; both can cause imbalance. Balance is key in the body; it is no different for the energy in the meridians.

Let me pay attention to the meridians of the head.

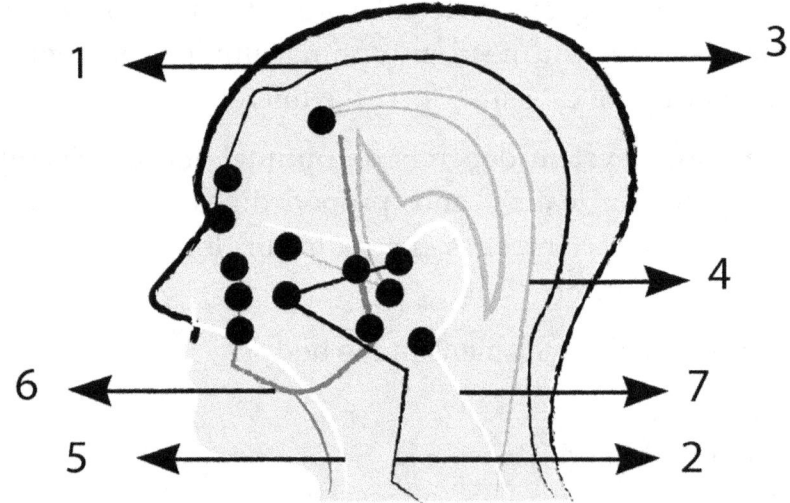

1. Bladder
2. Small Intestine
3. Triple Warmer (Tw)
4. Gallbladder
5. Large Intestine
6. Stomach
7. Pericardium/Sex

MERIDIAN	IMBALANCE	BALANCE
BLADDER	Lack of energy, fearful, resisting change, headaches, pain in eyes, colds	Calm and peaceful
SMALL INTESTINE	Sadness, "fed up", low mood, inactive	Joy, light and passion, easy digestion
TRIPLE WARMER	Disorders of throat, eyes, ears, disregulation of organs in thorax, abdomen and pelvis	Kind hearted, stable mind, emotion of joy
GALLBLADDER	Overstimulation of mind, muscular aches, rage, bitterness	Gratitude, kindness, compassion, awakening
LARGE INTESTINE	Guilt, shame, little self-worth, unable to "feel", constipation	Feeling worthy, feeling loved, self-respect
STOMACH	Hunger, greed, brain fog when eating too much sugar, fatigue	Feeling abundant, happy, tranquil
PERICARDIUM/SEX	Jealousy, sexual tension, regret, remorse, pericarditis	Soft state, generosity, relaxation, letting go of the past, relaxed muscles

NOTE: this is just a very, very short summary of the functions and dysfunctions of the organs. There are amazing books out there that you can read to learn more!

Emotional Alignment Is Easy

The teeth in the upper jaw are connected to the subconscious: *"negative emotions keep us busy"*.

The teeth in the lower jaw are connected to the conscious.

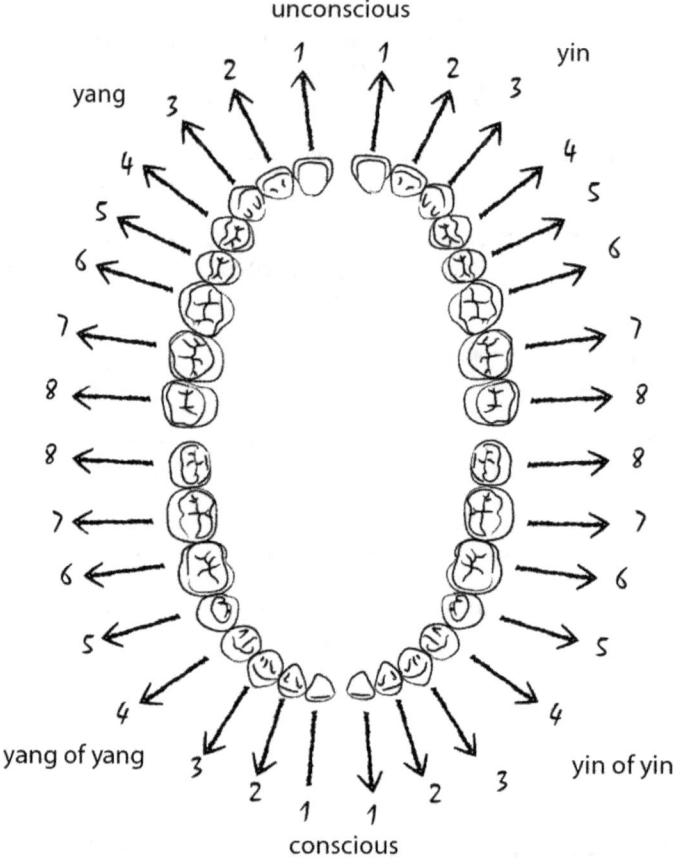

Tap into your canines

Teeth are infinite: they still can exist for thousands and thousands of years after the rest of your body disappears, just like your soul.

Crystals, the most orderly structures in nature (as they have the lowest amount of *entropy*, a measure of disorder), are able to absorb energy waves! Remember that your enamel consists of compact crystals.

Crystals are structured in such a way that they respond to the input of all the different energies around them, leading them to oscillate and emit specific vibratory frequencies. The energy is consistent because of the well-balanced crystal lattice; when dissonant energy is inputted it *will be* balanced and transformed into a harmonic energy.

Crystals can contain a huge amount of energy or information: this is why we use liquid crystals in computer and cell phones, for instance. Quartz (a type of silicate mineral) is used in watches and clocks to help them tell earthly time; it helps stabilize and regulate the flow of energy. A quartz crystal can be used to store data for up to 300 million years! So, if you would like to talk to your great-great-great-grandma, just tap into one of your canines :-).

What do crystals have to do with spiritual growth? Well, according to Nikola Tesla, energy, it is all about frequency and vibration. Crystals have their own vibration, as do the cells in our bodies as well as, of course, the chakras. So when we come in contact with a crystal, it interacts with the vibration of the cells.

Color or light therapy is the term used to describe the exposure of light to the human body. It has been used in Western traditional medicine only since the late 19th century, but has been known in Eastern medicine for thousands of years. In Eastern medicine, light therapy mainly focuses on the energy systems of the body, the various chakra zones, and meridian points.

Light is energy and our body is comprised of energy. When red light penetrates the skin, it tends to strongly promote healing, rejuvenation, and balance.

Red light is converted into cellular energy, thereby stimulating the natural processes of the body on a cellular level. This leads to a complete series of metabolic events, all to make your cells jump for joy!

Red light therapy will boost your lymphatic system, the most important part of your immune system. It carries all the "kill and attack-molecules". Some benefits of red light therapy include:

- Reduction of inflammation, the root cause of many diseases
- Formation of new small blood vessels (capillaries) (remember that teeth contain blood vessels...)
- Increase of ATP energy packs release straight from your mitochondria! (omg, teeth will jump for joy)
- Repair of soft tissue (your gums will thank you)

- Increase of oxygen flow (omg, let your teeth get oxygen before they fall out)

In Japanese Acupuncture Clinics, They Sometimes Use The Lumen Photon Light Therapy. They Use A Device with Seven Different Wavelength Settings. For Example, There Are Settings For:

- Nerve Pain (Herniated Disk/Gum/Tooth Pain)
- Joint Pain (Tmj-Jaw Joint)
- Muscle-Tendon-Ligament Pain (Total Oral Cavity!)

When will you let your light come in?

Let's get physical

In 2017 I decided to get braces because I wanted to look even better than I already did.

On the day of the appointment when I'd finally have my braces removed, I felt something strange on top of my gums. There was a lump!! Whattt? I had to stop at a traffic light and look in the rear-view mirror. I lifted up my upper lip to check… and I saw it… a little lump, kind of yellowish. I rubbed my finger against it. My diagnosis was clear.

My tooth needed to be pulled out!

Wouldn't you be devastated? Just finished an orthodontic treatment for two years and now your right front tooth has to be pulled out? A front tooth. As a dentist!

You may find it difficult to believe, but the opposite was true. I was totally relaxed, had no fear and the only thing I could think of was, "What is Spirit trying to tell me?". I felt a total resignation and expectation that the Universe or my Angels wanted to protect me from something worse than losing a front tooth.

Something worse which could have a dis-ease causing frequency, for when cells vibrate in a different frequency than their own, you will feel discomfort.

I was thankful for the message.

It turned out I had been _biting_ my way through life. I had been a very sensitive and caring child. I could "feel" so much as a kid but I never dared to share that. Parents are supposed to make you feel safe, but I did not have this comfort. As I've already explained, I have forgiven my parents for that; I know that they had their own issues, too. There is no such thing as "the perfect parent". Even the best parents have their own conditioning, beliefs and hurt. I attempted to solve their issues by trying to please and help them as much as I could and whenever I could. Unfortunately, pleasing them meant losing myself. I looked for love everywhere and I wanted to show how good I was.

Losing my tooth showed me I had to "let go" and not to "force life" but rather allow life to come through me.

We all have to let the <u>fear</u> out of our lives! Your life path has already been orchestrated like a movie on a DVD. If you start **_being_** and stop the frantic **_doing,_** all will be well.

Just follow your heart and follow your dreams despite what your parents, neighbors, sisters or teachers tell you. Remember, your blueprint wasn't made by them but by somebody else.

By the way, don't worry about me. I have a new front tooth...

Psychodontics

Have you ever wondered *why* your teeth:

* Are heavily filled?
* Have so many crowns?
* Are dead?
* Are missing?

Everything is energy (sigh... here we go again).

We need a good energy level to be able to have a well-functioning immune system. The cells' mitochondria are the energy suppliers.

As human beings, we are subject to bacteria, viruses, and fungi 24 hours a day. They invade our bodies through the mouth, through the air, liquids and food. So even at night when we snore, we are being attacked, LOL. So our immune system is never allowed a break from its duties. .

The better our energy, the better the immune system works for us. The less energy through the meridians, the less your immune system will protect you. The immune system is a system of cells. T and B-cells, neutrophil, eosinophil, basophil, monocytes, macrophage-cells and natural killers. I figured I'd throw a little science in here, to make sure you're concentrating!

Negative emotions steal a lot of energy from our bodies. Let me give you an example. Our first, top left molar (26), is connected to the stomach (sorrow/sick to the stomach). If a person keeps on hanging into their sorrow, the immune system of that tooth will weaken. Hence this system might not be able to attack the bacteria in an effective way and a cavity might be lurking around the corner (especially in the absence of proper dental hygiene).

An example:

The 26 (2nd quadrant, 6th element) molar stands for chakra V. It stands in YIN energy, and it carries the information of the energy of the past and the now! The 26 is situated in the upper jaw (unconscious). This means that problems with it can indicate that negative emotions are dominating our unconscious.

Archangel Michael

Why this chapter?

In my spiritual journey I discovered that we are surrounded by angels. They know our truth. There are many people who channel Angels. I met one of them and through her I met Archangel Michael. The questions I had were answered by him. In retrospect I came aware that all the answers were already present but I didn't believe myself or my intuition. Intuition is your truth.

Archangel (*"Chief of the angels"*) Michael, whose name means

"He is who is as God"

Is most often thought of as the angel of protection and the most powerful of all angels! He is considered a leader within the angelic realm and a patron angel of righteousness, mercy and justice. That is why he is usually depicted as a warrior, carrying a sword. Archangel Michael assists in situations where you are afraid, confused or fear for your safety. He helps us to release fear and doubt. He is the embodiment of compassion, the Earth's representative of the all-encompassing strength of the Divine.

He wants us to make positive changes in life and he is often said to work closely with those who perform healing work or provide spiritual teaching.

He can be of assistance with your courage, direction, energy and vitality, spirit release, worthiness and self-esteem.

Do you wish to talk with him? You can! Is he around? Yes! How do you know because you cannot see him? NO doubt he will give you signs; you will see evidence of Michael's presence. He is a clear communicator: he is your GUT feeling.

Don't tell me you have never seen *small flashes of light!* Don't get obsessed trying to **find** signs; rather, open your mind (crown chakra) and "sense".

Don't tell me you have never heard *"a voice"*, telling you something. That is Michael. Have you found the name "Michael" popping up more in your life? That could be him, too. The family for which I was au pair had two Michaels, the father and son. I didn't realize in 1984 that this was a sign of Archangel Michael's presence.

If you would like to talk with Archangel Michael and ask him for guidance, speak to him. If you don't know how, you, can contact an oracle.

An oracle is someone who offers advice or prophecies thought to have come directly from a Divine Source. Spiritual psychotherapist and intuitive medium Rev Lea Chapin is an inspirational spiritual counselor, teacher and oracle for the Ascended Masters and Celestial realm. She has 25 years of experience as a direct voice channel for Spirit and helps her clients understand the ROOT cause of their life challenges and soul lessons from a spiritual perspective.

I have told many people that in a former life I must have been a Native Indian woman living in America! I've always have felt that, and Archangel Michael confirmed this. He also confirmed my connection to certain animals, and he said that in earlier life I was a Shamanic healer of both animals and people.

As I have stated so many times in this book:

Body pains are linked to specific emotional states. Although I AM a being of light, I choose to be in this body and experience life on Earth. Hence Spirit will tell me what is the matter when I am in pain, or experience any other discomfort in my body.

What did Spirit tell me about my **back pain**?

As a dentist we sometimes bend over in miraculous ways to fix your teeth. Although this posture issue was part of the cause of my back pain, I knew there was a bigger one, and, yes, Archangel Michael confirmed that. He told me that because I am so highly sensitive, I pick up too much of the energy of my client.

Michael said: "Do weight training to strengthen the muscles of your back" (I have been doing this for five years now and my back has gotten so much better), and "clear the energy of every client when they leave your office".

What did Spirit tell me about my nail bed?

The nail bed of my left index finger was damaged. I figured it was from the curing light for the composite fillings; perhaps it overheated the tip of my finger. Growing more aware, though, I realized that Source was telling me something different. Source just needed this light and my nail to make me aware of something.

Michael said: "Your nail bed is weak, the opposite of what you are: strong. This is the only weakness left in your body. It is telling you to regain your powers in every part of your life."

This absolutely resonated with me! I did healing work for myself and my nail is going back to normal!

What did Spirit tell me about my left index finger?

Since the nail bed is a part of the finger...

Michael said: "The left finger is about inner power" and "you have to set your boundaries" and "or not knowing what you want."

He said he knew exactly what I want, and that I am very focused on any kind of work I do. I take no crap, and I have no time for nonsense. True. However, I still have work to do in boosting my inner power and establishing boundaries.

Oh my Michael, you were right again.

What did Spirit tell me about my left eye being different than the right?

I have what we call a "lazy eye". My left eye doesn't function as well as the right one. This minor loss of function has been with me ever since I was born. No worries; it does NOT inhibit me in performing dentistry, driving a car or any daily life function.

Michael said: "This lifetime is provided for you to balance your male-female energy. And you decided to not accept your female energy, so there is a blockage". (Remember that yin is female energy, and yang is male energy).

I can assure you that Archangel Michael is more than right.

This life I now live is for me to be a healer of humans as well as animals, according to Archangel Michael.

It is absolutely an honor and my passion to be of service to you!

Leslie van O, The Awakening Dentist Embodied Divine Goddess.

Aftermath

I am so honored that you have read this book, that you took the time to invest in Self and faithfully find your way Home. Our purpose here, on Mother Earth, is to learn knowledge of who we really are at a soul level, learn from past "mistakes" and/or why what is happening now relates to that.

I am so honored that such a tremendous number of people are reaching out to me to discuss life with or without teeth. I've also been thrilled to be a guest on many radio shows all over the world. Thank you, thank you for inviting me.

"What should I do?", is the most common FAQ. Just a few others are: *"Should I do a crown?"*, *"Should I have that tooth pulled?"*, *"Can I use coconut oil?"*, *"Do I have to undergo a root canal treatment?"*, *"What toothpaste do I have to use?"*, *"When does my child have to go to the dentist for the first time?"*.

The truth is that there are pros and cons to every kind of treatment.

Adding to the confusion, some people go to extremes, claiming that certain kinds of treatments are always wrong. This can lead to a number of dilemmas.

Amalgam is poison, but removing it is also poisonous. Root canal treatments block the chakras, but the pain is unbearable without one. Braces can cause terrible headaches but my teeth are crooked.

This implant is titanium but I want a new tooth. See all the "buts"?

The only thing you have to do is get your energy right, remember? If it doesn't feel ok, back off.

Ask your dentist for the technical and financial information, as well as all the pros and cons. If he or she doesn't want to provide this information, you know it is time for a different dentist.

Always be aware of your gut feeling! Be aware of your every 1/100th of an inch of your enamel for it will never grow back.

What does your dentist do to cherish your tissues?

Thank you for chewing on this.

'Who am I grateful for?' list

I thank you all so very much!
<u>Archangel Michael</u>, for you kept showing me the way!
Alan, for freaking me out :-)!
Andrea, for saying: you have no niche!
Berna, for reminding me I am Spirit.
Carolien: infinite love
Dirk, for watching over me, dad!
Dot, for being my friend, editor of my book proposal.
Edith, for being your only holy daughter.
Eef, for being my inspiring daughter!
Elspeth, for unlocking my soul.
Fitzpatricks, for infinite love.
God, for telling me: you can do it!
Jill, for reminding me #Iamtheboss!
Jose, for infinite Spring!
Keij, for being my amazing daughter!
Lea, for your Celestial messages!
Max, for being my brilliant son!
Patty, for believing in me!
Ronald, for taking such loving care of me!
Taz, for being awesome
You, for reading this book!!

About the Author

Leslie van Oostenbrugge is a passionate holistic dentist. She graduated from Dental School and the School for Physical Therapy with honors. She is a joyful, and empowering woman.

Leslie combines dentistry and spirituality in a new and authentic way. She has a holistic dental office in Vianen, the Netherlands. She teaches the principles of how the universe always has your back, and quite often, your front too!

She is known as "The Awakening Dentist" and her lectures have changed many people's lives—physically, spiritually, and financially.

She cannot emphasize enough how important oral health is to our overall health. "Teeth never lie" is her favorite empowering statement!

Leslie is the proud mom of two daughters and one son. She loves her physical workouts and her two doggies.

Leslie is the co-author of the book Time to Rise, a book on personal growth and professional transformation.

Life is all about realizing we are a soul having a bodily experience. Know your purpose and live your best life!

Visit Leslie online at www.TheAwakeningDentist.com

MAKE YOUR MARK GLOBAL

Get Published Share Your Message with the World

Make Your Mark Global is a branding, marketing and media agency based in the USA and French Riviera. We offer publishing, content development, and promotional services to heart-based, conscious authors who wish to have a lasting impact through the sharing and distribution of their transformative message. We also help authors build a strong online media presence and platform for greater visibility and provide speaker training.

If you'd like help writing, publishing, or promoting your book, or if you'd like to co-author a collaborative book, visit us online or call for a free consultation.

Visit www.MakeYourMarkGlobal.com or

Call +1 (707) 776-6310 or

Send an email to Andrea@MakeYourMarkGlobal.com

www.ingramcontent.com/pod-product-compliance
Lightning Source LLC
Chambersburg PA
CBHW070522010526
44118CB00012B/1049